PELICAN BOOKS

QUAKER BY CONVINCEMENT

Geoffrey Hubbard trained as a physicist and worked for some years in a large industrial research laboratory before joining the administrative Civil Service and embarking simultaneously on his career as a writer. He has written scripts for television series for young children and his plays for sound radio have been transmitted by the B.B.C. and by various overseas broadcasting organizations. In 1965 he published a study of Cooke and Wheatstone and the invention of the electric telegraph.

Geoffrey Hubbard is currently Director of the Council for Educational Technology. He has been a member of the Religious Society of Friends (Quakers) since the nineteen-sixties, having been, for all his previous adult life, a fairly humanist agnostic.

D1331750

QUAKER
BY
CONVINCEMENT

GEOFFREY HUBBARD

PENGUIN BOOKS

Penguin Books Ltd, Harmondsworth, Middlesex, England
Penguin Books Inc., 7110 Ambassador Road, Baltimore, Maryland 21207, U.S.A.
Penguin Books Australia Ltd, Ringwood, Victoria, Australia
Penguin Books Canada Ltd, 41 Steelcase Road West, Markham, Ontario, Canada
Penguin Books (N.Z.) Ltd, 182–190 Wairau Road, Auckland 10, New Zealand

—

First published 1974
Reprinted 1976

—

Copyright © Geoffrey Hubbard, 1974

—

Made and printed in Great Britain by
Cox & Wyman Ltd, London, Reading and Fakenham
Set in Linotype Georgian

Contents

Preface   7

PART I
A Brief History

1. *The Beginnings of Quakerism*   15
2. *Great Days and Great Trials*   25
3. *Consolidation*   40
4. *The Effects of Evangelism*   55

PART II
Fundamental Beliefs

1. *God and Man*   67
2. *The Quakers as Christians*   75
3. *The Necessary Minimum*   85
4. *Problems that Remain*   98
5. *Quakers and Other Churches*   105
6. *The Spiritual Experiment*   113

PART III
Belief and Behaviour

1. *The Moral Law*   121
2. *Quakers as Peacemakers*   127
3. *Materialism*   135
4. *Towards a Quaker View of Sex*   144
   A Note on Race and Colour   152
5. *Crime and Punishment*   155
6. *Religion and Social Order*   164

PART IV
Organization and Practices

1. *The Organization of the Religious Society of Friends* 177
2. *Meeting for Worship* 187
3. *Other Meetings, Other Worship* 203
4. *Entrances and Exits* 213
5. *Debits and Credits* 229

Suggested Additional Reading 245

Index 247

Preface

THE purpose of this book is to give the non-Quaker reader an outline of what Quakerism is today; of the religious beliefs that inspire and motivate Quakers, and of how they are moved to behave. Although the book starts with a brief history, this is only a background to the understanding of what Quakerism is; for the history of the Society of Friends is only important if the Society itself is still a living influence.

I have throughout been more concerned to convey the feeling of being a Friend than to represent all shades of belief, all aspects of Quaker activity. For anyone who tries to be scrupulous in attending to all varieties of Quaker experience attempts an impossible task. The Quakers do not have a defined creed; they are diverse in their beliefs, and in their way of carrying them into the world. Yet something binds them together, and makes them declare themselves Friends.

But what are they – Quakers or Friends? I have used both terms indifferently, as Quakers do among themselves. (We have already met our first example of Quaker peculiarity; capital 'F' Friends are Quakers!) We are concerned with 200,000 inhabitants of many countries, members of the constituent elements which form the Religious Society of Friends, and with an undefined number of people who are not formal members of the Society but do associate with Friends in their worship and other activities. I write as a member of London Yearly Meeting, the original element in the Quaker world family, and I write therefore primarily of Quakerism in Britain and in countries where it has followed the British model. I write, too, with the role in mind that it is capable of playing in the disturbed world of my time. If Quakerism were only a historical survival, a relic of the proliferating sects of seventeenth-century nonconformity, it might be better left in the decent obscurity of academic historical studies. But I see it as an insight, derived from but not constrained within the Christian tradition, about the relationship at the deepest level between man and his total environment, between man and man, between man and society, and between man and that intangible element which he has called God. Now this matter of relationship, in this broad sense, is at the heart of the malaise of our civilization. We are told that the trouble is materialism, or the collapse of traditional moral and religious beliefs. Perhaps so, but we cannot attain to a state of belief by an effort of will; our creed can only be the credible. Quakerism, as it seems to me, has the capacity to help direct modern man towards beliefs about himself and his relationship to the world, tangible and intangible, in which he lives. One is not required to suspend one's critical faculties on entering a Meeting House.

But what is required of one on entering a Meeting House? What typifies the Quakers; how do they differ from other nonconformists; how far are their generally known characteristics (their concern with social welfare, their non-violence) distinguishing features or merely subsidiary?

Much of this book explores such questions in detail. It may help meanwhile, to give some broad indications of what Quakers are, even if these indications must be accompanied by warnings, caveats and reservations to the effect that Friends are not a homogeneous body; their beliefs, practices and attitudes vary greatly.

Quakers are the inheritors of a line of development in religious attitudes and practices which started in seventeenth-century England, but had roots and parallels much earlier within and without Christianity. The starting point of Quakerism was the concept that God was directly accessible to all men, an idea which recurs continually in the history of religion. In Quakerism this led to, or became associated with:

The priesthood of all believers – they recognized no priestly caste, no individual or group set apart as the preferred channel of communication between God and man.

Rejection of the concept of a defined creed or statement of belief to which all members must subscribe.

Unprogrammed, silent worship, interrupted only by the ministry of anyone present who may find himself or herself moved to speak. This deserves a word more of explanation, since it is so very distinctive. Quakers meet for worship, usually on Sunday mornings, sometimes on other days, and this is one of the main activities, though not the only one,[1] in their Meeting Houses. Meeting for Worship (more fully described in Part IV, Chapter 2) is open to all; there is no form of service. Those present sit in silence, unless some one of their number is moved to speak. Most Meetings for Worship consist of more silence than talk; perhaps three or four people may speak, for a few minutes each, in the course of an hour's meeting.

Rejection of all formalized sacraments, such as baptism, confirmation or communion, in favour of an acceptance of the whole of life as sacramental.

This is a list of negatives – no priest, no creeds, no sacraments, no service – yet at the same time each negative rejects a limitation; no one priest, for all are open to the word of God; no defined creed, for each must find his own way of expressing his own experience; no sacramental rites, for all of life is sacramental; no prearranged service, so that our Meeting is open to God's message however it is expressed. It is this openness, shown in these more obvious and easily identified aspects of Quakerism, that give it a particular significance in our time, an ability perhaps to speak to those whom other, more formalized religions cannot reach.

Perhaps the title I have chosen deserves a word of explanation. Quakers have long given up their distinguishing costume, in fact the unmodified dress of an earlier generation,

1. Meeting Houses are not sanctified and set apart like churches; to the Quaker no day, no place is more sacred than any other. All places, all days, all actions are equally opportunities to find and follow the will of God. A Meeting for Worship can take place in a private house, a rented room or a consecrated church as well as in a Meeting House; equally Meeting Houses are used for a variety of purposes including non-Quaker meetings and conferences. I know of one which accommodated sessions of a juvenile court. Everyone seen going into a Meeting House is not necessarily a Quaker, therefore.

while clinging to a few curiosities of language which are equally vestigial survivals from earlier times. But whereas the clothes of the day before yesterday tend to be merely quaint, the corresponding language has more to recommend it, and Quakers describe those who come into the Society as 'Quakers by Convincement'. As a title, I hope it conveys that the book is very much a personal testimony and interpretation.

It remains to acknowledge the great help I have received in writing this book from many Friends who have read parts of it and given me most detailed and helpful comments, and from Friends and others who have greatly helped me in deciding which aspects of my subject are most important to those for whom the book is written. The emphasis may strike Friends as decidedly odd; but what we think important about ourselves is seldom what others think important about us.

I should like to thank particularly the members of Colchester Meeting, of Richmond upon Thames Meeting and of the Tuesday lunchtime Meeting at Westminster Meeting House, with whom I have worshipped and who have greatly influenced, helped and supported me. To name individual Friends seems invidious, since so many have contributed to this book both by written comment and in informal discussion, yet I must record the particular assistance of Eric Baker, Joe Brayshaw, John Brigham, Maurice Creasey, David Firth, William Fraser, George Gorman, Charles Hadfield, Harold Loukes, the late Brindley Marten, Walter Martin, Edward Milligan, William Sewell, Nicholas Sims, Phyllis Taunton Wood, and the late Alfred Torrie. My special thanks are due also to my wife Rochana who read and commented on much of the text and typed a good deal of it.

I should point out, meanwhile, that some of the most valuable comments came from those who utterly disagreed with me. Let me also make it clear that what I have written is in no way endorsed by the Society as a whole; it is a personal observation, written with deep affection but also inevitably with a strong personal bias.

When I joined the Society I was told that 'the Society does not make Quakers, it discovers them'. My hope is that this book may help some undiscovered Quakers to find themselves. I feel a dedication would be pretentious, but perhaps I may be allowed a quotation – which will recur in the text. It is from the works of George Fox; it must have been a favourite of his, for we have it in a number of versions. It was quoted at the first Meeting for Worship I attended, and convinced me that though I might be a bad Quaker, a humanist agnostic Quaker, I had found my spiritual home. It was: 'Walk cheerfully over the world, answering that of God in every one.'[2]

2. George Fox, *Journal*, ed. J. L. Nickalls, Cambridge University Press, 1952, p. 263.

PART I

A Brief History

CHAPTER I

The Beginnings of Quakerism

CHRISTIANITY, like other great religions, is a revelation of the original overwhelming truth of man's relationship to that which is greater than man. Its history, like the history of other great religions, is of a truth proclaimed, and first buttressed and then stifled by ritual and dogma. But truth will out, and there are always those who hark back to the spirit of the founder, regardless of the careful commentaries, the elaborate theology created by others. So the history of a religion becomes the history of its heresies, because it is among the heresies (which may include the most outrageous nonsenses) that truth will survive and flourish.

The heresy which is Quakerism started in seventeenth-century England from the spiritual experience of one man, George Fox. What was revealed to him, and what he proclaimed to and found echoed in others, can be seen either as a restatement of the Christian message, a return to the essential teaching of Christ, or as the recurrence of a perennial doctrinal error. It can also be presented as a facet of the thought of his time, as part of the complex of social revolutionary ideas which culminated in the overthrow of the monarchy, as a belated afterthought of the Reformation, an extreme aspect of Nonconformity, or even as a manifestation of Fox's undoubtedly idiosyncratic personality. The important thing is that the religious attitude which he stimulated has proved to be dynamic, capable of changing and producing change without losing its identity, so that today the history of Quakerism is not a closed chapter but a prelude, a prelude to the description of Quakerism today which welcomes new interpretations and seems almost to be patiently waiting for modern thought to catch up with it.

The essential idea of Quakerism then as now is of a direct awareness of God within man. It was not a new idea, indeed it is a perennially recurrent concept, not restricted to Christianity. But on the many earlier occasions on which it had manifested itself the Church had been triumphant, on the side of imposed hierarchical authority. This brief history will show how on this occasion the expression of this idea has survived, essentially the same but changing to match the temper of each succeeding age. To Fox and his companions it was the vital truth of Christianity underlined and re-inforced by the words of the Bible: for some of us today the phraseology of the seventeenth century and the words as-sociated with religion generally form something of a barrier, 'the letter that killeth'. But we should remember that the words which are now hallowed or hackneyed were then new-minted; what happened to Fox happened in a time of great social and intellectual ferment; the authority of the Catholic Church, for so long a supra-national authority, had been broken; the whole question of religion was wide open and sects proliferated all over an England where thought (pro-vided it was Christian and neither treasonable nor seditious) was free.

It was into this world that George Fox, the founder of Quakerism, was born. The opening of his *Journal* (in reality an autobiography dictated in later life) is both a concise record of what is known of his early life and also a revealing picture of the man:

That all may know the dealings of the Lord with me, and the various exercises, trials and troubles through which he led me in order to prepare and fit me for the work unto which he had appointed me, and may thereby be drawn to admire and glorify his infinite wisdom and goodness, I think fit (before I proceed to set forth my public travels in the service of Truth), briefly to mention how it was with me in my youth, and how the work of the Lord was begun and gradually carried on in me, even from my childhood.

I was born in the month called July in the year 1624 at Dray-ton-in-the-Clay in Leicestershire. My father's name was Chris-topher Fox; he was by profession a weaver, an honest man, and there was a seed of God in him. The neighbours called him 'Righteous Christer'. My mother was an upright woman, her maiden name was Mary Lago, of the family of the Lagos and of the stock of the martyrs.

In my very young years I had a gravity and stayedness of mind and spirit not usual in children, insomuch that, when I have seen old men carry themselves lightly and wantonly towards each other, I have had a dislike thereof risen in my heart, and have said within myself, 'If ever I come to be a man, surely I shall not do so nor be so wanton.'

When I came to eleven years of age, I knew pureness and righteousness; for while I was a child I was taught how to walk to be kept pure. The Lord taught me to be faithful in all things, and to act faithfully two ways, viz. inwardly to God and outwardly to men, and to keep to 'yea' and 'nay' in all things. For the Lord showed me that though the people of the world have mouths full of deceit and changeable words, yet I was to keep to 'yea' and 'nay' in all things; and that my words should be few and savoury, seasoned with grace; and that I might not eat and drink to make myself wanton but for health, using the creatures in their service, as servants in their places, to the glory of Him that hath created them; they being in their covenant, and I being brought up into the covenant, as sanctified by the Word which was in the beginning, by which all things are upheld; wherein is unity with the creation.[1]

Without questioning the pureness and righteousness of the child, we may see the mature man in the metaphysics of the last phrases.

Afterwards, as I grew up, my relations thought to have me a priest, but others persuaded to the contrary; whereupon I was put to a man, a shoemaker by trade, and that dealt in wool, and used grazing and sold cattle; and a great deal went through my hands . . .

. . . When I came towards nineteen years of age, I being upon business at a fair, one of my cousins, whose name was Bradford, being a professor [that is, one who makes profession of religious faith] and having another professor with him, came to me and asked me to drink part of a jug of beer with them, and I, being thirsty, went in with them, for I loved any that had a sense of good, or that did seek after the Lord. And when we had drunk a glass apiece, they began to drink healths and called for more drink, agreeing together that he that would not drink should pay all. I was grieved that any that made profession of religion should offer to do so. They grieved me very much, having never

1. George Fox, *Journal*, ed. J. L. Nickalls, C.U.P., 1952, pp. 1–2.

had such a thing put to me before by any sort of people; wherefore I rose up to be gone, and putting my hand into my pocket I took out a groat and laid it down upon the table before them and said 'If it be so, I'll leave you.' So I went away; and when I had done what business I had to do, I returned home, but did not go to bed that night, nor could not sleep, but sometimes walked up and down, and sometimes prayed and cried to the Lord, who said unto me, 'Thou seest how young people go together into vanity and old people into the earth, and Thou must forsake all, both young and old, and keep out of all and be a stranger unto all.'

Then, at the command of God, on the 9th day of the Seventh Month [September, since prior to the calendar reforms of 1752, March was the first month], 1643, I left my relations and brake off all familiarity or fellowship with young or old.[2]

He wandered southward to London, and back again to Leicestershire, occupying most of two years in the process. He must have worked from time to time, but he speaks only of temptations and despair and of going to many a priest to look for comfort but finding no comfort from them.

Among those he consulted was one Richard Abel of Mancetter in Warwickshire. Fox 'reasoned with him about the ground of despair and temptations, but he was ignorant of my condition and he bid me take tobacco and sing psalms'.[3] Dr Cradock of Coventry was asked about despair and temptations and how troubles came to be wrought in man; searching questions to which he replied by asking Fox who were Christ's father and mother. In the middle of this interesting if somewhat academic discussion 'as we were talking together in his garden, the alley being narrow, I chanced, in turning, to set my foot on the side of a bed, at which the man was in such a rage as if his house had been on fire. And thus all our discourse was lost and I went away in sorrow worse than I was when I came.'[4]

A third priest, John Machin of Atherstone 'would needs give me some physic and I was to have been let blood, but they could not get one drop of blood from me ... my body being as it were dried up with sorrow, grief and troubles ...'[5]

2. George Fox, *Journal*, 2–3. 3. ibid., p. 5. 4. ibid., p. 6. 5. ibid, p. 6.

Fox was in the grip of that utter despair which comes from finding no meaning in life, no purpose in living. His rationalization was in religious terms, despair at the evil in the world, despair that none did God's bidding, but it is fundamentally the same lack of understanding of the purpose of living which still leads to despair today, whether the rationalization is in religious or agnostic terms. And the response from the 'professors' who today are more likely to be doctors than priests is in many cases all too like that of Doctors Abel, Cradock and Machin – 'Take yourself in hand, get outside yourself, take up a hobby, I'll give you a tonic.' But, as Fox said, 'they could not reach my condition'.

About this time Fox began to have 'openings', as he called them, intuitive perceptions of the truth. The first such perception does not seem very fundamental today even though it was against the background of his time. He was convinced that 'being bred at Oxford or Cambridge did not qualify or fit a man to be a minister of Christ'.[6] By this he meant not so much a criticism of the universities but a criticism of the concept of priesthood as something to be acquired by worldly activity, by book learning and residence, and also an implied rejection of the special position of the clergy, whereby a modicum of education ensured a man preferential treatment, particularly at law. Instead, regardless of his learning, a man was fit to be a minister of Christ if he served Christ and followed his teaching.

Then in 1647 came a deeper revelation. Fox puts it in these words:

Now after I had received that opening from the Lord that to be bred at Oxford or Cambridge was not sufficient to fit a man to be a Minister of Christ, I regarded the priests less, and looked more after the dissenting people. And among them I saw there was some tenderness, and many of them came afterwards to be convinced, for they had some openings. But as I had forsaken all the priests, so I left the separate preachers also, and those called the most experienced people; for I saw there was none among them all that could speak to my condition. And when all my hopes in

6. ibid., p. 7.

them and in all men were gone, so that I had nothing outwardly
to help me, nor could tell what to do, then, oh then, I heard a
voice which said, 'There is one, even Christ Jesus, that can speak
to thy condition', and when I heard it my heart did leap for joy.
Then the Lord did let me see why there was none upon the earth
that could speak to my condition, namely, that I might give him
all the glory: for all are concluded under sin and shut up in
unbelief as I had been, that Jesus Christ might have the pre-
eminence, who enlightens and gives grace, and faith, and power.
Thus, when God doth work who shall let [i.e. prevent] it? And
this I knew experimentally.[7]

This was the turning point. Fox was no simple soul and his
very complexity led to his having periods of uncertainty and
depression which rendered him inactive from time to time
throughout his life. Nor was he man made perfect; he had a
certain stiff pride, almost amounting to self-satisfaction at
times, particularly when he considered the Lord had dealt
justly with those who opposed him. But from this time, in
his twenty-third year, the progress towards annihilating despair was stopped short, the whole process wiped out as if it
had never been. From this time forward human fallibility
might lead him astray, into uncertainty that stopped him in
his tracks. But only for a moment. Stopped, he would gather
himself and recall his vision; indeed one suspects that he did
literally recall it, calling it back until it existed once again.

The vision of 1647 was not unique and final, and Fox continued to have 'openings', sometimes profound, sometimes
of only temporary and local significance. The difference is
only one of degree, since Fox was responding to intuitive
promptings. Once the awareness was there, the intuition
could be awakened by and directed to an intense spiritual
need or an immediate action as when he looked on the
church of St Mary at Nottingham in 1649 'and the Lord
said unto me thou must go cry against yonder great idol and
the worshippers there in'.[8] These direct instructions are
relatively easy to assess; what is much more difficult is to
disinter the true meaning of the fundamental revelation.

7. George Fox, *Journal*, 1952, p. 7.   8. ibid., p. 39.

There is a long passage in the *Journal* which seeks to explain it, but we must remember that this was written twenty-five years after the event. At such a distance in time the inner voice that said 'go cry against yonder great idol' might be remembered, but the description of an experience which was by its nature indescribable is likely to have been heavily overlaid by years of interpretative preaching and pamphlet-writing.

Indeed the tone of the *Journal* reflects the time when it was written, when Fox was the leader of an organized Society and had emerged as its dominant figure. There is an air of assurance and authority which was surely not there in 1647, but came from having seen his words justified by time. Nearly thirty years had passed, the solitary visionary had gathered followers, first a handful and then a host, and they had survived the combined assaults of Church and state. One can understand, if not excuse, a hint of self-congratulation.

What Fox said in the *Journal* is mystical and symbolic, full of remembered snatches of vision expressed in biblical terms – 'a voice which did say "Thou serpent, thou dost seek to destroy the life but canst not, for the sword which keepeth the tree of life shall destroy thee." '[9] The theme that runs through it all is the inward love and power of the divine spirit, which Fox saw as God, the universal deity, interpreted to man through Jesus Christ.

My desire after the Lord grew stronger, and zeal in the pure knowledge of God and of Christ alone, without the help of any man, book or writing ... the Lord did ... let me see his love, which was endless and eternal ... and that love did let me see myself as I was without him ... I saw many talked of the law, who had never known the law to be their schoolmaster: and many talked of the Gospel of Christ, who had never known life and immortality brought to light in them by it ... The flesh would have its liberty and the spirit would have its liberty, but the spirit is to have its liberty and not the flesh. If therefore ye quench the spirit and join to the flesh, and be servants of it, then ye are judged and tormented by the spirit, but if ye join to the spirit and serve God in it, ye have liberty and victory over the flesh and its works.[10]

9. ibid., p. 13.   10. ibid., pp. 11–18.

The flesh here is not simply the fleshy lusts of Puritanism, it is the sense of personal uniqueness, the ego. This is made very clear in the writings of early followers of Fox; Stephen Crisp was convinced with his mind and intellect but felt the inadequacy of his state; at last, at a meeting he thought 'it was but in vain to sit there with such a wandering mind as mine was ... At length, as I thought to go forth, the Lord thundered through me, saying "That which is weary must die" so I turned to my seat'.[11] And what other death than the death of the will can Camm and Audland mean when they say 'Being faithful to the Light ... it will lead you to the Death upon the Cross, and Crucify you unto the world and worldly things and raise you up into the pure Life, to follow the Lamb whethersoever he goeth ... and therefore all come to the Cross and love it and rejoyce in it.'[12]

The interpretation that Fox put upon the Christian teaching brought him into fellowship with many who felt that here was the truth they had been seeking. From some of these groups, who had practised silent worship, Fox and the Children of Light, or Friends in Truth, as they called themselves, took their Meeting for Worship; sitting in silence, waiting upon God, until some member of the Meeting felt the compelling promptings of the spirit to spoken ministry. But as Robert Barclay said, '... though there be not a word spoken, yet is the true spiritual worship performed'.[13] The worship was so intense, the spiritual exercise so profound, that some shook and quivered under stress and earned for the Children of Light or Friends in Truth the nickname of 'Quakers'. The nickname has stuck.

It is important to remember that Quakerism was not in fact offering anything completely original. The essential insight was not new, and while the combination of beliefs and practices was novel, the elements were all to be found in earlier groups, particularly in the Anabaptists, the Particular Baptists and the Familists, the sect founded by

11. Stephen Crisp, *Journal*, 1694, p. 19, 'Collected Writings'.
12. Camm and Audland, *Works*, 1689, pp. 257-8.
13. Robert Barclay, *Apology*, 1678, Proposition 1, 155.

Henry Nicholas in 1530 in Holland whose writings were in Fox's library at his death.

The concept of the inward light was expressed by Nicholas in terms acceptable to any Quaker, and the Familists were very Quaker in their use of silence in their meetings (they were not alone in this), in their rejection of war and oaths and their insistence on plain speech. The Particular Baptists opposed tithes and 'Hireling preachers' and extended the functions of the laity to include women among their preachers; the Anabaptists rejected oaths and war; and even the Ranters, though they had a reputation for lack of balance leading to excess, contributed something of the doctrine of the free spirit, the indwelling God.

The mystical doctrine of the inward light was fundamental, but the outward practices tended to attract more attention, and to be given more importance than they deserved. These practices were all justified in theological terms, often with convenient biblical support, but there is a hint of plain radicalism in some of them. They must have struck a ready response in the independently-minded North-country people among whom the movement first grew; people who liked plain speech and plain clothes, and had no time for courtly flourishes and deferment to social superiors. Yet these practices attached themselves firmly to Quakerism and were seen as stemming directly and inescapably from the spiritual attitude.

In Fox's *Journal* there is an exposition which starts 'Now I was sent to turn people from darkness to the light that they might receive Christ Jesus . . .'; two pages later the mysticism gives way to a direct concern for the widows, the fatherless and the beggars, and then to:

And I was to bring people off from Jewish ceremonies and from heathenish fables and from men's inventions and windy doctrines by which they blowed the people about this way and the other way, from sect to sect; and all their beggarly rudiments, with their schools and colleges for making Ministers of Christ, who are indeed ministers of their own making but not Christ's; and from all their images and crosses and sprinkling of infants, with all their holy days (so called) and all their vain traditions, which they had gotten up since the apostles' days, which the Lord's power was against, and in the dread and authority thereof I was moved to declare against them all, and against all that preached and not freely, as being such as had not received freely from Christ.

Moreover when the Lord sent me forth into the world, he forbade me to put off my hat to any, high or low; and I was required to 'thee' and 'thou' all men and women, without any respect to rich or poor, great or small. And as I travelled up and down, I was not to bid people 'good morrow' or 'good evening', neither might I bow or scrape with my leg to anyone; and this made the sects and professions to rage.[14]

Indeed it did more than that; refusal to swear oaths, or to take off the hat or to use the second person plural as a sign of deference became the distinguishing sign of a Quaker and a frequent excuse for persecution. And the early years of Quakerism were indeed years of persecution.

14. George Fox, *Journal*, pp. 34–6.

CHAPTER 2

Great Days and Great Trials

Fox had his first great 'opening' in 1647. It was followed by a
period of coming to terms with his insight, and developing
into an itinerant preacher. He felt commanded to turn
people to the inward light, but at the same time this teaching
was in his mind completely associated with the rejection of
'men's inventions' ... (which included the separated priesthood, all sacraments and ceremonies, manners and customs)
and the need to

> cry for justice ... and in warning such as kept public houses ...
> that they should not let people have more drink than would do
> them good, and in testifying against their wakes or feasts ... and
> in markets I was made to declare against their deceitful mer-
> chandising, and cheating and cozening, warning all to deal
> justly, and to speak the truth, and to let their yea be yea and
> their nay be nay ... I was moved also to cry against all sorts
> of music and against mountebanks playing tricks on their
> stages. ...[1]

It was not therefore a simple matter of preaching a new doctrine, proclaiming a spiritual truth. The spiritual truth carried with it a programme of social reform, puritanical in its
rejection of feasts and fun and music as encouraging vanity
and looseness, but essentially concerned with justice and,
most of all, sincerity and integrity.

The first to share his outlook seem to have been some
former Baptists in Nottinghamshire; one of their number,
Elizabeth Hooton, is usually given as the first convert to
Quakerism, though it was many years before there was an
organized society and there can be no precision about who
was, or was not, a Quaker in those first years. Certainly
Elizabeth Hooton was an early and staunch supporter of
Fox. At this stage he was speaking mainly to the separatists
and Seekers, those small groups of concerned people who

1. George Fox, *Journal*, ed. J. L. Nickalls, C.U.P., 1952, pp. 37–8.

had broken all associations with the churches and the sects and were looking for a new insight. Many of these groups sat in silence, in hope that the pentacostal fire would descend and renew them; in such meetings Fox sat, and when he spoke it seemed as if their longings were fulfilled. From such a meeting, in Nottingham, he went down to the church and spoke out in the middle of the sermon, and was arrested for the first time, though on that occasion he was released without trial.

He was beaten, put in the stocks and stoned out of Mansfield-Woodhouse after speaking in church (the law allowed any to speak after the sermon, though Fox seems to have spoken whenever he was moved) and in October 1650 he was charged with blasphemy at Derby, and imprisoned for nearly a year. It was one of the magistrates at Derby who first applied the nickname 'Quaker' to Fox, in allusion to the quaking and trembling which came on those who were moved by the Holy Spirit.[2]

After his Derby imprisonment, his support in the Midlands fell away, and he moved into Yorkshire, though not before a mood of religious exaltation had caused him to walk without his shoes through the streets of Lichfield crying, 'Woe unto the bloody city of Lichfield.' In the north he found men and women of high quality: Richard Farnsworth, Mary and Thomas Aldam, and James Nayler. '. . . I was at the plough, meditating on the things of God, and suddenly I heard a Voice, saying unto me, "Get thee out from thy kindred and from thy father's house." And I heard a promise given in with it . . . that God would be with me, which promise I find made good every day.'[3] Nayler, like William Dewsbury, another early stalwart, found his way to the experience which was the heart of Fox's teaching before he met Fox, and this was perhaps the secret of the

2. And still comes; see 'On First Rising to Minister' in Part IV, Chapter 2, p. 197.

3. James Nayler, *A Collection of Sundry Books, Epistles and Papers*, 1716, p. 12, 'Christian Faith and Practice in the Experience of the Society of Friends, London Yearly Meeting of the Religious Society of Friends, 1960, § 22.

rapid spread in those early years, that Fox's words and power found a ready answer in those who had already gone a good part of the way by themselves.

For those who had gone no part of the way, for most of the priests and many of their congregations, Fox and his followers were a manifestation of error, and they were set upon by mobs, and sometimes arrested and imprisoned. But still the message spread, as one after another left home and family to travel and preach.

In the May of 1652 Fox crossed the Pennines and spoke at a meeting on the open hillside of Pendle Hill; in June, he met with the Westmorland Seekers, preaching in Sedbergh in the open churchyard, and addressing large gatherings on Firbank Fell. In this community centred at Preston Patrick, the leaders were Francis Howgill and John Audland; to them also Fox came as an illumination of their pre-existent condition. Great numbers of people were convinced; those few weeks of 1652 turned Fox into the leader of a movement, into a permanent influence in religious and social history. The Westmorland Seekers were men well grounded in the Bible, men of courage and independence who had refused to go along with accepted beliefs that were meaningless to them. They brought spiritual and intellectual strength to the movement, and they also contributed the silent Meeting as a framework in which the individual could minister as the spirit moved him, though we should not be deceived into imagining that the Meetings in the north were anything like a Quaker Meeting today. Fox might sit in silence for some long time '... in which time of silence F(rancis) H(owgill) seemed uneasy, and pulled out his Bible and opened it, and stood up several times, sitting down again and closing his book, a dread and fear being upon him ...',[4] yet when he did speak, it might be for three hours together.

From Preston Patrick, Fox went on to Swarthmoor Hall, near Ulverston. The owner, Judge Thomas Fell, was away, but his home was known as a place of resort for ministers and religious people, and his wife, Margaret Fell, was a

4. *The First Publishers of Truth*, edited for the Friends Historical Society by Norman Penney, 1907, p. 244.

Seeker, though she also attended church at this time. It was Margaret Fell who received Fox, and the next day, when he came into the church and spoke, she was deeply moved. Some weeks later Judge Fell came back from circuit to find his wife and household convinced and his neighbours in high alarm at the whole episode. Fell showed his character in the days that followed; despite the fervent emotionalism in which it was expressed, he recognized the inherent quality of the teaching, and after quiet and sober consideration, he invited the Quakers to use the Hall. From that time forward it was the pivot of the organization, though Judge Fell himself never moved from his position of sympathetic observation.

Throughout the following years, the movement grew in the northern counties, though not without opposition, sometimes from mob violence, and sometimes from the magistracy, frightened at this disturbing manifestation and often urged by the priests to convict for blasphemy. And blasphemy was easily found in Friends' attempts to put into the language of orthodox seventeenth-century religion the concept of the indwelling presence of God. Fox, asked by the magistrates of Carlisle if he was the son of God, replied 'Yes', and replied 'Yes' also to the question whether he had seen God's face. It was hardly surprising that he found himself back in prison, where also went many of his companions, committed for a variety of offences and, as the Commonwealth became more of a police state, for no offence in particular.

Fox himself met Cromwell, and impressed him; the Protector was never violently anti-Quaker and on several occasions intervened to moderate the attacks on members of the sect or to secure their release. He was, however, first and foremost a political leader and he did not let his sympathy for independent religious thought influence his trend to authoritarian government. Nor was it easy to maintain a liberal attitude towards a movement which gathered large Meetings, generated an enthusiasm which spread like a bush fire, and gave rise to excesses such as 'going naked for a sign', for which, for example, two young women Quakers were whipped at Oxford in 1654. At the same time, missionaries from the North were carrying a message over the rest of Britain, and setting up strong Meetings, particularly in Bristol and in London.

Over the later years of the Commonwealth, Friends were in Ireland, North and Central America, the West Indies, and Holland, and missions also travelled to Jerusalem and to see the Sultan of Turkey, who received Mary Fisher very considerately, listened to what she had to say, and commented that it was the truth, and that he felt great respect for one who had come so far with a message from God. A less charitable reception greeted two other Quaker travellers, John Perrot and John Luffe, at the hands of the Roman Catholic authorities in Italy. Luffe was hanged and Perrot spent some three years in prison and the madhouse.

One of the saddest episodes of this time occurred in 1656 when the first wave of persecution was declining. James Nayler, one of the first to join Fox, was the victim of a group of unstable disciples who played upon his emotional temperament. After a brilliant ministry in London, he seems to have become physically and mentally overwrought. After some extravagant episodes at Bristol, Friends persuaded him to go to Launceston to see Fox, who was once again in gaol; but Nayler was thrown into prison at Exeter. Here Fox came, on his release from Launceston, exhausted from eight months of rigorous imprisonment. No wonder that emotions were strained to breaking point, destroying all hope of a reconciliation. Nayler, on his release, returned towards Bristol, entering the city on a horse, with his followers singing 'Holy, holy, holy, Lord God of Israel' in a miserable parody of the entry of Christ into Jerusalem. The thousand or more Bristol Quakers took no part in this episode; and Nayler and his six companions were immediately arrested.

Nayler seems to have taken a negative attitude throughout these events. One suspects that his mental exhaustion and physical privations had led to an apathy in which he allowed the exaggerated imaginations of his companions to cast him for the role of the new Christ. The strangest part of this strange tale is that, instead of a normal trial, Nayler was taken up to London and tried by a Committee of Parliament, being finally sentenced by the House, quite unconstitutionally, to a barbarous composite punishment involving the pillory, several whippings, branding on the forehead and boring through the tongue with a hot iron, and subsequent imprisonment.

The effect of this incident on public opinion was to strengthen the distrust of Quakerism and the tendency to identify it with extremist sects such as the Ranters, and with politically subversive movements. It also gave rise within the movement to divisions, self-questioning and doubt.

At the same time, while Nayler was in prison and British Friends were generally in some disarray, Massachusetts passed a law against the Quakers, who were to be banished, and hanged if they returned. A first group (including Mary Dyer of Rhode Island) was banished, whereupon William Robinson and Marmaduke Stephenson went to Massachusetts, were banished, and together with Mary Dyer, returned to challenge the law. The men were hanged and Mary Dyer was reprieved at the last moment, but six months later she went once more to Boston and shared their fate.[5]

Meanwhile, in May 1660, with the Restoration the King had come into his own again. All was to be changed; there was to be no more Puritanism, and no more Presbyterianism. Very shortly, there was a strong effort on the part of the Established Church to put down dissent, and on the part of the new government to suppress all manner of plots against the state. Once again, the Quakers, more than other dissenters, came under pressure, particularly through the Acts of 1662 and 1664 which made all meetings for worship of more than four people (other than Anglican services) illegal. There followed a period of persecution, more persistent and systematic than in the days of the Commonwealth. Meetings were broken up, often violently, and Friends were repeatedly fined, in an effort to destroy them economically. But the few

5. Is it an example of Charles II's wry sense of humour that when his attention was drawn to the barbarities of the Massachusetts authorities he chose as the bearer of his displeasure a New England Friend who had been banished from Massachusetts?

intervening years of relative peace had given the movement a chance to work out its attitudes. The marathon preaching, the evangelism, the singing and shouting which were not unknown in the early period were now replaced by a quiet conviction. Friends could still preach to win if the occasion demanded and the spirit moved them, but before attacks by sheriff's officers they sat quiet with their hats on, if necessary while the building was pulled down round their ears. If their Meeting House was destroyed they met in the streets; if the men were imprisoned the women and children still met; on occasion, first the men and then the women of the Meeting were arrested, but the children still continued the illegal assembly. From 1662 until the Toleration Act of 1689 the movement continued and grew against a background of persecution. At least 21,000 Friends suffered fines or imprisonment, many of them more than once, and at least 450 died in prison or as the result of their sufferings in prison. But whatever was done to them the Quakers held firm.

Although the movement had gained its first strength from the yeomen of the north it reached to all classes of society. Mary Fisher, who visited the Sultan of Turkey, had been a servant; Isaac Penington, author of some of the most attractive Quaker writings, was the son of a Lord Mayor of London; and William Penn, the courtier son of the Admiral Penn of Pepys Diary, became a leading figure after his convincement in 1667. It was this wide social range which in part alarmed the authorities; it prevented them from treating the Quakers as just a bunch of ignorant religious eccentrics and gave credence to the idea that there might be plotters among them. To the religious establishment the threat was more real. There was a fundamental threat from the doctrine of direct inner experience of the divine, the theme of God in every man, and the more practical threat of a belief which found no place for the university-trained priest. Much of the attack was associated, of course, with misrepresentation, both in that the formulations which the Quakers, in the fire and glory of their first experience, used to describe the divine presence, were seen as blasphemy (as in the case of Fox at Carlisle) and in that their insistence on God's presence in the living individual was seen as a denial of Christ.

In fact, early Quakers spent much time trying to convince their contemporaries that they were true Christians, that Quakerism was primitive Christianity revived. They could in truth be none other. They had found the one true source of spiritual strength, and since they lived in a Christian civilization they saw their experience in Christian terms. (To say that they lived in a Christian civilization is not to say that Christianity in any sense prevailed, merely that its mythology was an integral part of the mental furniture of every man. This much at least was true of the western world until recent times.) More recently, much of their writing has been scrutinized and worked over in an effort to establish that Quakerism is only properly so called if it is tied to a particular view of the role of Christ. Discussions of this nature are of limited interest; it is enough for the historical perspective to say that the early Quakers did not see their experience as conflicting with the essential teachings of the Christian faith or the words of the Scriptures; having established these negative points they were more concerned to preach the inward light which they described as stemming from Christ, being Christ the Light.

[Christ] . . . hath given us a Light, which is the Life in himself; and saith believe in the Light so we Believe in that which Christ has given us . . . namely the Light, which is the Life in him, by which we may see him . . . and this light shining in our hearts, it gives us the knowledge of the glory of God in the Face of Christ Jesus . . . having the witness in ourselves that God is true in all his Promises and Prophets and Types and Shadows in the law, concerning his Son, Christ Jesus . . .[6]

That example from Fox is a fair example of the tautological rondo form in which their beliefs were so often described. The important part is not of course the common heritage of Christianity but the uncommon element which alarmed the establishment; the recurrent heresy of direct

6. George Fox, 'Concerning the Antiquity of the People of God called Quakers', quoted by Maurice Creasey in 'The Quaker Interpretation of the Significance of Christ', _Quaker Religious Thought_, Vol. I, No. 2, 1959.

knowledge of God. Whether or not the Light was Christ, the dangerous thing was to see the Light, and to follow it.

For all that this was the essential conflict between the Quakers and authority, there were also similar conflicts within the movement. The first of any significance involved John Perrot, who had been locked up by the Italian authorities. He spent only a short time in England after his release, and then, having been imprisoned here too, accepted release on condition of leaving the country and went to Barbados. During the period of his short stay he rallied some support for the view that there was no necessity or rule that the hat should be taken off when praying or preaching, that this too should be left to the working of the spirit. Orthodox Quaker practice was that one took the hat off to speak to no man, but one uncovered to speak with God. The point itself may seem trivial but there were deeper differences beneath the surface and the controversy of the hat produced many corrosive pamphlets. Later, from 1675 onwards, came the Wilkinson-Story controversy, a matter of somewhat greater importance, though still, at root, concerned with the conflict beween liberty and authority.

The origin of this dispute was in the resentment felt by Preston Patrick Friends when they were criticized, in the persecution following the Second Conventicle Act of 1670, for meeting in 'ghylls, woods, and unaccustomed places'. The Act offered inducements to informers, and Preston Patrick Friends saw no virtue in putting money into such hands by meeting openly. Yet Friends generally put great store by open steadfastness at whatever cost, and criticized the Preston Patrick Meeting accordingly; which resulted in a coolness between them and the rest of the Society. An added irritation was the bad feeling between Margaret Fox[7] and John Story, leader with John Wilkinson of the Preston Patrick group.

This difference developed over Fox's setting up of separate women's business meetings (which were intended to bring women into the business side of things by giving them

7. Judge Fell had died in 1658 and in 1669 George Fox had married Margaret Fell.

special charge of matters affecting women and children,
marriage to non-Friends and finding places for Friends who
were servants), and also over Fox's general organization,
which, they argued, was giving the opportunity for authoritarianism to develop. Wilkinson and Story favoured appointed delegates for business meetings, possibly because
without such a system the emerging élite of the Society
could too easily dominate. They also took a less rigid attitude on tithes, as against a tendency to ask for a declared
refusal to pay as a condition of participating in business
meetings, and saw no reason to carry steadfastness against
persecution to the lengths of enriching informers. They opposed, too, the 'groaning, singing or sounding' while another
spoke or prayed.

The Yearly Meeting of ministers came down firmly
against Wilkinson and Story, even to the point of approving
'serious sighing, sensible groaning and reverent singing'. But
all this, as in the earlier 'hat' controversy, was really subsidiary to the basic question of authority and the individual.
Increasingly, Friends were losing touch with the essential
experience, were seeing their outward testimonies and organization as things of value in themselves, where once the
value had been in the inner experience, and the outward testimonies had been an inevitable consequence. Now, it was
not the light within that drove a man to refuse to pay tithes,
it was a rule if he was to be counted a Quaker. Wilkinson
and Story put the issue plainly when they asked whether 'all
God's people ought not to be left to the manifestation of His
Spirit and truth in their own hearts, and whether, since there
were diversities of gifts, a judgement given forth by part of
the members of Christ's body could be a bond upon any
other part further than their understandings were illuminated thereby'. The true answer was Penington's – 'The
Light, Spirit and Power in the Church is never contrary to
the Light, Spirit and Power in any member, but always one
with it and a cherisher and preserver of what God begets and
which answers His witness in any.'[8]

8. Isaac Penington, *Works*, 1681, Part II, p. 435, in W. C. Braithwaite, *Second Period of Quakerism*, C.U.P., 1955, p. 348.

The outcome of the controversy was a fairly balanced position, not too far from Penington's attitude, neither strongly authoritarian nor wildly individualistic. In a way it was a lost opportunity; perhaps, because the leaders were ageing and worn by persecution, the basic point of dispute was not argued through and the movement took into the next century a leaning towards imposed discipline which was incompatible with the doctrine of the inner light. This is the reason for describing internal conflicts in the movement when its growth and spread during the same period makes so much more invigorating a story; for this same conflict was to recur over the years.

Nevertheless, the growth and spread were considerable. In 1671–3 Fox, with twelve other Friends, travelled to America and the West Indies, meeting with Friends and with the Indians. Elizabeth Hooton was one of the party, but she died soon after reaching Jamaica; the first of Fox's followers could follow no more. The journey was adventurous but triumphant, giving a great injection of strength to several scattered communities. In 1682 William Penn took a grant of land in the New World and set up the state of Pennsylvania, an experiment in the application of Quaker principles to government. Pennsylvania was a Quaker state for eighty years; under its government, no cheats were practised on the Indians, who had equality with colonists by law, and here, in 1688, German settlers first urged the inconsistency of Quakerism and slavery. Without giving the full history of the 'holy experiment' it is worth pointing out that Pennsylvania *worked*; the Quaker propensity for applying their principles where they could, against the general view that principles are best kept pure and unapplied, developed early.

In England, meanwhile, another wave of persecution broke out, mainly directed to extorting fines and penalties. Penn emerged particularly as a champion of civil liberties – those same liberties he was enshrining in the Pennsylvanian Constitution – and under his influence the Quakers moved from an other-worldly disregard of the law to its use as a weapon of policy. The Meeting for Sufferings, subsequently the executive committee of the Society, was set up not merely to relieve the sufferings of Friends, but 'to endeavour for relief by the Law of the Land to stop the destroyer'. These first steps in lobbying led to greater understanding in political circles of the Quakers' position, and to increasing general sympathy for them.

Although James II himself had been a friend of Penn and well disposed to Quakers, it was not until the accession of William and Mary, in 1689, that the passing of the Toleration Act put an end to intensive persecution of Quakers. There still remained the conflict over tithes, for non-payment of which Quakers were to have their goods distrained upon, and were to be imprisoned on occasion, for many years to come; equally they were to be imprisoned for refusal to serve in the militia and, at a later stage, for refusing call-up under the Military Service Act. But persecution for meeting, for not taking oaths, for keeping one's hat on, for using the second person singular, for what was called blasphemy – persecution, that is, out of sheer bloody-mindedness, because Quakers were different – was at an end.

So also was the first great period of Quakerism. Fox died in 1691, having made two trips to the continent of Europe in 1677 and 1684, and most of the other leaders of the early days were dead by the end of the century. William Penn lingered on, burdened with the problems of his colony and the complexity of his personal affairs – he was naïve in his judgement of people and over-trusting in worldly affairs, and towards the end of his life his mind clouded. Margaret Fox lived on at Swarthmoor, but only until 1702. Nayler, Penington and Dewsbury were all gone, and many others with them, worn down by years of travelling, by repeated imprisonment and by violent handling from the mob.

The full history of the first fifty years is not to be compressed in a handful of pages. I have chosen to stress the development of the message and the conflicts over its interpretation, rather than the actions and sufferings of the individuals, because this aspect is more relevant to the general approach of this book. It is important to remember that the message was received and declared throughout the most troubled period of English political history, and that the background to the growth of the movement from one man and his insights to some 40,000 or more was that of continued arrest and imprisonment in appalling conditions; often in medieval dungeons or roofless holes in the walls of old castles, at the will of magistrates dominated by fear of papists and plotters, and in the custody of gaolers who beggar description. There was one mitigating circumstance, which prevented the persecution from being inhuman; it was inefficient, generally unorganized and waywardly erratic. Although Acts of Parliament were passed proscribing assemblies, the way in which they were applied was at the discretion of the local authorities; although punishments were barbarous they were sometimes mitigated, as when during the final stages of Nayler's sentence a Friend was allowed to hold the executioner's hand so that the lash of the whip fell lightly. Prisons were vile, but prisoners were allowed some freedoms; visitors came pretty well as they pleased, meetings were held in prison. For all this, and even if (apart from the Massachusetts hangings) there were no judicial killings, the record of sufferings endured is an irrefutable evidence of the strength and validity of the inner experience which flooded the early Quakers. Even their persecutors were impressed. When the King asked the Governor of Dover whether he had dispersed all the sectarian meetings, the Governor was forced to admit 'the Quakers the devil himself could not. For if that he did imprison them or break them up, they would meet again, and if he should beat them, and knock them down or kill some of them, all was one; they would meet, and not resist, again.' And what of the 144 Friends who petitioned the House of Commons in 1659?

We, in love of our brethren that lie in prisons and houses of correction and dungeons, and many in fetters and irons, and many have been cruelly beat by the cruel gaolers, and many have been persecuted to death, and have died in prison, and many lie sick and weak in prison and on straw, so we, in love to our brethren, do offer up our bodies and selves to you, for to put us as lambs into the same dungeons and houses of correction . . . and do stand ready a sacrifice for to go into their places . . . that they may go forth and that they may not die in prison as many of the brethren are dead already.

They were one for one for every Quaker in prison at that time, and many of them had already suffered on their own account.

Nor was the faith apocalyptic that sustained these men and women; it was not the promise of joys to come, of a new heaven and a new earth. It was a present experience, a self-validating experience, an awareness and conviction that could not be denied. 'All things were new, and all creation gave another smell unto me than before, beyond what words can utter,' said Fox. 'Be patterns, be examples in all countries, places, islands, nations, wherever you come, that your courage and life may preach among all sorts of people, and to them; then you will come to walk cheerfully over the world, answering that of God in every one.'

And Francis Howgill:

Why gad you abroad? Why trim yourselves with the saints' words, when you are ignorant of life? ... Return home to within, sweep your houses all, the groat is there, the little leaven is there, the grain of mustard seed you will see, which the Kingdom of God is like ... and here you will see your Teacher not removed into a corner but present when you are upon your beds and about your labour, convincing, instructing, leading, correcting, judging and giving peace to all that love and follow him.[9]

And in 'some fruits of solitude' from William Penn:

The humble, meek, merciful, just, pious and devout souls are everywhere of one religion ... the less form in religion the better, since God is a Spirit; for the more mental our worship, the more adequate to the nature of God; the more silent, the more suitable to the language of a spirit.[10]

And finally, the last words of James Nayler:

There is a spirit which I feel that delights to do no evil, nor to

9. Francis Howgill, 'The Dawnings of the Gospel Day', *Works*, 1670, p. 46, 'Christian Faith and Practice', § 176.

10. William Penn, *A Collection of the Works*, 1726, Vol. I, p. 842, 'Christian Faith and Practice', § 227.

revenge any wrong, but delights to endure all things, in hope to enjoy its own in the end. Its hope is to outlive all wrath and contention, and to weary out all exaltation and cruelty, or whatever is of a nature contrary to itself. It sees to the end of all temptations. As it bears no evil in itself, so it conceives none in thoughts to any other. If it be betrayed, it bears it, for its ground and spring is the mercies and forgiveness of God. Its crown is its meekness, its life is everlasting love unfeigned; it takes its kingdom with entreaty and not with contention, and keeps it by lowliness of mind. In God alone it can rejoice, though none else regard it, or can own its life . . . When I was weak Thou stayedst me with Thy Hand, that in Thy time Thou mightst present me to the world of Thy strength in which I stand, and cannot be moved. Praise the Lord, O my soul. Let this be written for those that come after. Praise the Lord.[11]

11. James Nayler, *A Collection of Sundry Books, Papers and Epistles*, 1716, p. 12, 'Christian Faith and Practice', § 25.

CHAPTER 3

Consolidation

ONE of the last public actions of Margaret Fox was to protest against the growing tendency among Friends to rigid rules on dress and behaviour, to framing themselves 'according to outward prescriptions and orders, and deny eating and drinking with our neighbours [at christening feasts and funerals] in so much that poor Friends is mangled in their minds ... we must look at no colours, nor make anything that is changeable colours as the hills are, nor sell them, nor wear them, but we must be all in one dress and one colour: this is a silly poor Gospel.'[1] For what had been an outward expression of an inward prompting, an eschewing of ornament and show the better to serve God by devoting effort to his work without bothering with fashion or wasting time and money on finery, had begun to fossilize into a rule of plain dress, and that the plain dress of the period already past.

In part, this was an inevitable consequence of second-generation Quakerism. In place of those who had themselves experienced the inward revelation, the movement now consisted of their children, who had been brought up in the faith, and who had not necessarily had a corresponding experience themselves. They looked for forms and rules that would preserve the faith, and in so doing they moved towards the institutionalization which the founders had protested against. Other influences helped in this direction. Thus, though the vocal ministry in Quaker Meetings was (and is) free for all to share, it was recognized that some Friends had a greater gift in the ministry than others. These Friends, known as 'publick Friends' were often un-acknowledged leaders; but problems of unacceptable ministry led by the 1720s to regulations for the formal 're-

1. MS. quoted in 'Christian Faith and Practice in the Experience of the Society of Friends', London Yearly Meeting of the Religious Society of Friends, 1960, § 401.

cording' by Monthly Meetings of the gift of ministry. Moreover, elders were being appointed 'to advise and counsel ministers', and with the establishment by the middle of the eighteenth century of a hierarchy of Meetings of ministers and elders (Yearly, Quarterly and Monthly) the spiritual life of the Society had been handed over to an élite which tended, like most élites, to conservatism. By the latter part of the century Quakerism had been much affected by quietism, and leading ministers preached the worthlessness of reason, and the need for the mind to be emptied, like an Aeolian harp through which the winds of God might blow unhindered. This in turn led to a belittling of the vocal ministry and to the cult of absolute silence in Quaker ministry.

Nor were the recording of ministers and the appointment of elders the only evidence of formalization. In 1660, when the justices and captains had come to break up a general meeting at Skipton they were shown the accounts of collections for the poor 'that none of them should be chargeable to their parishes' and were made to confess that the Quakers did their work for them 'and so they passed away lovingly and commended Friends' practice'. But Quakers were human, and argued as hotly as parish overseers as to which Meeting should give relief. The result of such disputes was a series of efforts by Yearly Meeting to provide administrative guides, culminating in the 1737 'Rules of Settlement' which bore a marked similarity to the old poor law. The following year saw *Christian and brotherly advices*, a substantial and authorized volume of official advice and regulation approved by the Yearly Meeting. All this was a necessary response to the demands of the situation, but at the same time it tended to make the Society more and more preoccupied with the minutiae of procedure. Through the queries, answered in writing four times in each year by Monthly Meetings, the Yearly Meeting kept a watchful eye on departures from the norm, and the discipline required disownment for a whole variety of offences from marriage before a priest (the only way, when it came to the point, in which a Quaker could marry a non-Quaker) to paying tithe, hiring a substitute in the militia or bankruptcy.

Another characteristic of the period was the movement away from the land. Though direct persecution had ceased, Quakers were still at risk through their refusal to pay tithes. It is difficult to be sure how far this stemmed from religious motivation and how far from the egalitarian roots of Quakerism; objection to compulsory support of the parson is deep-rooted in the character of the English yeoman. 'We've cheated the parson, we'll cheat him again, for why should the blockhead have one in ten?' sing the chorus in Purcell's *King Arthur*. The Quakers found support in such texts as Matthew x, 8 – 'You received without cost; give without charge'; they linked their refusal to support the Established Church with their insistence on freedom 'for any person, moved by the Holy Spirit of God, to preach the doctrine of the glorious gospel of our Lord and Saviour Jesus Christ freely'.[2] There were repeated urgings to steadfastness, and warnings against entering into arrangements, such as paying an increased rent in return for exemption from direct tithes, and innumerable cases of distraint and forced sale. However, tithes pressed more heavily on agricultural communities than on those engaged in business, and so inevitably, since adherence to the testimony would ultimately ruin a farmer, more and more Friends moved off the land.

Another principle, that of letting your yea be yea and your nay be nay, led them to adopt fixed price dealing, and so to contribute to the decline of haggling over prices. This was gratefully welcomed by those who dealt with them, who also came to recognize the advantages given by traders whose integrity could be relied on. Hence Quaker traders were successful, and they also became trusted keepers of other people's money. The great banks, Barclays, Hoares, Lloyds and Gurneys in particular, were Quaker houses. As it happened, the early eighteenth century was not a bad time to leave the land. Trade was expanding, America was being opened up, and the increasingly close-knit Quaker community spanned the Atlantic. Some of the best-known Quaker names are associated with the cocoa and chocolate trade, built on the interest of Joseph Fry, an apothecary,

2. *Book of Extracts*, 1802, p. 185.

in the dietary use of chocolate. Quaker shippers, millers, brewers, ironmasters (the Darbys of Coalbrookdale were Quakers), smelters of silver, lead and zinc, middlemen in the textile trade – together they form a considerable part of the history of the Industrial Revolution.

This background of formalization, of the development of a closed society that was numerically at first static and then declining, but growing in wealth and dynastically inter-linked, must be kept in mind when considering the develop-ment of the Society in the eighteenth century. It is often spoken of as a period of quietism, under the mistaken im-pression that quietism is the same as lethargy. Even if it were, the phrase would not be apt. It is true that many Meet-ings were silent, that due caution became excessive caution, so that even the most ordinary utterance was hedged and conditioned to guard against any word which might, on mature reflection and deeper inquiry, seem to be, or to have the possibility of being, less than the truth. The Quakers' plain dress became obsolete dress, their plain speech became archaic speech, and guidance from within was almost sub-merged under admonition from without. For all that, it was not a stagnant period; much was done of great value, and the essential flame was kept alight.

At the beginning of the century, John Bellers was fol-lowing Penn's lead in exploring the application of Quaker principles to political and social organization. He had no colony to practise on, and therefore left only a number of pamphlets, setting out advanced schemes for the employ-ment of the poor, for the treatment of criminals and – a theme that Penn had already considered – the bringing together of nation states into an international organization for the avoidance of war. Beller's direct influence was small (though the Clerkenwell workhouse, founded on his prin-ciples, later became, after various vicissitudes, Friends' School, Saffron Walden). But his vision probably helped to direct Friends towards a deeper concern with the nature of society. The development of such a trend was also a probable consequence of growing involvement in trade and the move-ment away from agriculture.

Another concern developed before the turn of the century was the mainspring of Friends' activity for nearly one hundred and fifty years. It was German Friends in Pennsylvania who had first gone beyond Fox's paternalistic attitude to slaves, and had questioned the whole moral basis of slavery. If it was wrong to enslave the American Indians (and Penn had founded Pennsylvania on dealing with Indians as equals) was it not equally wrong to enslave the African Negro? This feeling of concern arose first in America, where the evil was most apparent, but slavery was increasingly censured in England too, from early in the eighteenth century. By the middle of the century, the movement against slavery was growing on both sides of the Atlantic. In New England Tom Hazard, given a farm by his wealthy father, had refused to accept the slaves who went with it, and John Woolman, one of the most gentle and saintly of American Quakers, had been brought to a crisis of decision by being asked to write a bill of sale for a Negro woman. He wrote the bill – but protested his objection to the principle, and from this grew his writing and preaching against slavery which was a keystone of the Quaker protest in America.

By 1761 London Yearly Meeting had decided to disown Quakers involved in the slave trade. The latter half of the century saw the disentangling of American Friends from slavery. It also witnessed the building up of the abolitionist movement, which led to the Acts of Parliament forbidding slave trading by British subjects and ultimately to the abolition of slavery in British dominions. Without rehearsing the details, it is worth pointing out that this was a classic piece of social lobbying. It started with the consciences of individuals, became a matter of the conscience of the Society of Friends, and then of the conscience of the civilized world. The Quakers were the core of the movement, but they joined with all types of liberal opinion. One in particular, Thomas Clarkson, came to know Quakers so well that, when the struggle was done, he wrote a *Portraiture of Quakerism*,[3] for he could not envisage any later issue giving a better

3. Thomas Clarkson, *Portraiture of Quakerism*, Longman, Hurst, Rees & Orme, 1806.

opportunity for an outsider to come to know and understand these separated people.

If, in the history of the Quakers, the campaign against slavery was a central feature of the century, it was not their only social activity. The Clerkenwell workhouse was not altogether successful, but in 1779 Dr John Fothergill brought about the foundation of Ackworth School in Yorkshire to offer a boarding education for children 'whose parents are not in affluence', and in 1796 William Tuke founded The Retreat, the first hospital to treat the mentally ill with kindness and love rather than whips and chains.

Inevitably, the eighteenth century tends to be looked on as a dull period of Quaker history. Its major figures are not heroic bringers of new vision like Fox and his associates, but gentle, persistent saintly John Woolman; capable, businesslike John Fothergill; William Tuke and his beautiful and dignified wife Esther; or the successful industrialists who built the new industrial England, the Darbys, Spencers, Rawlinsons, Hanburys, Lloyds and Reynolds, or the earnest middle-class ministers who travelled incessantly and preached, usually at some length and with much quotation from Scripture. To their specially 'appointed meetings' hundreds and, on occasion, thousands would flock. But although their influence on the spiritual state of the country must not be underestimated, numbers within the Society were static or declining, for it was much easier to offend against the increasing rigidity of Quaker discipline and be disowned than to enter the Society by convincement. The fire seemed to have passed into other hands, particularly those of John Wesley and the Methodists, who were establishing the foundations of the evangelical movement.

Yet the Quakers were a living force, as their social impact shows. What is difficult is to establish the real balance between these two aspects: to define the true nature of the Society at the end of the century and to see how far it was dormant, quietist, inward-turning and obsessed with preserving its own formalized heritage, and how far it was still a vehicle for the original creative force, with its emphasis on subjective awareness of the inner divine will, and on the outward expression of that will. Two documents show how the balance lay; the *Book of Discipline* as it stood at the end of the century, and the *Portraiture of Quakerism* as drawn by Thomas Clarkson.

By the 1780s, many meetings found the manuscript *Christian and brotherly advices* issued by Yearly Meeting in 1738 difficult to use on account of subsequent additions and deletions. A thorough revision was undertaken, approved in 1782 and printed the following year, its cumbersome title *Extracts from the Minutes and Advices of the Yearly Meeting of Friends held in London* being shortened to *Book of Extracts*. A further revision took place in 1802.

The variety and excellence of the matter contained in the *Book of Extracts*, entitle the collection to attentive and repeated perusal; there is instruction for the inexperienced, and confirmation for the more advanced Christian; and while it teaches the letter of our discipline, it bears abundant testimony to the spirit in which it should be conducted – the spirit, temper and habitude of mind, which ought to be the continual clothing of such as undertake, in any way, to be the advocates of the Lord's cause.[4]

Let us see what that spirit was.

First, it consists of forty-seven articles, mostly containing a number of separate extracts from epistles and advices, filling over two hundred handsomely printed pages. Of these articles, a dozen or so are concerned with the organization of the Society; with the different levels of business meeting and with Meeting for Worship, with disciplinary procedures and appeals against them, with the form of affirmation allowed by law whereby Quakers could maintain their testimony against others without coming into conflict with the civil power, and the procedures to be followed (again in accordance with stated law) at a Quaker wedding.

Another substantial group of articles covers the distinctive testimonies of the Society, the issues on which they held different views and followed a different course from society at large. There is also a section on 'Days and Times': 'That all friends keep to the simplicity of truth, and our ancient testimony, in calling the months and days by scriptured

4. *Book of Extracts*, 1802, Introduction.

names and not by heathen' (1697). This was made more complicated by the calendar revision of 1751–2, whereby the beginning of the year was moved from March to January, and hence the numbering of the months, used by Quakers in place of the heathen names, needed revision. Yearly Meeting 1751 advised 'friends to be sound in the observance' of the direction to omit the eleven days and took the opportunity to write an essay on the pagan origin of the month names and the need to maintain a testimony against all 'remains of idolatry and superstition'.

The objections to gaming and to gravestones (held to be a vain custom) are recorded, as are the more substantial objections to war, militia service, oaths and tithes and the successive stages of the objection to slavery.

The article on 'Plainness' is of interest, both in the development of its approach and in its generality. The first extract, of 1691, advises 'that friends take care to keep to truth and plainness, in language, habit, deportment and behaviour; that the simplicity of truth in these things may not wear out or be lost in our days, nor in our posterity's.' Friends were also warned 'to avoid pride and immodesty in apparel, and all vain and superfluous fashions of the world.'

By 1739, Friends are being instructed 'to beware of adorning themselves in a manner disagreeable to the plainness and simplicity of the truth' with extensive quotations from Scripture; in 1743 they are urged to exercise plainness of speech without respect of persons, and in 1753 'it is a matter of grief and concern ... to observe how far that exemplary plainness of habit, speech and deportment ... is now departed from'. Yet, in all this there is no actual definition of plainness, or any schedule of what constituted the uniform of a Quaker. Moreover, there are surprises in store if we have accepted the stereotype view of the eighteenth-century Quaker. Under 'Mourning Habits', in addition to the expected advice against the vain custom of wearing or giving mourning and all extravagant expenses in connection with the interment of the dead, we find that Friends were cautioned against the custom of discouraging the female sex from attending the burial of their relatives, this being a 'decent token of respect, which, if health permits, it becomes both sexes to show'.

The other major group of articles is on behaviour and conduct. Friends are advised to use arbitration among themselves rather than go to law; to stay clear of involvement in politics or the corrupt and immoral practices of elections; not to defraud the revenue (though refusing to pay tithes, of course); to be careful in conduct and conversation – one delightful extract beseeches them, in their ordinary conversation, to 'let your words be few and savoury' – to eschew hunting and shooting for diversion, but to spend their leisure in serving their neighbours, not in distressing the creatures of God for their amusement.

A change of attitude towards convincement can be seen developing. At first, the emphasis is on helping those who wish to join the Society, but by the mid century there is the warning to 'lay hands on no man suddenly, nor speedily admit any ... into membership. Let the innocency of their lives and conversation first be manifested and a deputation of judicious friends be made, to inquire into the sincerity of their convincement ...'

Liberality to the poor and love and unity are enjoined. In the advice on marriage, if there is an emphasis on parental approval and wise choice, there is also a warning to parents not to make a large settlement their first and chief care. There is also a growing rigidity against marriages with non-Quakers, ending in a registering of the 'great inconsistency and pernicious effects' of marriage by a priest, and advice to Monthly Meetings to be careful in accepting acknowledgement of repentance by those who offend. The rule of disownment for marrying-out was being established.

Warnings against excessive drinking appear in the mid eighteenth century, though Friends were by no means abstainers – the list of stores put on board for three Friends sailing for Philadelphia in 1756 would have done credit to a superior grocer's shop with an off-licence. By 1797 the warnings extended to frequenting public houses: 'be cautious of remaining in them, after the purpose of business, or of refreshment, is accomplished; but to make them a resort for any other purpose – may it never need to be named among a people who profess the practice of Christian sobriety!'[5] In the section on Scripture there are good Puritan warnings against romances, playbooks and vain, idle and irreligious books.

There is a substantial section on 'Trade', but while some extracts are directed at those who are too much involved in the world ('it is not unusual ... for our gain and our convenience to clash with our testimony'), there are also cautions against running into debt, and advice for dealing with bankruptcies, a reminder that not all Friends were Gurneys or Frys. Many Quakers, having been forced out of agriculture and unable (through their objection to oaths, which closed the Universities to them) to follow professions, struggled and failed in the commercial environment.

All in all, the impression one gets is of a sober, gentle, well-intentioned people, moving towards a certain pious heaviness. It was not until 1818 that the young were warned, not simply against frivolities such as frequenting playhouses, but even against action in the cause of religion, and in promoting the Lord's work on earth; by then they were indeed becoming a peculiar people.

Let us turn now to Clarkson, writing in 1806 with a great desire 'to do them justice; for ignorance and prejudice had invented many expressions concerning them to the detriment of their character, which their conduct never gave me reason to suppose, during all my intercourse with them, to be true'.[6] He defines Quakerism as an attempt, under divine influence, at practical Christianity; and he stresses the importance the Quakers attach to their system of moral education, and to the maintenance of a coherent and consistent morality that allows of no deviations for reasons of expediency. He also emphasizes the effects of this morality when

5. A while since, I was in a public house (for the purpose of refreshment) during the lunch-break of a one-day Quaker conference. My companion, a weighty Friend, commented, 'I never thought to see the day when I couldn't get to the bar for Quakers.'

6. Thomas Clarkson, *Portraiture of Quakerism*, Vol. I, p. ii.

applied in a self-contained community as the most significant influence on the young, and enforced by a rigid disciplinary system.

Clarkson also notes that gaming, cock-fighting, cards, music, the theatre, dancing, novels, and field sports are all forbidden. In this he is more specific than the book of discipline, but we can, I think, assume that he depicts accurately the practice of his time. He lists in detail the objections to each activity; while one could predict most of them it is interesting to examine those to music, if only because today we find it difficult to see any. The most unexpected is that the practice is sedentary and harmful to health, giving rise to weak and languid constitutions and hysteria, and disqualifying the females addicted to it from becoming healthy wives and healthy mothers or the parents of a healthy progeny. The more rational objections are that it takes time from spiritual activities, that the words of songs are worldly and depraved, that its consolations are superficial and, in times of distress of spirit, can stand in the way of more deep and true consolations, and that it leads its adherents into the company of the world.

In his general comments on all these prohibitions, Clarkson points out that the Quakers base them on the spirit of Christianity, and on the conflict between worldly and spiritual pleasures, and insist that all prohibitions of what they see as evils are accompanied by an endeavour to fill the minds of their children with love of virtue. He draws attention to the success of Quaker educational methods:

... 'it is difficult to put old heads on young shoulders'. The Quakers, however, do this more effectually than any other people. It has often been observed that a Quaker-boy has an unnatural appearance ... of age above the youth of his countenance, or the stature of his person. This, however, is confessing, in some degree, in the case before us, that the discretion of age has appeared upon youthful shoulders.[7]

Clarkson describes Quaker discipline in terms of all members of the Society watching over the actions and atti-

7. Thomas Clarkson, op. cit. Vol. I, p. 169.

tudes of each other. He counters the argument that it is a system of espionage by reminding us that it was aimed at preserving virtue, and that it was accepted by those to whom it applied; and he emphasizes that it was applied without distinction, and that the action following on any backsliding – starting with private admonishment and leading in the extreme to disownment – was directed to reform, not punishment. In describing the business meetings, he draws attention to the fact that issues are decided 'not by the influence of numbers but by the weight of religious character ... And so far do the Quakers carry their condescension on these occasions, that if a few antient and respectable individuals seem to be dissatisfied with any measure ... though otherwise respectably supported, the measure is frequently postponed, out of tenderness to the feelings of such members, and from a desire of gaining them in time by forbearance.'[8] The same is still the case today. Moreover, Clarkson points to the participation of the whole Society in its business as the reason for the acceptance of its disciplines; the rules the Quakers accept and apply to themselves are of their own making.

Many of the 'Peculiar Customs' of the Quakers recounted by Clarkson we have met already, but his comments are here particularly illuminating. Their dress he describes as by no means uniform, though generally simple and serviceable: '... the primitive Quakers dressed like the sober, steady and religious people of the age ... and that their descendants have departed less ... than others from the dress of their ancestors'.[9] He describes the absence of framed pictures in Quaker homes, but says that some had collections of prints in books or portfolios. In addition to the use of the second person singular, he reports other singularities of language – not using words such as 'lucky' or 'fortunate', or the expression 'Christian name' for a first name, or wishing another 'Good morrow' or 'Good evening', for all days are equally good. While the world supposed the Quakers a stiff and reserved people, Clarkson found them attentive and kindly, free of affectation and their manners, if not polished,

8. ibid., pp. 240–41.   9. ibid., pp. 273–4.

nevertheless agreeable. He draws attention particularly to their wishing their visitors to ask for what they want openly, and to their never regarding visitors as an impediment in the way of their concerns. 'If they have any business or engagement out of doors, they say so and go, using no ceremony, and but few words as an apology.'[10]

They did not talk politics or scandal, and on occasion a pause in the conversation would grow to a silence, which might give way to spoken ministry, being followed by a further silence before general conversation was resumed. If this is something now unknown among us, the short period of silence as a grace before meals still happily survives.

While Clarkson's description of Quaker theology is of little interest today, he does give a valuable picture of Meeting for Worship. 'They endeavour to be calm and composed. They take no thought as to what they shall say ... The creature is thus brought to be passive, and the spiritual faculty to be disencumbered, so that it can receive and attend to the spiritual language of the Creator.' 'If the minister engages in prayer, he kneels, and the whole company rise up and the men with the minister take off their hats ... If he preach only, they do not rise, but remain upon their seats as before, with their heads covered. The preacher, however, uncovers his own head upon this occasion and stands.' 'In the beginning of their discourses they generally utter their words with a slowness ... which sometimes renders their meaning almost unintelligible ... As they proceed, they communicate their impressions in a brisker manner; till at length, getting beyond the quickness of ordinary delivery, they may be said to utter them rapidly.'[11]

After defining the 'Great Tenets' of Quakerism – the insistence that conscience comes before law and that the Christian must be prepared to suffer for conscience, the objection to war and violence, the insistence on a universal ministry and hence the objection to professional ministers and to tithes for their support – he goes on to set out the good and bad characteristics of the Quakers. The good ones

10. Thomas Clarkson, op. cit., Vol. I, p. 363.   11. op. cit., Vol. II, p. 279.

are benevolence, concern for the spiritual, resistance to councils of expediency, calmness, courage, independence and integrity. The bad ones are more interesting because more unexpected, though Clarkson was so well-disposed to his subject that he finds most of them attributed to Quakers by the world through lack of understanding.

First comes lack of learning, particularly of philosophical learning, which he ascribes to the nature of Quaker education, with its strong emphasis on moral teaching. In fact, the Society was to produce more than its fair share of scientists in the nineteenth and twentieth centuries, and the Quaker schools were certainly not backward in moving towards a scientific education. Yet it is still true today that Quakers are often accused (usually by their own members) of lack of intellectual rigour, particularly in theology. This aspect will arise in Part II of this book; briefly, my view is that intellectuals, and particularly academic and theological intellectuals, often attribute lack of rigorous thought to others where the truth of the matter is that simple thought appears inept to those given to complexity. Real rigour is more dependent on a grasp of fundamentals; the creator of complex intellectual structures cannot forgive those who disregard the edifice and cast penetrating glances at the foundations.

The accusation of being superstitious was founded on the conditional nature of Quaker undertakings. They would do things 'if they had liberty to do them'; that is, they accepted the uncertainty of temporal affairs. Furthermore, charges of superstition were also based, according to Clarkson, on some members of the Society having fallen for 'animal magnetism'. Quakerism has a strong mystical element, and members sometimes pursue ideas not commanding general support; just at the moment, those of us concerned about pollution of the environment, natural husbandry and so on are finding with some relief that we are no longer classed with believers in animal magnetism. But today, as in Clarkson's time, a few of us do fall for minority ideas which never achieve respectability. Obstinacy is easily understood – I am strong minded; you are obstinate. Undue desire for money Clarkson had to admit as a fault in some, for it was picked out for censure, as we have seen, in the *Book of Discipline*. He argues from this that the providing of wealth and independence for young people is an evil which is compounded, for the Quaker youth, by their being sheltered from the world in their formative years, so that they come into money without experience of its dangers.

The world also accused Quakers of coldness, slyness and evasiveness, 'though they will not swear, they will lie'. This Clarkson finds quite untrue. 'I know of no people who regard truth more than the Quakers';[12] the world's opinion was due to a failure to understand the importance attached by the Quakers to absolute honesty, and their refusal to meet the world by making frank, open statements which were untrue.

I hope that this description of the Society as it saw itself, and as it was seen by an outsider who had come to know and love it, will have given a fair picture of the Quakers at the end of the eighteenth century. It represents a closed and self-sufficient community, preoccupied with the spiritual virtues, and deriving from this preoccupation a great strength, which after achieving substantial social ends, was being turned to maintaining the *status quo*. But if the fire of Fox and his companions had been banked down, it was not yet extinguished; if the organization was becoming authoritarian it had not completely rigidified. The eighteenth-century Friends handed on a heritage capable of vigorous and sustained revival.

12. Thomas Clarkson, op. cit., Vol. III, p. 282.

CHAPTER 4

The Effects of Evangelism

THERE are two aspects to the history of Quakerism in the nineteenth century. One is the continuing and broadening of the social witness, the continuation of the anti-slavery campaign (slavery is still not banished from the world today), the developing of relief activities in peace and war, the concern for the under-privileged and the carrying on of foreign mission work. The other is a sadder and drearier story of theological controversy, and of separation and division. But it needs to be told, since without it neither the activities of Friends in the world nor the nature of the Society today can be seen in context.

The controversy was linked in some respects with the earlier disputes, being concerned with conflict between the authority from without and the authority from within. It was accentuated by the religious temper of the times; and by the emotional climate of the evangelical movement, with its emphasis on man's inherent sinfulness, the authority of Scripture and salvation through the crucifixion of Christ. Evangelical Christianity brought new life to the moribund churches; to Quakerism which, though spiritually quiet, was by no means moribund at the end of the eighteenth century, it brought discord and division.

There is no point in rehearsing in detail the growth of the dispute. The essentials are that, under the influence of Joseph John Gurney and other Friends, an evangelical theological outlook was gaining ascendancy in London Yearly Meeting, and parts of America. Uneasiness at their ministry was typified by the reactions of Elias Hicks, then an elderly and respected member of New York Yearly Meeting. His theology was centred round the inner light; he made a complete separation between the historical Christ and the Christ he described in terms of 'an eternal principle in the soul, and nothing else can be Christ our Saviour'. For Hicks, the whole duty of man was to be still and attentive to that of God in him, and by following and serving the inner light to do God's will. His attitude was consistent with the inherited Quaker view, but utterly in conflict with the evangelical attitude. The conflict came to a head in 1827, when the Philadelphia Yearly Meeting split. Numerically, the followers of Hicks greatly outnumbered their opponents.

While the issues in dispute were theological, one curious feature was that those controlling the government of the Society, that is the body of ministers and elders and the membership of the powerful Meeting for Suffering which then as now was the instrument of discipline, were orthodox in a general rather than a Quaker sense. This means that they sided with the evangelical influence and wished to impose on Friends more dogmatic beliefs which differed little from those held by the organized churches. They were, in fact, moving in the direction the other churches had taken, and for the same reason, namely that a defined creed assisted the maintenance of an imposed authority. This became apparent in their treatment of liberal Friends, who were disciplined and ruthlessly disowned.

A further split occurred in 1845, when a smaller body led by John Wilbur seceded from the orthodox party in New England. This group became known as 'Conservative' Friends: they maintained the practice of early Quakerism – or at least of the somewhat static eighteenth-century period – but the theological division was slight.

Thus, by the middle of the nineteenth century, there were three main groups in America: the 'orthodox' Yearly Meetings, with whom British Friends were in official correspondence and which were sometimes referred to as 'Gurneyite' by their opposers; the small group of 'conservative' Yearly Meetings (with many orthodox Philadelphia Friends in sympathy) clinging to the mystical rather than the evangelical aspect of Quakerism, but preoccupied also with minutiae of plainness of speech, behaviour and apparel; and the 'Hicksite' Yearly Meetings, separated since 1827–8 and shunned as unsound by orthodox and conservative alike. But now, as Quakerism spread through the Middle

West with the advancing frontier and with the Great Revival of the 1860s, many of the orthodox Meetings became impatient with much of traditional Quakerism. Step by step, Meetings became churches, revivalist hymns found their way into worship, shared ministry gave way to set sermon, belief in a universal priesthood to a paid pastor. Inevitable, further 'conservative' separations occurred. By the end of the century some British Friends began to wonder whether they were not in at least as great a spiritual unity with the conservatives as with such orthodox meetings as had programmed worship and a pastoral system.

In Britain, disparities also existed, but the outcome was less clear cut. Whether this was a good or a bad thing is still not altogether apparent. A small body of excessively evangelical Friends left the Society in 1836, and after a few years of separate existence, joined with the Anglicans or the Plymouth Brethren. In 1869 a more significant division occurred when a body of Friends, disturbed at the steadily more evangelical and doctrinal tone of London Yearly Meeting (had the separatists of 1836 waited a little longer they might never have gone at all) left the Society to form a separate Yearly Meeting at Fritchley in Derbyshire. This body maintained its independence until 1968, when Fritchley and London Yearly Meetings were reunited.

What can we discover from kicking over the dry bones of these long-dead controversies? Something of the historical perspective, of course; otherwise the complexity of the American scene can hardly be comprehended. Something also of why the greater number of Friends in the world – East Africa Yearly Meeting; its parent body, the evangelical Friends Alliance in the U.S.A.; and part at least of the Friends United Meeting which developed from the orthodox division – worship in ways closer to the manner of the nonconformist churches than to the manner of Friends elsewhere.

But the consequences of the evangelical influence went further and deeper than this. In Britain, as we have seen, there was no major split; the body of the Society absorbed the new influence. As a result, the attitude of Friends in

Britain today still contains the remnants of an unresolved conflict, as will become apparent in our discussion of contemporary Quaker beliefs. Yet for most of the second half of the nineteenth century, and on into the twentieth, the effect of evangelism was beneficial. The extreme withdrawal from the world was halted and reversed; Friends had a message which it was their duty to share; they had a stimulus to service, and a sense of personal discipleship which led them back into the active role and made possible social and educational activities of the greatest consequence. Fortunately the better part of their heritage was nonetheless preserved; the modern sense of creative conflict stems from a need for reconciliation of the best in the strands comprising modern Quakerism.

We can turn now to the less arid aspects of nineteenth-century Quakerism. At the beginning of the new century, the anti-slavery campaign was at its height, and moving towards the outlawing of slavery in British colonies. In America, however, an uneasy truce developed, with Friends eschewing slave-holding themselves, but doing little about abolition, and indeed being decidedly equivocal in relation to those who supported it. In 1817, social activity took a new turn in England, meanwhile, when Elizabeth Fry visited the women prisoners in Newgate and began her life's work which was to transform the treatment of criminals. Friends began to take part in local and national politics* and to take office as magistrates, though not without much questioning by conservative Friends as to whether such activities were consistent with their principles.

In the mid thirties, Joseph Sturge, one of those able determined Friends who move on from one superhuman endeavour to another without apparent pause, discovered that the conditions of freed slaves in the West Indies under the 'apprenticeship' system which had followed abolition

---

* Joseph Pease, son of the Edward Pease who backed George Stephenson and built the Stockton and Darlington Railway, became the first Quaker member of Parliament in 1833, despite his refusal to offer bribes or even to solicit votes.

was as bad as or worse than outright slavery. Nobody wanted to know; the abolitionists had triumphed, and to suggest that things were worse rather than better was tiresome and implied that their great victory was hollow. But Sturge persisted, went to the West Indies to compile an irrefutable case, and, largely by his own efforts, informed and influenced public opinion and Parliament until the necessary reforms were achieved.

Friends' activity in the mid nineteenth century has a difference of quality from earlier periods, in that their social and philanthropic endeavours, in prisons, through politics and in education and welfare, were now turning outward. They were aware of, and concerned with, the poor, ill-treated and deprived sections of the community outside their own numbers, whereas previously their actions had been more directly related to providing for their own. This was a consequence partly of historical development in the Society and partly of inescapable pressure from the outside world. The Industrial Revolution had offered the Friends a chance to apply their honesty and industry; many had grown rich and had, on the whole, dealt generously with the less fortunate among them. At the same time, the same revolution had disrupted and shaped the community, and the process as a whole was not in the hands of Friends. A gigantic machinery of exploitation had grown up, and vast numbers had been forced by economic pressures into industrial slavery. Few noticed the condition of the poor, and fewer still thought it anything other than a regrettable by-product of an inevitable and desirable process. But some Friends, sensitized no doubt by their part in the anti-slavery campaign, were among those who recognized the avoidable human misery nearer to hand, and were impelled to seek ways of bettering conditions. Among the means envisaged, however, they did not include any radical change in the structure of society; then as now, perhaps, they were too much the prisoners of their essentially bourgeois environment. But within that limitation – that is, as ameliorators rather than reformers – they devotedly worked for prison reform, the abolition of capital punishment, the spread of peace, the succour of the oppressed and hungry, the education and care of the ignorant and the deprived.

Yet at the beginning each of these praiseworthy efforts was likely to be opposed by the conservative elements in the Society of Friends itself. It was felt that the time was not yet right; Friends should 'gather to that true quietude of mind'; there were a variety of phrases for expressing the view that nothing should be done, other than the enforcing of the discipline which fossilized Friends in practices and attitudes without contemporary significance, bearing the badges of a peculiar people.

These attitudes also brought about a decline in numbers. The Quakers were possibly the only religious body of any standing in Victorian England whose numbers actually declined. Apart from the disownment of those who failed to meet the increasingly rigid standards of adherence to the testimonies, disownment for marrying-out drove many younger members from the Society, so that its marriage rate was only one fifth of that for the population at large. Since there was no doctrinal bias against marriage – indeed a generally wholesome attitude towards the family was combined with plentiful examples of rewarding marriages – one must assume that Quakers found mates as frequently as other folk, but found them more often outside the Society than within it, and hence were disowned on marriage. As John Stephenson Rowntree commented in an essay on the causes of decline in Quakerism, published in 1859, 'Rich indeed must be that church which can spare such members for such a cause.'

The essay came at a turning point, and the restrictive discipline was modified, but only just in time. At the end of the seventeenth century Quakers had numbered one in every hundred and thirty of the population of the British Isles; by 1800 the ratio was reduced to about one in five hundred, by 1860 to one in eleven hundred. (Today the ratio is more like one in two thousand two hundred, for our growth, healthy enough in a time when most other churches face a steady decline in numbers, has still not kept pace with the growth in the population.) At about the same time, the disinclination to look outward became less and, urged on by the evangelical spirit, Quakers began to take a hand in missionary enterprise. Nevertheless the first Quaker missionaries went about their work unsupported by any organizational backing, and protracted debates were held as to whether such activity was too worldly.

One incident of this time shows how the Quaker tradition continued, through all the internal conflicts. In America, in 1869, when General Grant became President, he put the administration of Indian affairs largely in the hands of the Quakers. Despite tension between the different Meetings, for ten years American Friends conducted the management of major Indian reserves and built the beginnings of a policy of fair dealings and peaceful relations with the Indians. It is not an aspect of how the West was won which attracts the makers of films, but then the Quakers were not given to the quick drawing of six-shooters. On the other hand, the Associated Executive Committee of Friends on Indian Affairs is alive and celebrating its centenary, with centres serving the Seneca-Cayuga, the Osage and the Kickapoo Indians.

The impulse which gave rise to mission work was also behind the growth of the adult school movement. This had particular emphasis on Bible study but no specifically doctrinal basis, and was directed to the education of adults at a time when many had received only a rudimentary education in childhood. The movement was one of the many initiatives of Joseph Sturge, who started the Severn Street Adult School, Birmingham, as early as 1845, and reached its maximum period of influence in the last part of the nineteenth century and the years before the First World War. At the present time there are many elderly Friends still alive whose vigorous, well-informed and wide-ranging minds are a tribute to the benefits the Adult School movement brought to intelligent men and women denied any great measure of formal education. The movement did not proselytize, but through it the Society did gain many valuable members.

Victorian England saw no war, but the American Civil War had its due proportion of Quakers ill-treated and tortured for their refusal to bear arms. The Franco-Prussian War was the occasion of a major relief effort, which laid the foundations of the service called forth, on a much greater scale, by the infinitely greater holocausts of our own time. Thus by the end of the century Quakerism had become closely associated with service to others, both at home and abroad, under the impulse of the evangelical spirit. Even where the theological temper was not overtly evangelical, there was an outward-going movement and the day of Quakerism as a Society separated from the world was over everywhere, except possibly among the relatively isolated communities of the Conservative (Wilburite) Friends in the United States.

One great Victorian controversy seems to have had little effect on Friends. They had never stood apart from science and technology, and Darwin's *Origin of Species* did not disturb them as it did others. (Though it is sometimes suggested that they were too deeply engaged with evangelical and specifically Quaker doctrinal issues to give much attention to minor matters such as the complete overthrow of the fundamentalist attitude to the creation.) Certainly at a conference in Manchester in 1895 it was roundly declared that there was no need 'to accept the Hebrew Chronology or the Hebrew cosmology as a necessary part of an all-rounded and infallible word of God', and moreover that the doctrine of the total depravity of the human soul was no part of Quakerism. That this last needed saying indicates how far Quakers had moved from walking cheerfully over the world answering that of God in everyone. Yet the movement back was well under way, from the long, perennially silent Meetings and often total inactivity of the early part of the century to the evangelism and fervent preaching of the second half, and so to an extended period, lasting to the present, of seeking a viewpoint for our day. This search is active and often confused; some seek among the historical roots, forgetting that what Quakerism was in 1660 is not evidence of what it is today; others try to construct a completely new conceptual structure, forgetting that no one can disown his history. Most Friends look perplexed when asked what Quakers believe, and talk instead about what Quakers do; and perhaps that is the right line to take.

*

The history of Quakerism does not stop abruptly at the end of the nineteenth century, nor at the more natural terminal point of the outbreak of the First World War. But the later stages will be referred to in other parts of this book; at this point it is enough to say that Quakerism has remained a living and growing force, increasingly active in the world and particularly well adapted to reach out to those who find the teachings of orthodox Christianity irrelevant. That is why this particular book has had to be written, though there are many excellent books already available.

For the same reason, this book differs from most of the general books on Quakerism in being something other than a history, in being more concerned with current beliefs, organization and activities and, as a history, including only the brief sketch in the preceding chapters. I should emphasize that this sketch is a sketch and no more. Quaker history is rich, particularly in anecdote, and anyone who wishes for more than he finds here will be well served by the major works of the Rowntree Series of Quaker Histories. There are also a number of single-volume studies (notably Neave Brayshaw's) on the sect's general history and many books on its specific aspects. In this book I have concentrated on helping an understanding of Quakerism today; hence the omission of many names and incidents highly regarded by Friends.

So individualistic a faith writes its history through the lives of individual men and women; but the plan of the book does not allow of their all being remembered. Let me say only that as I have met them, read their writings and their stories, and tried to marshal the events through which they lived their faith into some sort of order, I have grown increasingly aware that in becoming a convinced Quaker I have added an inadequate recruit to a great company of steadfast and noble predecessors.

PART II

Fundamental Beliefs

CHAPTER I

God and Man

WE have seen how the history of what is now the Religious Society of Friends starts with a seeking for the truth about the nature and function of man; how that seeking was answered by an 'experimental' knowledge, an appreciation from inward experience of the truth, and how the Society has built its life and works on that inner experience. While the history of the Society can be shown in these terms, as three hundred years of growth stemming from a point of realization, for each individual member of the Society the road must be travelled afresh. There is no creed, no set form of words to be read over and accepted or rejected; only the living experience of other Friends to be compared with one's own experience. Hence these chapters, which are an attempt to set out Quaker beliefs, cannot be categorical. They try to draw a map of partially explored territory rather than to describe the celestial city at the journey's end.

A religion without a creed is not the contradiction in terms it might appear to be. Religion is about matters which are not susceptible to proof, and a creed, a definite statement of beliefs, is in some ways incompatible with religion. For to say in the noble Latin of the Mass or the equally noble seventeenth-century English of the Prayer Book 'Credo in Unum Deum', 'I believe in one God, the Father Almighty' is to beg a great many questions in a handful of words. Why does one believe this, what does one mean by God, in what sense is there *one* God, and in what other sense is there a Holy Trinity? Are these statements of fact, are they symbolic, or do they refer to factual and historical matters which are also symbolic? The further one goes the more unanswered questions arise. Now Friends are not without a concern with theology; indeed they are sea-theologians as others are sea-lawyers, and they enjoy a disputation on a religious theme almost as if it were an art form. Perhaps this

is the right simile. Their disputations are a search for agreement, an intellectual exploration; but at the same time they
are generally agreed that theology is a secondary concern,
more a gloss on their beliefs than the substance of them.
Some Friends occasionally suggest that a creed might help
to clarify our thoughts and remove the penumbra of wool-
liness of which we are often accused. At this suggestion the
majority close their ranks, and hold firm to their beliefs,
which are not to be contained in the strait-jacket of a creed.
All this is very well, but it is decidedly vague and, it must
be admitted, woolly. What are the beliefs which are so firmly
held, which are common to all Friends and bind them in
their Society? If they cannot be expressed in the words of a
creed, can they be expressed at all? Are they anything more
than a general well-meaning concern with human values,
liberal humanism dressed up with a few archaic con-
ventions; orthodox Christianity diluted to such a degree that
there is no perceptible flavour left in the brew? To attempt
to answer these eminently reasonable questions, to conduct
an inquiry into Friends' beliefs, is a perilous exercise. One
needs to emphasize repeatedly that it is an inquiry and not
a statement. The result resembles a spectogram when the
light of the sun is passed through a prism: a continuous
band of light passing from the invisible ultra-violet through
the full range of visible colour to the invisible infra-red,
crossed by a number of defined bands which show the presence of certain elements. Not a bad analogy, perhaps, if we
recognize that our inquiry is directed at the light of truth
refracted through the membership of the Society.

Essentials first, then. It is the *Religious* Society of Friends.
Though its members are active in the world, leading their
own working lives, engaged often enough in voluntary social
welfare activities as well as in running a Society with a minimal paid central staff and no full-time Ministry, yet the dynamic is religious. They live as they do, and do what they do,
because of a conviction about the non-material element in
life, a conviction derived from personal experience; subjectively authenticated though not susceptible of rational
proof.

Now religion is usually concerned with man and God, though I suppose essentially religion is concerned with the spiritual aspect of life which does not necessarily involve the concept of God. But a good starting point of our inquiry is the nature of Quaker views of God. Here a certain restrained dogmatism is possible; here we can pinpoint the common ground on which Quakers have something approaching an agreed view. They believe that there is that of God in every man.

For some, this is an extension of the Divine presence into the human existence; a linking of man with God through the presence in every man of the Holy Spirit, the still, small voice. For others, this is not quite their view, nor their experience. Nevertheless, those who express their experience in very different terms identify a basic shared belief, knowing that they are finding words for the transcendental, that the experience on which belief is based is fundamentally non-transferable. I shall try to explain this belief from the viewpoint of one who was an agnostic, who had a training in natural science and who came only reluctantly to recognize a different dimension. This is not necessarily the best viewpoint, or the truest or the most revealing; but it is the one I understand best, and the one which may interest those who find the plain statement at the end of the preceding paragraph baffling, or intriguing or even ludicrous. To those who are already sure in a belief in God (however defined, in whichever orthodoxy) the Quaker view is in some ways easier of access. An exploration of its implications to them would require a separate treatment of the beliefs of each other religion and would take us deep into the realms of academic theology. Adopting the viewpoint of the agnostic allows us to take nothing for granted. And if what we are discussing has any reality, then the viewpoint and manner of approach does not matter. The truth we describe may be shown in different forms, as drawings show different aspects of a building; but we will begin to see as we study one description after another, the truth underlying them all.

If we set out from the agnostic position, we are not much concerned with the question of how the world started, nor can we assume a pattern and purpose in the Universe which is there for us to discover. All we can assume is that we are here, now. Speculation on the origin and ending of the universe, however fascinating, does not promise answers to the vital questions of why we are here, now; or of what purpose our life has, and how it should be directed.

What manner of creature is man? Well, man is an animal with an intellect. This is a very powerful tool which enables him to find out in increasing detail the nature of the mechanistic world in which he lives and to recognize that however far he pushes the discovery of that world there will ever be greater realms undiscovered. He recognizes his own intellect and is already well on the way to mastering its mechanism, through newly created branches of science and medicine. We can describe the structure of the brain, identify the seat of certain types of thinking and even modify, by chemical or psychiatric treatment, certain abnormal functionings of this complex apparatus. Yet the more one is concerned with the nature of man, the more the advances of science in this field as in others seem to emphasize by their very extent a curious omission. When it comes to the point, a description of my thinking equipment, no less than an anatomical description of my body, fails to describe me. I am something more.

From the moment one becomes conscious of this something more, there is an urgent curiosity to discover more about it. It is something to do with individuality, with being me and not you. It is something to do with free will, with creativity, with being able to initiate. It is the inner objection to any idea of life as a strictly mechanistic system, to the ultimate rationalism of 'When we know enough we shall be able to predict everything.'

If we persist, as persist we must, with this examination, we pass through stage after stage of identifying and rejecting parts of ourself which are not the essential self we seek. We are like Peer Gynt peeling away skin after skin of the onion (and like him we risk finding nothing at the centre). The intellect, which is our keenest weapon in this attack on ourselves, seems to penetrate only to destroy; the more we know about ourselves the less significant that knowledge seems. We are inflating our egos at the expense of minimizing our purpose; the 'I' we are discovering has no function except to be itself.

This is a fairly commonly described condition. It is perennial, and it was the condition of George Fox in his early wanderings. It has been the condition of myself and of others I have known intimately. It can lead to simple despair, or even to mental unbalance or suicide. One asks – if the purpose of life is just this, to be, and to be me, why should I live it? In T. E. Lawrence's words, 'Indeed the truth was I did not like the "myself" I could see and hear.'

To this condition there is an antidote. It is to be quiet, not just physically but mentally. If, instead of using the mind, instead of thinking, instead of referring everything to the standards of the intellect, we suspend this continuous argument in our head and become still, then we have a new awareness. We are aware of a sense of unity with the whole creation, aware of the very sense of being which has so far escaped us. We have discovered, in plain terms, the spirit which is in us. The spirit is not the flesh, the spirit is not the mind, it is coexistent with the body and the mind; and since I cannot (being a man) conceive of anything except through my body and mind, I cannot tell by direct examination whether the spirit lives independently of the body and the mind. But I can tell that it lives in me, and the recorded experience of others, Quaker and non-Quaker, Christian and non-Christian, tells that it has been found by and within men and women of all times and all conditions. So, with some assurance, we can indeed walk cheerfully over the world, answering that of God in every one.

The nature of the divine spirit would seem to be this, that it is not in the working of the mind, which is mechanistic, but in the motivation which directs the mind. It is personal, in that each of us is a channel for it and can be aware of its power; and yet it is universal, in that the divine spirit in you is the same as the divine spirit in me. Here is the explanation of the difference between the intellectual analysis of man's nature, which leads to the destruction of any sense of worthwhileness and to ultimate despair, and the discovery of the spirit within which gives purpose to living. Intellectual analysis increases our sense of separateness; the discovery of the spirit brings with it the discovery of an underlying identity and universality.

The agnostic may here object that if what I say is true it is very wonderful, and would be a key to religious and mystical writings of all faiths and all times, but that I have not proved my case. I have described a spirit which, if it be as I describe it, may truly be called divine, and I have stated that this spirit dwells in every man. But I have not proved anything.

To this I can only reply that no one can prove this to anyone else, but each of us can prove it to himself. The barrier to knowledge of God – and why should we shy at using that name; the divine spirit is God and God is our name for all that is truly non-material and truly creative in life – the barrier to knowledge of God is fear, which manifests itself in the fear of loss of identity, which is pride. What one has to do is to stop the relentless operation of the mind, be still, be quiet, be nothing. It is as simple as that; very simple and very difficult. One way of attempting this most difficult and worthwhile operation is by joining in the silence of Quaker worship. There, all about you are engaged in the same effort, and God grows and strengthens in all.

I have attempted to sketch one view of the nature of God, that least dependent upon historical tradition, and therefore most accessible to the modern agnostic who rejects the traditional teaching. But this concept of the indwelling presence of God can come equally from an understanding of the traditional teachings of Christianity, as the early Quakers found and as many Quakers find today. Moreover there is a way of understanding through action – many of us have started out with no other motive than compassion or simply guilt, inability to ignore the sufferings of others and recognition of one's own good fortune. From this comes service to others, and in that service comes a realization of a deeper community, of a one-ness that is something more than 'common humanity'. From whatever starting point we set out and along whichever road we travel, the knowledge of the indwelling Divine Presence is ultimately what, as Quakers, we share.

We hold varying personal views of what God is, but we do not find these differences a barrier to common worship or common endeavour. Our experience of God must be within ourselves; where we differ is in our theorizing as to what this personal experience reflects. For my part, I do not extend my theorizing very far, being content to know what I can know through my own experience and to recognize the limits of my own knowledge. Others may see their inward experience as an aspect of a divine being, whose totality is much greater than that experience, so that they are aware of an outward God who yet permeates our existence. It is unnecessarily arrogant to suggest that one view is right and the other wrong, since our intellectual formulations about God, who is above all a spiritual entity, are projections of a reality which the mind cannot know. In Plato's *Republic* there is an analogy of chained prisoners who see only shadows cast by the fire they cannot themselves see. This analogy is archetypal and will bear many interpretations, but certainly it is a true symbol of our knowledge of the reality of God. We should not be surprised that our individual concepts are varied, but should concentrate on the agreed qualities which show that the flickering shadows we see are projections of a common reality.

Let us recapitulate the ideas about the nature of God which Quakers are agreed on. By God we mean a spiritual, non-material force or entity which may or may not have a separate existence away from the material man, but which dwells indeed in the inmost heart of every man. This spiritual entity is not uniquely personal, but is universal, so that there is a bond between us all which is stronger than any physical bond. In our unity in God we are part of one another.

One thing more needs to be said. Belief in God, in this sense, means experience of God. Nobody can say, 'Yes, your argument has convinced me; before I did not believe in God, now I do.' Conviction can only come through being still, and quiet, and without personal ambition or desires, being for however short a time devoid of individuality, and hence aware of the divine spirit within. (It is significant that Quakers speak of those who decide to join them as members 'by convincement'.) It follows, therefore, that Quakers are, in a general sense, mystics; mystics, that is, in the sense of the dictionary definition – 'One who seeks by contemplation and self-surrender to obtain union with or absorption into the Deity, or who believes in the spiritual apprehension of truths inaccessible to the understanding' (*Shorter Oxford Dictionary*).

I would only make two comments on that definition; the first 'and' might well be 'or' and the last 'or' might well be 'and'. I would hope also to have shown that mysticism is not a matter of spiritual apprehension of truths inaccessible so much as spiritual conviction of truths beyond logical and intellectual proof. With those corrections, Quakers stand convicted of being mystics.

CHAPTER 2

The Quakers as Christians

THE explanation of the heart of Quaker belief, as I have given it in the preceding chapter, might seem to be complete, and sufficient in itself; the direct awareness of God is surely the highest attainment possible to man; how can any other belief add to it? And yet every religion does add to it, in one way or another. What is added is generally a structure of belief which often expands into a codified morality and a ceremonial worship. It is these elements which distinguish the different great religions and their different sects; the profound and fundamental truth of God in man is to be found in them all, though often concealed in the writings of mystics or expressed in symbolic terms. But the beliefs, the moralities, the ceremonies diverge into an awesome variety, so that the task of seeking unity even among the churches of one religion is too much for us.

Within the Society of Friends there exists a very wide diversity of belief, accompanied by an absence of codified morality or ceremonial of worship. These conditions are so unusual in any religion that they lead to suspicions (among Friends themselves sometimes) that the Society is no more than a comfortable club, that its members have really no common bond and only coexist because they do not apply themselves to the questions which might divide them. In fact nothing could be further from the truth. Friends frequently examine these questions, and have done so from the early days, always finding that the bonds that bind them are infinitely stronger than the differences which might divide them. They have re-affirmed repeatedly that they are a Religious society and a Christian society; they have accepted into membership people whose declared views cover an exceptionally wide spectrum, including a substantial number who specifically will not concede any uniquely divine character to Christ; and their conviction that such divergence is compatible with Quakerism has been justified over and over again.

To explain this, it is necessary to look first into the reasons for belief, and for this the starting point is the nature of experience of God, which is wholly other than anything else we know or can know. This is easy to appreciate when one is thinking of the saint, whose life of mystical contemplation only touches our everyday world fleetingly; it is more difficult to reconcile with the twentieth-century commuting man. Yet it is true; embark upon this way, still your thoughts, open yourself, and if you achieve spiritual experience, your awareness of God will be wholly different, not in degree but in intrinsic quality, from anything else you know. For most of us we only achieve this awareness spasmodically, for brief intervals of time, but once achieved, however briefly, we know it as essentially and utterly different.

Merely to say it is different does not convey the true quality: listen to Isaac Penington:

> But some may desire to know what I have at last met with. I answer 'I have met with the Seed.' Understand that word, and thou wilt be satisfied and inquire no farther. I have met with my God, I have met with my Savior, and he hath not been present with me without his Salvation, but I have felt the healings drop upon my soul from under his wings. I have met with the Seed's Father, and in the Seed I have felt him my Father; there I have read his nature, his love, his compassions, his tenderness; which have melted, overcome and changed my heart before him ... I have met with the true peace, the true righteousness, the true holiness, the true rest of the soul, the everlasting habitation which the redeemed dwell in. And I know all these to be true in him that is true, and am capable of no doubt, dispute or reasoning in my mind about them, it abiding there where it hath received the full assurance and satisfaction.[1]

In the poetry of his words, there is indeed some measure of the overwhelming nature of this experience.

Now such an experience needs to be moderated if it is to

1. Isaac Penington, *Works*, 1681, 'Christian Faith and Practice in the Experience of the Society of Friends', London Yearly Meeting of the Religious Society of Friends, 1960, § 28.

be lived with. We are not, generally speaking, clear, whole personalities free of stress and free of faults. We are the inheritors of our human past and the product of our human environment. We have become what we are in the struggle to survive, and we have been more than a little battered in the process. To have awareness of God, to live in the direct light of that glorious Sun, is too much for us. We must moderate the experience if we are to survive, and the nature of that moderation is commonly a structure of belief.

Most of what I have written must be admittedly such a structure. The experience cannot be communicated, so I am forced to write instead about how the experience may be related to mundane life. In so doing I am of necessity writing about a subjective matter, about the integration of my experience of God in *my* life. It is here that the divergence creeps in, for although you and I may be able to see enough similarity between our faltering description of our experience to recognize it as aspects of a single truth – if only because we agree on its otherness – you and I are different people, with different personalities; and beliefs which are meaningful for one may not be so for another. Thus if we understand that these beliefs are the moderating force through which our experience is brought within the capacity of our fallible and essentially human limitations, so that we may live with it and through it, we can understand how they will be different for each one of us. Sometimes the differences are small enough to pass unnoticed; sometimes they are great enough to divide a whole people. But they are not reflections of deeper differences, nor are they the difference between the true and the false. The beliefs which enable me to dwell with God are true for me, and those which are true for you will enable you to do likewise; there is nothing here to divide us.

To say this is not to say that we may believe what we please. Rather, it is to say, as Jesus said, 'Ask, and you will receive; seek and you will find; knock, and the door will be opened.' As you go towards God, you will be led to the beliefs which answer to your personal need. Accept them, hold them steadfastly – and do not try to ram them down the throats, of others whose needs may be very different. God in his infinite universality will minister to them also.

It is this attitude towards belief, explicit or implied, which enables the Society to be so tolerant. It is within the very broad range which this attitude allows that the Society can claim to be Christian.

A marked difference from other churches is the absence of any dogmatic creed, though not for lack of attempts to urge such a definitive statement of belief on us from time to time. But consciously, and I think courageously, Friends reject these attempts, and stay with a few fairly general statements that affirm the God-centred nature of our common experience, and relate this to the life and teaching of Jesus. One interpretation of Christianity we can all accept: we recognize Jesus as a man through whom the divine light shone undimmed, 'totus Deus sed non totum Dei', wholly God yet not the whole of God. We can accept his teaching, in so far as we have it, and seek to follow it as best we can. We are all his disciples, all weak and imperfect but all convinced that he showed the way, and that we must follow.

At this point the pragmatic nature of Quakerism begins to show. 'Hold fast,' said Fox, 'to that which is eternal.' We do that; we cling to our direct experience of the eternal, we find this absolute worked out in living terms in the teaching of Jesus, and then we turn our whole being to trying to follow that teaching. But as to the explanation of the nature of Jesus, the rationalization of the incarnation, crucifixion and resurrection, the uniqueness of the divine revelation – these are all fine Latin-based words, strictly for schoolmen. Individually we need the belief structure, as I have suggested, in order to live with our experience. Individually we will find the belief which is true and meaningful for us. But collectively we can agree on the simple but profound experience of God and the example of Jesus; this dictates a way of life for us, which must be lived in answer to our own individual inner guidance. Our beliefs both sustain us individually and warn us against forcing our own ideas on others; we can show them the way to God, but he will show them the pathway of belief, and since they are not the same person as we are, their belief may well be different from ours to match their personal need. Besides, if we have reached the point of accepting and seeking to follow the teaching of Jesus, for the simple and unanswerable reason that we know it to be right and that it accords with the deepest level of our being, then we have a life's work before us. When we have achieved our aim, and left all that we have and followed Jesus, then in the Quaker view, we shall have time enough for theological dispute as to whether he was the unique manifestation of God, on the true and precise nature of other revelations and on the historical validity of the traditional life of Jesus. Our feeling is that the more one turns one's life towards God, the less time or inclination there is to indulge in theory – one is too busy trying and, alas, failing to live up to the standard set by the founder of Christianity, extended as it is into every corner of life by the living presence, the still, small voice within.

The actual range of beliefs inside the Society is very wide, and far more complex than appears at first sight, or from a study of Quaker writings. These give an impression of sturdy orthodox nonconformity, an unsophisticated faith and trust that could offend no one. Friends are, I think, too inclined to present themselves in this light, both in writing and at Meeting, because they are very sensitive of other people's feelings, and consider simple faith acceptable to all. Within the Society, we all put our own gloss on the homely piety; but to those outside I think it gives a wholly misleading impression of near simple-mindedness. The outsider asks, 'How can intelligent men and women, many of them graduates and of high standing in their professions, go and listen to and take part week after week in Meetings whose content is so intellectually modest?'

The answer is simply that we do not go to Meeting for intellectual pleasure, but for shared worship, and this worship is tied very firmly to shared experience. Our beliefs do not obtrude themselves very strongly, and can be expressed, if at all, in fairly neutral symbology because they are important primarily to the one, not the many. But in discussion groups, both formal and informal, where we seek to deepen our understanding, we are able to consider our differences of view openly, knowing that the oneness in Meeting overspreads all the varieties of individual belief.

We start from the indwelling presence; on this we are agreed. That of God within us is the one aspect of which we can be sure of. But then, moving outwards, we are unable to agree about the nature of the manifested God, God made man; and of course we realize and accept our inability to comprehend the totality of God, the transcendent Deity.

Now, let us look at ourselves. Some of us are reluctant deists, temperamentally opposed to all suggestions of divine intervention in the material world, grudgingly admitting what we cannot deny, but anxious to limit our admissions as far as possible. We include followers of Jung, who find that the most penetrating of that master's insights into the collective unconscious have carried us to a level which we must recognize as divine rather than human. We have peeled the onion and found, almost to our consternation, the Holy Ghost.

At this same extreme are those of us who sometimes wonder whether we would not be better classified as humanists, except that we cannot stay away from Meeting for Worship. Our awareness is centred on our fellow men; we are practical people, who feel the hurt of others' suffering and have to go out and do something about it. All we ask of Christ is his teaching, the message of love which finds its echo in our hearts.

Yet at the other extreme there are those of us who have found not a teaching but an example, not an example but a presence. To us, there can be no truth in an abstraction; the truth is to be found in a living presence, someone to follow, someone to worship, someone who by his very being sets the standard for us all. And this presence we find in the unique historical and risen Christ, who lived in Palestine two thousand years ago and lives today in the hearts of those who own him as their Lord.

I have written as if I myself came in each of these groups, and of course there are many intermediate positions I have not described. Yet when it comes to the point, the various attitudes are incompatible. Individually, we cannot believe more than one of them, and to believe one to be true is to hold the others to be untrue.

Or is it? Have we not got here a classic example of exclusivity, of the desire to classify as either/or? We know, by experience, something of God, and we know that this is a shared experience. We can hardly conceive of there being, so to speak, several prospectuses of God, of which one is true and all others are false, with no distinguishing feature whereby one can tell the true from the false. Our limited direct knowledge of God prevents us from accepting any of the theologies which imply a salvation limited to the elect. Whatever else it is like, the Kingdom of Heaven is not like a 'rights' issue on the Stock Exchange, available only to existing shareholders.

But if we cannot reconcile our direct knowledge of God with the exclusivity of many of our thoughts about him, can we not now reconcile the diversity of our views with the diversity of ourselves? We, the bodies and brains in which the Holy Spirit is planted and through which God must work, are the product of complex evolutional and environmental processes. We are – as we know – all different from one another, alike only in this essential centre where we own God. So, I suggest, God is available to us in the form in which we need him, in whatever form is reconcilable with our individual defects of understanding. The totality of God embraces all forms, and all symbols and all appearance; for any individual there is only one aspect of this totality which carries meaning, which strikes to the heart, and so God is manifest to him in that form.

Let me make it clear that I am not suggesting that God is whatever we want him to be, or that we imagine him in whatever form we please. I am suggesting that we should recognize the message of our own inward experience and the teaching of all great religious masters. God is not this, not that; not limited and specific but universal. And this universality is the quality of transcending space and time, of not being constrained within the dimensional framework of the material world. Moreover this God, we know, is love, and desires that all creation be brought into unity with him. When I say we 'know' this, I do not mean that we are told it in Scripture or that it is preached at us, but that we know it directly, from any awareness of God we attain, however limited. Is it not then conceivable that God will be aware (and these anthropomorphic expressions are utterly inadequate) of what are the needs and limitations of our individual personalities, and will offer himself in a form we individually can recognize and turn to? This form, moreover, may change as we change, always leading us closer to the transcendent reality.

I have spoken of 'forms' and this might be interpreted as phantoms, appearances, non-real. Nothing is further from the case. As F. H. Bradley pointed out, anyone who asks for a reality more than that given in religious experience does not know what he is seeking. If we are able to say that the living Christ is with us, that presence is more real to us and closer to us than the man sharing our seat on the bus. But what I must emphasize is that if two of us are able to say, the one 'I am aware of the presence of the living Christ and this to me is the heart of my religion' and the other 'I cannot understand what you mean by the living Christ; I admire the example of Jesus, and seek to follow his teaching, but my absolute standard is the still, small voice of God within' they are far closer in essentials than they are separated in appearances. The manifest God they recognize is in each case a projection into their world of a greater and unified whole.

We must guard against the idea that, though God is manifested in different ways to match our differing apprehensions, nevertheless our own appreciation of God is in some way closer to the truth than all the others; that other people may at present be satisfied with something other, but in the end, if they progress along the path of true wisdom they must come to share our own deeper and more profound understanding. This is nothing more nor less than spiritual pride. A more truly humble attitude finds a measure of the Divine, and an indication of how far the Divine transcends the human, in the infinite diversity of its appearances, and in the precision with which those appearances are matched to the needs of each one of us.

Having said so much in general terms about belief, we should perhaps turn to a specific example to show just what this attitude means in terms of range of permissible attitudes. The heart of the Gospel story is the crucifixion and resurrection of Christ; let us examine how Friends see this. Is it a historical fact, which shows the Son of God dying that we might be saved, bearing our sin and redeeming us by his sacrifice, and then rising from the dead to live eternally in the presence of God; a promise of salvation that awaits those who believe in him? Or is it expressive of the love that is God shining through a man who lived his life in that love, and showing how we are saved by love, even in suffering; the resurrection a symbol and a vision of the presence of God with us in the world, now and forever? Or is it just a myth, of uncertain historical validity, showing, insofar as it shows anything, what harm can be done by an efficient bureaucracy and an institutional church, and worthy of study because of the light it throws on the nature of man, that will have such myths, and the symbology of myth which is so significant to man?

All these views are to be found coexisting within the Society, and moreover, there is also a fairly wide acceptance that these different views are not alternatives; that the one episode exists in a multiplicity of forms, all of equal significance. To say, 'I see the crucifixion as a symbolic myth' or 'I see it as a literal event, and the crowning intervention of God in the life of man' is to make different statements about ourselves, not about the crucifixion. Fox told us to seek to find and answer that of God in every man; we have learned to recognize that it is not always the same aspect of God, so we do not look to others to mirror our own beliefs, but to show God in their own way. The mirrors of the soul are tarnished and distorted; no two show the same image, yet they all reflect the one God.

What I have written is in line with the views of many Friends; of a Society so determinedly non-dogmatic one can say no more with certainty. It corresponds at least with what

I have observed of Friends in action, of the way in which they work together, admitting and accepting their differences. It makes the Society of Friends what it says it is, a Religious Society; and it makes it a Christian church in that its members follow the light of Christ. In the words of the seventeenth-century Quaker George Bishop, 'By the word Light, and the Light within, we mean Christ the Light.'[2] What we mean by 'Christ the Light' is indeed a more subjective matter, and we cannot as a Society subscribe to any exclusive doctrines in relation to Christ. But it is sufficient for us to know God inwardly, and to find his message to us lived out by Jesus in the Gospels, by those who have knowingly and sincerely followed him, and by others who have never known him but have independently followed the same path.

Our task is to conform with that knowledge and follow the example of that life – not quite an impossible undertaking but requiring of us our complete devotion and submission. We will not willingly let aspects of belief come between ourselves and others who share that task.

2. George Bishop, 'Vindication of the Principles and Practices of the People Called Quakers', 1665, quoted by Maurice Creasey in 'The Quaker Interpretation of the Significance of Christ', *Quaker Religious Thought*, Vol. I, No. 2, 1959.

CHAPTER 3

The Necessary Minimum

THE two preceding chapters have shown that in seeking the essence of Quakerism, one is constrained to a very simple formulation of the awareness of the Divine within us. Beyond that formulation, the attitudes diversify so much that to identify even their range is difficult. Certainly it is impossible to offer any set formula, any doctrine of the type normally called religious, that can be attributed to Quakers as a whole.

Yet there are some attitudes which are specifically Quaker. They are not of the type normally called religious; that is to say, they do not relate directly to ideas about the creation of the Universe, the status and authority of sacred writings, sacred persons or the Church itself. They are not explicitly doctrinal, and nobody is required to subscribe to them formally. Nevertheless they are, more than any strictly religious beliefs, the attitudes which mark out a Quaker, and which we usually find in applicants for membership.

First of these is sincerity. If the essence of Quakerism is the concept of that of God in every man, the essence of the Quaker way of life is the sincere following of the consequences of that concept as we individually see them, in the circumstances in which we live. Religious beliefs, as we understand them, are not something for Sundays, not a comfortable personal and private matter, but must dominate our whole lives and influence our every action. This is not a matter of formal observances, of morning and evening prayers and thanking God for our good bank balance, but of continually seeking understanding of the divine will, and of striving to live in accord with it.

It could be argued that such an attitude, if followed through, would lead to all Quakers being poor, having given all they possessed to others, and all working among the outcasts of society. This is clearly not so. Yet observing Friends as objectively as I can. I see them as, in a materialist world, quite incredibly sincere in following out their religion in practical living. Individually they will all refute this hotly, pointing out the ways in which they are falling short, the comfortable circumstances to which they cling, their inadequacy as compared with the Naylers and Dewsburys of the seventeenth century. Yet they are in fact models, each in their own manner, of how one can strive in a basically non-Christian world towards living the Christian life. Perhaps the best measure of this is that nobody has ever said to me of a Friend, that his actions belie his words; and it is only Friends themselves who question, often and urgently, the extent to which the Society as a whole is consistent with its principles.

A second characteristic is regard for the integrity of others, regard for their individuality, for their needs and their strengths. This is of course a direct outcome of the basic concept of 'God in every man'; if you are seeking God in every man you cannot treat any man as a client, a case or a statistic. And most of all you cannot treat them, in domestic or professional relationships, as people to be manipulated or exploited, nor can you give their opinions, beliefs or feelings less regard than your own.

A third characteristic is that which gives this chapter its title. Rufus Jones expressed it in the pungent phrase 'No infallibilities, except the infallibility of the guiding spirit';[1] it could be represented as a devotion to Occam's razor, a deep-seated objection to classing anything as an absolutely required belief or a necessary and inescapable requirement. There is one such inescapable requirement, that imposed on me by my own awareness of God. From that there is no escape, but it is imposed on me, not on anyone else, and however absolutely it leads me to certain beliefs and actions, it does not lead me to force them on anyone else. This is not historic Quakerism, which as we have seen has had its strongly held and enforced tenets, but it seems to me a characteristic of Quakerism today. I am at variance with

1. Rufus M. Jones, Introduction to *The Beginnings of Quakerism*, W. C. Braithwaite, Macmillan, 1919.

many Friends on issues of great importance – particularly perhaps on the issue of the centrality and uniqueness of Jesus – and many will disagree with a great deal of this book; but I doubt very much whether I shall find myself disowned in consequence.

Where then is the source of any discipline in the Society? First of all in the self-discipline which comes from the sincere attempt to follow out in practice what we have discovered for ourselves. To become a Friend is to make a commitment, not to the Society but to God and to living our lives in the light he shows us. Yet, if this seems unduly individualistic, the Society gives us a frame of reference in which we live, in that we are a Society of Friends in the simple meaning of those words, supporting and sustaining each other in our endeavours.

There is, moreover, the sense of corporate testimony, a unity of action stemming from a deeper unity. We have seen[2] that there was a division among the early Quakers as to whether 'a judgement given forth by part of the members of Christ's body could be a burden upon any other part further than their understandings were illuminated thereby'. The conflict there revealed was never wholly resolved; yet in the process of living with it the Society has gained a valuable insight, an insight which to this day it does not always appreciate fully. I have already quoted Penington; in today's language L. Hugh Doncaster has observed that 'It is a fact of experience that faithful following of the Light leads us into unity with those who also seek to follow it.'[3] It is this unity which we call our corporate testimony.

What Quakers believe is not, in any sense, dictated by the majority view. It is not that if, say, ninety-nine out of a hundred Quakers hold to a particular belief or course of action, the hundredth is bound to agree with them. Indeed, I would say that though ninety-nine disagree with him, the hundredth is bound to follow the Light that 'illuminates his understanding'. The obligation is not on him to disregard

2. Part I, Chapter 2, p. 34 et seq.
3. L. Hugh Doncaster, *God in Every Man*, Swarthmoor Lecture, 1963, George Allen & Unwin.

his personal convictions and fall into line, nor with the majority to compromise in order to achieve a spurious unity. But the obligation rests on all to reconsider their positions, to ask themselves whether they are indeed following the Light; whether from pride or laziness they are not allowing themselves to stand in the way of the Light. From such an examination it is then possible to move on towards a true unity of testimony.

This sense of corporate testimony has a double value for the individual. If he finds himself in accord with the testimony of Friends, but on a matter on which the rest of the community thinks differently, it is a cohesive and supportive influence, as in the case of the many whose non-violent principles have brought them into fellowship with Friends. It is a great source of strength to be able to say 'I know this is the right course, and Friends take the same view, so I will stick to my principles.'

If, however, the individual finds himself at variance with Friends then he is forced, as are the majority, to a more careful examination of his own attitude. This, you may say, is a pressure towards conformity, yet it is rather more of a protection against wild enthusiasms and personal whims masquerading as the will of God. It becomes part of one's attitude of mind to stop short and think again when one finds a marked difference between one's own belief and the corporate testimony of Friends. One stops short and thinks again; one does not always change one's attitude.

I have said that this is not a pressure towards conformity. There is evidence of this in the way in which some corporate testimonies survive and strengthen, while others fade away. Many of the seventeenth-century testimonies – the use of the second person singular, not taking off the hat, not wearing a sword – have lost all relevance in a changed society. The early peace testimony, though under continual pressure from Friends who see the need for modified formulations and attitudes to match our own time, remains widely acknowledged. Temperance, in the form of total abstinence, was almost universal among Friends in the second half of the nineteenth century, but is now maintained only by a minority, the corporate testimony being, if anything, a testimony of true temperance and moderation in place of abstinence. The one-time testimony on slavery has re-emerged, modified to suit the problems of our time, in our concern for community and race relations.

How do these modifications of testimony come about? Not, clearly, by a majority vote on a resolution at an Annual Conference – there are no votes at Yearly or any other Quaker Meeting. They result, instead, from the life and power of the Meeting – from a growth of common attitude in the Society that is rooted in our common worship. The more interesting aspect is perhaps not how a testimony takes hold of the Society – usually one or more members feel a strong personal concern over a certain issue and their concern spreads and informs the whole – but how a strongly established testimony is modified or eroded.

We can see a number of examples of this in the Society's history. First the process is slow; at times painfully slow. There is always a great force towards retaining an old attitude. Many Friends will feel deeply that the particular testimony is an inherent part of our beliefs and that not to maintain it would break faith with our predecessors (many of whom suffered great hardship in maintaining this very testimony). Often, too, the voice of caution and conservatism is heard much more clearly than the counter-suggestion that the testimony no longer commands Friends' willing support, and that we are uncertain whether the divine will requires this particular testimony any more. Friends are on the whole very 'tender', very considerate of the feelings of others, and outspokenness is often thwarted by a small number of manifestly sincere conservatives (who are sometimes less inhibited by these same considerations since they feel they are voicing the underlying conviction of all and merely strengthening the corporate testimony against the assaults of the world). But the movement grows until the voice of reform cannot be stilled, even by consideration for the feeling of the most weighty traditionalist. And so, in time, the testimony is modified or dropped. It is not a question of the Society declaring that this or that is no longer the testimony of all;

testimonies are what the Society shows to the world as its common belief and if the Society does not show a common attitude on a particular issue, then that, not any historically endorsed doctrine, is its testimony.

The practice of issuing Epistles after Yearly Meetings and of publishing collections of extracts from them, has led in recent years to the compilation of the *Book of Christian Discipline*.[4] This document does give the Society as a whole an opportunity from time to time to decide what it does corporately accept. The two halves of this book – Christian Faith and Practice in the Experience of the Society of Friends' and 'Church Government' – are available to the outside world (and 'Christian Faith and Practice', an anthology of Quaker writing, deserves to be better known as one of the noblest books of guidance, encouragement and consolation in the language). But as a guide to our corporate testimony they are more illuminating to ourselves than to others. As the concluding minute of the special Yearly Meeting in 1967, which completed the most recent revision, observed 'We have discovered again in experience the nature of this discipline we lay upon ourselves and corporately accept. It is not something imposed from without, a discipline of law, but it is a quality of the spirit.'

The concept that our testimony to the world is what we act and believe has interesting overtones. We are accustomed to thinking of the 'Great Tenets' of Quakerism in this context, the beliefs on which we have traditionally shown a united front to the world. But we should also recognize the importance of those areas where we are not united. For the purpose of the Society's testimony is surely not simply in its value to the individual, in 'the help that the group gives the individual in his search for discipleship' as a support and defence in his fight for personal moral integrity, but rather that it demonstrates the power of God working in the world. To speak of the difference that the power of God or awareness of the divine will could make in this world, is of proved

4. *Book of Christian Discipline of London Yearly Meeting of the Religious Society of Friends*, London Yearly Meeting of the Religious Society of Friends, 1968.

ineffectuality; men have preached Christianity for nearly two thousand years without much obvious progress towards the new Jerusalem. But to show that power, in the lives of individuals, and to see its effect on a handful of people, not separated from but integrated with the rest of the community, this has its effect, and would have more if each of us individually came closer to recognizing and following the inner light.

However, if the function and purpose of our lives and actions in showing our beliefs to the world is to demonstrate the power of God, then we should not be surprised if the particular attitudes we find ourselves driven to demonstrate are modified with time. For there are two requirements, first that the testimony should show the nature of God and the quality of the life lived in his spirit, and second that it should do this in such a way as to strike home to others and 'speak to their condition'. Now what may have been a very impressive demonstration to one generation of the power of God to change men can be completely without effect on another; thus we have lost any urge towards maintaining the early distinctions on manners and dress. We see, too, that these, maintained after they had ceased to function as a demonstration of the power of God, became, instead, evidence of man's capacity to hold to what he knows, to fail to surrender completely, and to refuse to recognize that what is required of us is continual attention to the voice of God and continual responsiveness to what we hear, even if it requires us to change course.

Thus, if we return to Hugh Doncaster's words, 'faithful following of the Light leads us into unity with those who also seek to follow it'. But in some areas, particularly in the theologically crucial area of the Quaker attitude towards Jesus, and the question of how far modern Quaker thought should be called 'Christian', while we cannot question the sincerity of all those involved and their honest desire to follow the Light, the result is *not* unity of belief. I would however suggest that it is unity of a different sort – and this other unity is where the Light leads us and is what shows God's power to move men. This unity is the community of

worship and action transcending diversity of beliefs and
understanding. In crude terms, the need today is for a demonstration that however divergent men's beliefs may be,
they have a common spiritual source and centre; and resting
on that alone they can build a caring community.

After all this diversity, it is comforting to find that a few
clearly expressed attitudes find widespread acceptance, for
example the view of the Bible as a record written by men
from their spiritual experience rather than as an absolute
authority – 'And the end of words is to bring men to the
knowledge of things beyond what words can utter. So, learn
of the Lord to make a right use of the Scripture: which is by
esteeming them in their right place and prizing *that* above
them which is above them'[5] – and the rejection of any bind-
ing credal statements – '. . . all such attempts are provisional
and can never be assumed to possess the finality of ultimate
truth . . . Among the dangers of formulated statements of
belief are these:

1. They tend to crystallize thought on matters that will
always be beyond any final embodiment in human
language;

2. They fetter the search for truth and for its more
adequate expression; and

3. They set up a fence which tends to keep out of the
Christian fold many sincere and seeking souls who would
gladly enter it.'[6]

But even when the Quaker attitude appears to be defined,
one must be careful in interpretation; for example our non-
ceremonial form of worship, the silent unprogrammed meeting, might lead to the deduction that Quakers reject the
concepts of sacraments and of priesthood, yet the truth is
more that:

5. Isaac Penington, *Letters*, ed. John Barclay, 1828, pp. 39–40, 'Christian Faith and Practice in the Experience of the Society of Friends',
London Yearly Meeting of the Religious Society of Friends, 1960,
§ 204.
6. 'The True Basis of Christian Unity', report to London Yearly
Meeting, 1917, 'Christian Faith and Practice', § 205.

The kingdom of Christ, not being a kingdom of this world, is not limited by the restrictions which fetter other societies, political or religious. It is in the fullest sense free, comprehensive, universal. It displays this character, not only in the acceptance of all comers who seek admission, irrespective of race or caste or sex, but also in the instruction and treatment of those who are already its members. It has no sacred days or seasons, no special sanctuaries, because every time and every place alike are holy. Above all it has no sacerdotal system. It interposes no sacrificial tribe or class between God and men, by whose intervention alone God is reconciled and men forgiven. Each individual member holds personal communion with the divine head. To him immediately he is responsible and from him directly he obtains pardon and draws strength.[7]

And that excellent exposition of the Quaker attitude is drawn from J. B. Lightfoot, later Bishop of Durham.

It puts forward what is perhaps another of the general characteristics which replace beliefs as the distinguishing characteristics of a Quaker; namely, an awareness of and concern with the universality of the spiritual element. It is not to be found only in certain places at certain times, nor recognized only in certain people, but at all times in all places and in all people. We cannot say, of any situation, 'Don't let's bring religion into this' because it is already there. Everything we do, or fail to do, every thought we think, has a spiritual significance. Every time I fail to do what I know is required of me I need forgiveness – not to clear my spiritual bank account or to ensure ultimate admission to Heaven, but to liberate me from the burden of guilt and failure so that I can go forward to the next moment and the next action free; able to devote all my energies to the present test. Whether I derive that forgiveness from formal absolution, from prayer in the accepted sense or from an unformalized awareness that God does not blame and that forgiveness is in my hands is a question of what sort of person I am, not of what sort of God God is.

It is this awareness of the underlying spiritual element in every man and every situation that results in another Quaker characteristic, the developed social concern. Every

7. J. B. Lightfoot, *The Christian Ministry*, Macmillan, 1901, p. 1.

Quaker is not deeply concerned and participating in every activity to improve the condition of the world and make it a loving, caring community; but few are without some involvement; if it is not working for peace it is care of the aged, or education or help to the developing countries.

From this picture of the caring individual, seeking through a curiously unstructured worship for the divine will, helped in distinguishing his proper path by the corporate testimony of his Friends, aware of an underlying spiritual element in all things, we do not get a precise picture of Quaker attitudes to the great theological issues; indeed we might say this is more a description of a moderately good man than of a follower of a particular religion. But then all herrings are not kippers – if all Quakers have the characteristics I have described, all men with these characteristics are not Quakers, nor even Christians. And it is only an egocentric desire to make our set better than all the rest that leads us to the essentially fatuous claim that such people are 'really' Christians, or Quakers, or of any other specific religious description.

I must make it clear at this point that some Friends would disagree vehemently with my approach, not denying the characteristics I have set out, but insisting that to define a Quaker in such terms, without a supporting theology, is insufficient. But I think my proposition is logically defensible; I have put down the characteristics which *are* to be found in some measure in all Quakers, not those which some Quakers consider *should* be found in all Quakers. And since it is an observational approach, let us not try to construct a self-consistent theoretical structure of Quakerism, but let us instead write down the observed characteristics. For whatever the theorist and the theologian may say, Quakerism today is not defined by what is found in books but by the judgements of individual meetings in accepting applicants for membership. And their judgements have been so liberal that, observing the resultant membership, one has to say that on questions of Christian theology the Quakers do not have a unified observable attitude – in other words, their range of opinions is as wide as that of a broad liberal slice of the general population.

While I believe this diversity to be a more profound and effective testimony than any doctrinal unity could be, I know that Friends in general find it difficult to accept; difficult to accept that the diversity is there and certainly difficult to accept that it should be lived with and that we should not be devoting our efforts to trying to eliminate it. But a few quotations, all written in the summer of 1969, will show what I mean.

The Society has never required its members to conform to a particular view about Jesus, holding that the only valid test of a Christian is whether he lives in the spirit of Christlike love, and not what he says he believes.[8]

If we remove the word Christlike from this sentence is the meaning altered? Surely not.[9]

In so far as we are led towards a general consensus of the kind I have indicated by the terms Christ-centred radicalism or radical Christ-centredness, I believe there are several very relevant and important things we shall be entitled to say. We shall be entitled, for example, to say that the Society of which we are members can testify, out of an experience of more than three centuries, that it is possible for men and women to find meaning, purpose, deliverance from anxiety, fear and enslavement to convention, and to enter into deep and satisfying relationships and to find true community. We shall affirm that such things have been given us on the sole condition of our willingness to be gathered in obedience to the 'Presence in the midst', whether we describe it, with Paul, as 'God's spirit', 'the Spirit of Christ' or 'the Spirit of him who raised Christ Jesus from the dead' or even find it necessary to use quite other terms. Furthermore we can say that, in order to know this experience, we do not find it essential to depend upon the ministrations of any specially ordained persons or to follow any prescribed liturgical pattern of worship. But we do find it essential to look for and relate ourselves to the Christ who is to be encountered in every man, who is to be min-

8. George H. Gorman, *Introducing Quakers*, p. 18, Friends Home Service Committee, 1969.

9. Michael J. Alcott, 'Do Friends Need Jesus?' *The Friend*, Vol. CXXVII, No. 26, 5 September 1969.

istered to in every situation of need, suffering, deprivation or injustice.[10]

From time to time, in *The Friend* as elsewhere, I read phrases such as 'encounter with Jesus Christ as a living reality', 'the experience of the Living Christ'.

I am not clear what is meant, how much is metaphor, how much is deduction? What is meant more than 'a deep spiritual experience?'

I would be helped if someone who speaks in such terms could explain.[11]

With that sort of range in relation to the crucial distinguishing feature of Christianity in its accepted sense, there is no point in going on to discuss the Quaker attitude to other doctrinal attitudes such as the significance of the Trinity, the crucifixion or the resurrection. There is in truth no one Quaker attitude on these matters. My only regret is that we are, in my view, a little less than clear sighted about what our doctrinal anarchy stands for, and about what we are showing forth to men by this. For, as I have suggested earlier, whether we like it or not our whole lives are our testimony, and if we demonstrate a wild diversity of doctrinal disorder, that in itself is a sort of witness.

It seems to me that survival as a Society, in spite of differences of belief enough to shatter a dozen churches, is in fact a declaration of the supreme authority of the divine, as against the human. Nobody is going to tell a Quaker what is true or what he has to do, because he takes his instructions from God. And the acceptance of each other's heterodox opinions is rooted in the shared experience of being so instructed. Herein also lies the small but significant distinction between the most undoctrinal Quaker and the humanist. When the humanist says 'I can see no higher law than that we should work together for the general good, loving our fellow men', the Quaker says 'my experience is of a higher law from which that law derives'.

10. Maurice Creasey, *Bearings*, Swarthmoor Lecture, Friends Home Service Committee, 1969, p. 80.

11. Norman Passant, letter in *The Friend*, Vol. CXXVII, No. 26, 5 September 1969.

There is no disputing this, because there can be no basis for argument about an experience which is only to be known inwardly and subjectively. Nor is there any reason for dispute, whether between Friend and humanist, between Friends and other Christians, or between Friends and those of other faiths, while we find ourselves, whatever our starting point, living the same sort of lives to the best of our abilities.

CHAPTER 4

Problems that Remain

A RELIGION so essentially simple as Quakerism, so free of accretions, ceremonies, dogma, has relatively few difficulties to
argue its way out of. Being non-authoritarian, it does not
have to expound a particular body of doctrine, or make any
particular formulation credible. The individual Friend believes what he can; the Society strives through its educational activities to improve his capacity for understanding
but not to dictate what he shall understand.

We are not faced therefore with the greater part of the
problems of theology – those concerned with the reconciliation of the teachings of Scripture and of the churches with
man's understanding of himself and the world in which he
lives. We may proceed, indeed, with explorations in this field
as far and as fast as is helpful to our spiritual understanding.
But even of questions which have been held to be crucial by
other churches – the doctrine of the Holy Trinity, for
example – we may say 'I am not yet ready to go into that
question; I may never be ready.' On the other hand, there
may come a moment, perhaps when one is reading in a quite
different field, studying Jung on the religions of east and
west, or Joseph Campbell's great work on mythology, *The
Masks of God*, or in quiet contemplation and prayer, when
one is ready, when some particular issue is brought into
focus, and the meaning enshrined in the myth is made apparent.

Yet certain problems cannot be put on one side. They are
implicit in the human condition, rather than in any formulation of belief. They obtrude themselves upon us, whether
we like it or not, and some discussion of them is necessary. It
can only be a discussion; Quakerism does not endorse any
specific answers.

The first of these intrusive problems is the question of
divine purpose. We have come one way or another to recog-

nize the presence in the world and in ourselves of the Light, the Holy Spirit; of what C. F. Andrews described to Hugh Doncaster as 'three words (which) are almost interchangeable: God, Christ and Love'.[1] It has been usual to attribute to God such things as omnipotence and omniscience: such attributes are not necessarily implied by our direct experience and raise more problems than they solve. Nevertheless, we are forced to ask ourselves whether this God we are aware of has a purpose, or whether indeed it is appropriate to use such words as 'purpose' in relation to God. The third of C. F. Andrews's interchangeable words, after all, does not require a purpose, but is an end in itself; if we know what love is we do not need a reason for loving. So one might say that to know anything of God is to know that we must seek him and do his work. My own feeling, insofar as my own experience goes, is that awareness of God is the same as love, and that this is the one self-validating experience of life, the only experience which does not require an aim or a purpose outside itself.

Yet where is this leading us? Is it no more than a question of being, not becoming, as the Oriental philosophers put it? That, I think, is part of the truth, but only part. There is a western tradition of God making a covenant with man, of a promise of salvation; and the teaching of Jesus is not only a morality, but also a reiteration of the promise, and indeed a declaration that it is made good here and now, not at some distant future time. What is the nature of this compact? On man's part it is that he should do God's will, and should become aware of the presence of God within him and be directed by it; by countless examples we know that the direction so given is to the good life, a life of love and kindness to others, of service and integrity. On God's part the compact is (or at least this is how it has been expressed by those who seemed most sure of it) to sustain us, not to try us beyond our strength, and to gather us to himself. We can but try our part, which is its own justification, and see whether the rest

1. L. Hugh Doncaster, *God in Every Man*, George Allen & Unwin, 1969, p. 73.

follows. 'Set your mind upon his kingdom, and all the rest will come to you as well.'[2]

Unfortunately, man creates God in his own image; the moment we start talking of 'him' and 'his' attributes we impose upon the divine a whole range of human characteristics – will, purpose and so on. These may be characteristics of God, but we have no reason to assume them; what we may attribute to God is not the collection of characteristics we would like him to have but those which our experience can vouch for or which are vouched for by those whose experience we can accept. I suppose that in a sense all the expressions of divine purpose, whether in terms of individual redemption or the gathering of God's people, are but symbols for the searching of the individual towards spiritual truth, in whatever form it is available to him, and the effects of that search upon him. One thing on which most of the evidence agrees is that the divine in some way is not bound by the limitations of time and space which circumscribe our material world. By evidence I mean of course the evidence of spiritual leaders and seekers. If we find this evidence acceptable, then we can begin to see that purpose, in the human sense, is time-dependent, and is not relevant to a concept of God which is outside of time. But we are time-dependent, at least unless we achieve complete submission to and immersion in the divine will, and so it is our nature that finds a divine purpose necessary.

How far this discussion is sufficiently rigorous to satisfy anybody I do not know. The most I would hope is that, without deploying the full apparatus of metaphysics or theology, it may show how individual purpose can be accepted without implying or requiring that we know the divine purpose. It may also open the way for discussion of another question of continuing difficulty, the problem of pain and suffering.

This problem is simply stated. If God exists, and if his nature is good, why does he permit so much suffering in the world? There are, once again, considerable amounts of writing on this subject from the standpoint of orthodox Christianity. But here, too, the point of departure has been the

2. *New English Bible*, Luke xii, 31.

need to construct a logical system reconciling the world as it is with the tenets of the faith, and the results are singularly lacking in conviction. To put it bluntly, I do not know of any exposition on this theme which would have any chance of convincing a mildly critical agnostic.

Perhaps we should start by looking a little more closely at the problem. It involves a number of assumptions; first, that our happiness or unhappiness, pain or pleasure, is a matter of concern to God, second, that he has the capacity to alter our material condition at will or to devise our material circumstances, and, third, that having this capacity he will use it. But these ideas belong to a wholly egocentric view of the universe, in which the whole machinery is built round us and our standards. Moreover, it assumes a rather old-fashioned view of God as the architect and chief engineer of the universe. If we still speak of God as the creator, we surely mean it in a symbolic sense; rather that he is the all-pervading basic source of values in the universe than that he is in any mechanistic sense the creator. As to creation and its consequences; we know much and learn more every year about the origins of our world; but we appreciate that however much we learn we will always have to ask 'and what happened before that?' But to be able to point to the limit of our own knowledge is not to have found God; and there is no reason at all to associate the experience of God which we may find within ourselves with the 'God of the gaps', the postulating of God as the excuse for and origin of everything we cannot explain.

If then we do not make assumptions about God's responsibility, but simply accept that we know very little about him, and that little mainly in terms of subjective experience, we can make a slightly different approach to the problem of pain. We can in fact try to accept that pain is as much a part of the world we live in as pleasure; we know it has a physiological function, for physical pain is the way in which we are warned of damage to our bodies, and it may well have some similar psychological function. But the pain and suffering is there, that is an established fact; We all have sufficient experience and observation to vouch for it.

From there we can go on to divide suffering into evitable and inevitable, into that caused by man and that beyond his control. Of the man-made suffering there is little to say; it is our doing and we can prevent it and we must not therefore try to put the blame on God. Our task is simply to right wrongs, to prevent or ease suffering and pain wherever we can; time enough when we have prevented the preventable and cured the curable to ask profound questions about the remaining part.

Of that inevitable remaining part, I would only say that I see it as being as much a part of the natural order as the rain and the stars. The rain performs its part in the complexity of the universe, a complexity which is its own explanation. If the various elements did not dovetail in a way which some thinkers have seen as evidence of the divine hand, the system would not survive – the hands only go round on watches which are working. So also the inevitable pain is part of this pattern, and part of the framework in which we are placed and have to make all our efforts, including the efforts we may make towards the divine. And if we do that, there are the lives and works of many to show us how they have accepted suffering and sought for a closer approach to God through suffering. But, for myself, this is never an argument that God sends us suffering in order that through it we may come closer to him. Rather, there is a way to God in all things, even in suffering.

Both the question of divine purpose and the problem of pain throw into relief the question of how far we can see the world and what goes on in it as God's work, and how far we have to accept the evidence that the world is as we find it and try to see God in the context of and against the background of a mechanistic world which is not of his making. This, which can be represented as a throwing overboard of one of the vital attributes of the divine, is a concept increasingly to be found in modern religious thought. As a way of expressing our awareness of God, it is probably more appropriate than the traditional mode to our time and our way of thought. Neither is 'true' – in the sense of being a complete and exclusive statement of the truth – each has some elements of truth in it. In a time when we see clearly the evolutionary nature of the physical world, when we begin to appreciate the inevitable nature of the design process that we call natural selection, and the systematic consequences of truly random events (for example, the sorting out by natural selection of genetic mutations produced by the random bombardment of cells by cosmic rays), it is understandable that we should find ourselves more in sympathy with a model which makes God coexistent with the material world than with one which attributes to him its creation and operation. It is, however, important to remember always that we are talking about models, about symbolic representations, because what we know about God in the world is really only the fragmentary experience of individuals – which is why it is so stupid to press the claims of one dogmatic and comprehensive theology and cosmology against another. It is like a man with a street map of Bath and a man with a London Underground map disputing as to which was best qualified to do an Ordnance Survey of the whole of Europe.

One of the greatest areas of our invincible ignorance is as to whether that part of man which can attain to some knowledge of the divine is itself in some sense immortal; whether it lives after the body dies and, if so, in what manner. As the aphorism has it, the trouble with life after death is that those who know don't talk and those who talk don't know.

The concept of the indwelling spirit of God must incline us to see resurrection as symbolizing the death of the ego-self and the rebirth in awareness of God which can happen to us in this life. It also inclines us to accept death as breaking the link between the physical body and the divine light within us, letting that of God which is in us return back to complete unity and absorption with the totality of God. This makes of death a full realization of what we seek in life, yet in a sense so different from our life experience that it must be a complement rather than a substitute. The living-out of life in searching for and finding, however inadequately and spasmodically, God in life, is too rich, and too clearly the course required of us, for us to give it up in favour of the possibility of instant union with the divine through death. Death, which may bring that union, that resurrection, is another experience. Living in search of God is a present fact.

One thing is quite certain. Quakers today would not ever offer the next life as either reward or punishment or consolation for the life on earth. And in my observation, they find this subject of little interest, preserving by-and-large either a robust conviction or a cheerful agnosticism, which as they get older may sometimes moderate into a quizzical curiosity.

'Not expecting but hoping that the Resurrection
Will not catch him unawares whenever it takes place.'[3]

3. John Heath-Stubbs, *A Charm Against the Toothache*, Methuen, 1954, p. 35.

CHAPTER 5

Quakers and Other Churches

'THE unity of Christians never did nor ever will or can stand in uniformity of thought and opinion, but in Christian love only.'[1] Fox found his first followers mainly among the Seekers, those who had already dissociated themselves from other religions and who sought the truth, not knowing where they would find it. But very soon Quakers began to attract members from existing churches, and until comparatively recently this has been the main source of replenishment of membership. Today the position is once again that most new members admitted to the Society on convincement come from the ranks of the seekers – from those who have rejected other churches and religions; from the great multitude of concerned agnostics.

The Society's ability to speak to those who reject other churches is the result of its lack of dogma. The seeker is not asked to accept and proclaim doctrines concerning the nature of God and the historical Christ which may raise logical and theological problems for him. Instead, he is offered a concept of the inner light, of that of God in every man, which is exemplified in the teaching of Christ and for which, if he is so inclined, he may find support in ancient religions and modern psychology. But he is not asked to accept this concept as an act of faith. Instead, he is invited to come, through the Meeting for Worship, to experience of it. This experience is not limited to those who say a particular creed, nor could it ever be seen as a restricted benefit. The all-pervading love of God is there, in every human soul, for every man who can accept it.

So Robert Barclay, in the seventeenth century, was able to say,

1. Thomas Storey, 'Discourse at Horsleydown', 1737, 'Christian Faith and Practice in the Experience of the Society of Friends', London Yearly Meeting of the Religious Society of Friends, 1960, § 221.

The church [is] no other thing but the society, gathering or company of such as God hath called out of the world, and worldly spirit, to walk in his light and life ... under this church ... are comprehended all, and as many, of whatsoever nation, kindred, tongue, or people they be, though outwardly strangers, and remote from those who profess Christ and Christianity in words, and have the benefit of the Scriptures, as become obedient to the holy light, and testimony of God, in their hearts ... There may be members therefore of this Catholic Church both among heathens, Turks, Jews, and all the several sorts of Christians, men and women of integrity and simplicity of heart who ... are by the secret touches of this holy light in their souls enlivened and quickened, thereby secretly united with God, and there-through become true members of this Catholic Church.[2]

It would be idle to claim that Barclay and the early Quakers implied by this a recognition that the truth could be found in other religions; certainly as regards the heathens, Turks and Jews, some Quakers have been quite sure that they themselves had to proclaim the truth without any equivocation or any suggestion that there were valid alternatives to Christianity. This attitude was the foundation on which Quaker missionary efforts abroad were built. But as regards other Christians, the Quakers are not given to poaching, and generally have been happy to work with any who follow Christ's teaching in bringing others to the same way. The differences, from the seventeenth century onward, have been over what constituted Christ's teaching.

The issues facing those working for Christian unity in, for example, the Councils of Churches, have always been somewhat artificial to Quakers. Discussion tends to be on credal matters – the Quakers have no creed – and on questions of sacraments and procedures, which to Quakers are not worth arguing about. It is worth stressing that the barriers against a Quaker participating in the offices or sacraments of any other church can only come from that church; the Society itself makes no objection.

As Isaac Penington observed in 1659:

2. Robert Barclay, *Apology*, 1678, pp. 181–2, 'Christian Faith and Practice', § 224.

Even in the Apostles' days, Christians were too apt to strive after a wrong unity and uniformity in outward practices and observations, and to judge one another unrighteously in those things; and mark, it is not the different practice from one another that breaks the peace and unity but the judging of one another because of different practices ... Men keeping close to God, the Lord will lead them on fast enough ... for he taketh care of such and knoweth what light and what practices are most proper for them ...[3]

However, the Quaker attitude can produce its own difficulties in relations with other Christian churches. At the foundation of the World Council of Churches in 1940, the Quakers were unable to accept membership because it involved acceptance of a statement of belief; their membership of the British Council of Churches was made possible by the 'exceptive clause' in its constitution, which permitted membership of bodies represented on the formative Commission but which were unable to accept the Council's basis of belief. Both Quakers and Unitarians, who had been on the Commission and had played a significant part in the setting up of the Council, were thus able to accept membership.

Some years later, in 1964, the British Council of Churches proposed the adoption of the revised basis of belief of the World Council of Churches without the exceptive clause. There was, perhaps, an initial failure of communication; the other members of the Council, used as they were to working in harmony with the Quakers, were not fully aware of the nature of the objection to the basis – namely, an objection on principle to any formal intellectual acceptance of a definition of faith, rather than to any particular statement or wording. When this was understood, the proposed constitution was reworded to allow for associate membership for those previously covered by the exceptive clause. Associate members have full rights of membership apart from being unable to vote on changes of the constitution.

This is, for Friends, a position which is not easily accepted

3. Isaac Penington, *Works*, 1681, Part I, pp. 240–42, 'Christian Faith and Practice', § 222.

or very comfortable. We are aware that the rules have been modified to allow us to remain on the Council; that it is a modification for existing members only; and that if we were a new applicant we would be expected to accept the basis. From a logical viewpoint, we should perhaps carry our objection to intellectual statements of faith right through to objecting even to a formalized exception in our favour. But against that, we have worked in the Council of Churches for a quarter of a century; we know that the words may divide us but the spirit joins, and so we gratefully accept the continued opportunity to play our part.

It is salutary to see in this incident the two sides of the coin; the difficulties produced by an insistence on dogma and the corresponding difficulties produced by an equally rigid opposition to dogma. It is also reassuring to see both overcome by the exercise of understanding and loving concern on all sides.

Of course the constitutional difficulties have had no bearing on working together locally, and in this the ecumenical movement has gathered strength in recent years. There are two ways of operating and both are adopted. The more formal is the association of the Friends Meeting with the local Council of Churches, and, through this body, with collective social and community action. But cooperation also occurs through individual members of different churches joining a specific social service agency – for example, it takes all sorts to fill the Samaritans' duty rota.

One area where Quakers and the churches have been able to help each other greatly is in exploring the thought of Teilhard de Chardin and writers of the 'New Reformation', such as Paul Tillich, Dietrich Bonhoeffer and their successors.

If we consider primarily the writers of the New Reformation rather than de Chardin, whose visionary insights are in a different category, they are in fact engaged, in the title of Tillich's book, in the shaking of the foundations. They are vigorously engaged in pulling away the columns of the temple, to see at what stage the roof comes in. This is not done from an idly iconoclastic motive, but as a controlled experiment, to establish how much of the structure is redundant and how much essential.

Many Friends have found this whole movement very helpful in their own search for truth. While mainstream Christian theology, and particularly Protestant theology, moved only sluggishly, remaining academically remote from other aspects of modern thought, the Quaker was encouraged to a certain complacency; without much intellectual effort he could reasonably lay claim to an outlook more in keeping with his times than that of any other sect. But with the New Reformation, the concepts of theology have been rigorously re-examined and the comforting differences eroded. The Quaker is forced to the same healthy, if disturbing, examination of his own attitudes, and has to compare his personal interpretation of religious experience with mainstream theories.

An aspect of this reassessment is a concern with the validity of Quakerism as an independent movement. If mainstream theology turns away from a 'God out there', if we are to contemplate a God we can do without, a Father who genuinely wills his children's emergence into complete independence; if the mythic elements of the life of Christ are to be accepted for their mythic and symbolic value, their historic validity not proven and not relevant, how far is a separate Quakerism still significant? Could not Quakers go back to the churches, as radical protestants within the fold?

For some individuals this may be possible and the right course. For the Society as a whole, however much we wish to see the man-made barriers between the churches dismantled, we must recognize that reabsorption into institutionalized protestantism is a long way off; there are so many differences still between the different denominations, and Quakerism is still something different again. But from this examination does come a renewed concern with what Quakerism stands for, and with what it has to offer and to whom. Its particular value for our time is in its ability to make contact with those who are seeking for a meaning in their lives but cannot be helped by more orthodox, more credal religions, and in its showing to the world an examplar of a socially conscious religious society.

Others, from different viewpoints within the Society, have come to conclusions similar in content, if differently expressed:

The alternative that the Quaker vision opposes to institutional Christianity is not the 'church withdrawn' but a church which has discovered the true nature and source of world-redeeming power. It should be the task of the heirs of the Quaker vision to witness for the church of the cross and to make this genuine alternative to institutionalized Christianity a live option in this present age.[4]

I see Quakerism as having a greater opportunity at the present time of speaking to the condition of contemporary men and women than it has ever had since the seventeenth century. It can do this, not only because it understands and sympathizes with much in their mood of radical questioning, search and protest, but also because it knows, in its corporate experience over three centuries, the reality of a presence and a power which focuses, to their mutual enrichment and harmony, the experience of worship, community and service, and thus 'answers that of God in every man'.[5]

The reason for the separate existence of the Society can be seen thus as functional rather than conceptual. By being the type of Society we are, we can speak to those who are otherwise isolated. This indeed gives an insight into a unity which does not depend on the absorption of different churches into one or on a common creed or a common worship, but rather

every one learning their own lesson, performing their own peculiar service, and knowing, owning and loving one another in their several places and different performances to their Master, to whom they are to give an account, and not to quarrel with one another about different practices. For this is the true ground of love and unity, not that such a man walks and does just as I do, but because I feel the same Spirit and life in him, and that he walks in his rank, in his own order in his proper way and place of

4. Lewis Benson, *Catholic Quakerism*, published by author, 1966, p. 73.

5. Maurice Creasey, *Bearings*, Swarthmoor Lecture, Friends Home Service Committee, 1969, p. 87.

subjection to that; and this is far more pleasing to me than if he walked just in that track wherein I walk.[6]

However, a further element of challenge rests at the heart of the ecumenical movement. If one allows that the Christian Church should be one, that differences of formulation reflect the imperfections of man rather than any absolute characteristics of God, then why is the boundary drawn round the *Christian* churches? Could it not be that God has revealed himself many times through many prophets and divinely inspired teachers, and that man has created the small change of his religions out of the treasure which ever and again he finds hidden in the field? Ought we to recognize the same Spirit and life in the Buddhist, the Moslem and the Hindu, in the esoteric sects which spring from the soil of India and take root on the West Coast of America, the dream culture of the Ulu and the dying mystical life of the Kalahari Bushmen?

I find that this concept is labelled syncretism, and is viewed with great sympathy by many Friends, who see their own spiritual experiences reflected in other religions, and who have conducted mutually helpful discussions with adherents of these other faiths. Understandably, however, syncretism is viewed with grave distrust by those for whom the Christian quality of Quakerism is inherently derived from concepts of the historical and universal Christ. Yet it is difficult in the modern world to accept a view of God which is limited to the Judaeo-Christian tradition, or even to take the attitude that all other religions have a shadowy insight into the truth but that Christianity alone reveals all. Better perhaps with Penington to recognize that 'All Truth is a shadow except the last, except the utmost, yet every Truth is true in its kind. It is substance in its own place though it be but a shadow in another place (for it is but a reflection from an intenser substance) and the shadow is a true shadow, as the substance is a true substance.'[7] Or, in Geoffrey

6. Isaac Penington, *Works*, 1681, Part I, pp. 240–42, 'Christian Faith and Practice', 1960, § 222.

7. Isaac Penington, *The Life of a Christian*, 1653, 'Christian Faith and Practice', § 1B.

Heawood's words: 'The truth does not lie in the superficial half-truth that all religions are one, nor in the complementary truth that we have something to learn from each. It lies, surely, in the discovery of the differing needs of men, and the differing ways in which God seems to meet them . . . the great overall truths are simple and universal, the search is individual.'[8]

8. Geoffrey L. Heawood, *The Humanist Christian Frontier*, Society for Promoting Christian Knowledge, 1967, p. 85.

CHAPTER 6

The Spiritual Experiment

I MAY have surprised many readers, and possibly will have surprised many Friends, by writing so much about beliefs. Friends, by and large, tend to discuss beliefs only among themselves, and to see them as best advertised by action. Indeed, the growth of Quaker public relations work, of any attempt to reach out to non-Quakers, has had to overcome the conviction of many that a Christian life speaks for itself, and has no need of the worldly arts of publicity. This attitude, however, is now fading; we do not see why the cigarette manufacturers should have all the best posters. In the modern world it is not simply a matter of showing an example of Christian life to those who seek Christ, but of making contact with those who do not know what they seek and perhaps hardly know that they seek at all.

At this point, when contact is made, a difficulty arises. The inquirer listens to what is said to him, observes the lives and outward attitudes of Quakers, perhaps says, 'Yes, all this is admirable. You are admirable people leading admirable, socially beneficial lives. In your work for the community and your concern for others you remind me very much of my good friends the liberal agnostic humanists. The difference is that you relate all that you do to a belief in God and a discipleship of Christ, and you spend an hour or more a week, when you might be doing something useful, sitting in your Meeting for Worship in silence. This seems to me odd; please explain it.'

An explanation, in terms of a theology, is likely to be forthcoming; I have tried to set one out in the preceding chapters. But any such explanation leads back in the end to the central fact of experience of God, awareness of the living Christ, being possessed of the Holy Spirit. To have that experience is to be convinced, not in the limited sense of becoming convinced of the truth of a particular doctrinal framework but in the widest sense of all, convinced and ever after aware, of a non-material dimension to life.

It has always seemed to me a great pity that Friends will discuss theology, or morality, or social action or Christian unity, at any time and in any place where they are not actually engaged in the silence of Meeting for Worship, but they are loath to discuss the actual experiment by which they convince themselves of the existence of God and the love of God. I can understand this reluctance. It is an experience quite unrelated to the material world; it is mystical; and it is therefore likely to be met by others with incredulity and mirth. Worse, it is likely to make people think of us as a little queer, not altogether reliable. Even among ourselves we are hesitant – perhaps for the other reason; through thinking that our experience is not the real thing, that others have a much deeper experience, that they don't suffer as we do from back-sliding and lack of faith. When, from time to time, usually late at night after a conference, we get down to exchanging notes, we usually find an encouraging amount of common ground; and yet, next time someone asks us what happens at Meeting we talk about silence, and vocal ministry and reading the 'Advices and Queries'. We don't usually manage to talk about the presence of God; we all have a sizeable element of the blessed Saint Peter in our make-up.

One advantage of writing as a means of communication is that one does not actually have to face one's reader. Safe behind the impersonal printed word one can risk making a fool of oneself by attempting to describe the spiritual experiment, in terms of an experiment in natural science; attempt, so to speak, to set down the methodology.

First the hypothesis to be tested: that there is, coexistent with the natural world, a non-material entity; that this entity, which we call God, inter-penetrates us, being both accessible to each of us individually and common to us all collectively. Also that the knowledge of God is an awareness of universal love, which we find to be the essential teaching of Jesus Christ.

To this main hypothesis can be added many subsidiary

deductions as to the effect of spiritual awareness on our material life. But for the purpose of the main experiment we are seeking only to test the concept of the nature of God and whether it is possible to become aware of God. The further stage, having reached this awareness, of observing its effects, is relatively straightforward – almost a simple piece of psychological or sociological experimental work. Many people record the results of this secondary experiment when they look at a group of Quakers, or any other believers in a living faith, and comment that they seem to radiate a certain inner conviction and happiness; there must be something in it. But our aim is to reinforce this deductive approach by a positive God-seeking experiment.

The hypothesis to be tested proposes that the divine spirit is in us, and we therefore seek it in ourselves, rather than in others. There is really no other experimental apparatus, except a quiet place. This is readily found in a Friends' Meeting House, or a church out of service hours, but can equally be the quiet of a wood, a garden or a private room.

Our theoretical analysis suggests that the divine force we are seeking must be essentially different from the normal everyday world. The experimental method we propose to use is that of withdrawing from the material world, and ceasing all preventable activity and participation. We know that what we call God is something different in nature from our everyday selves; if we strip away all we can of ourselves we should be left either with nothing, or with something we recognize as the vestigial remnants of our own personality, or with something quite different. If we find this last then we have found something which may be what we seek; whether it is or not we can only consider when the experience is there to be examined.

The experiment is conducted as follows. One sits quietly in the chosen place. Let it be a place and time when you will not be disturbed, and if you can make the experiment with friends by all means do so.

The benefit of the group is obvious in terms of helping one to be still. It is endorsed, too, by Scripture and experience; yet one must admit that it apparently introduces a possibly misleading mechanism. Little though we know of the human mind, we have sufficient indications that one mind, in suitable circumstances, may influence another by non-sensory means. Could not the group lead therefore to some apparent perceptions which were no more than a form of mass-hypnosis? If the whole group is trying to find God, could not the very effort of the group create the experience they search for? It possibly could, yet the experience itself must be the final arbiter. The purpose of this experiment is to create the conditions in which we are open to the experience, not to assess the experience or to try to establish by logical analysis what it might be. If it is what we are looking for it will be self-validating; we may never be able to say how it arises, or what is its ultimate nature. But that does not matter once we have established, for ourselves, its existence. From the point of view of setting up the experiment, the most advantageous situation is the group, and particularly the group containing members who have already experienced what we seek. Sitting quietly, in silence, without any physical activities other than those of the involuntary systems essential to life, the mind should be directed to considering who one is, and how awareness of oneself is maintained. It is maintained by thought; awareness of time and awareness of self both come from the continuous procession of thoughts. Now the next stage is to cut down, and ultimately cut out, thought. This is the simple, yet intensely difficult, key.

I can only suggest ways in which it may be attempted, because this is an intensely personal aspect, and the way in which one person progresses may be quite useless to another. The essential element is perhaps willingness to sacrifice the individuality, to be prepared to see the sense of uniqueness which we have prized and exalted swept away into a more universal awareness. When we read about this in a book it does not seem a very significant threat, a mere metaphysical form of words. But when in fact we start to get near to giving up, even momentarily, our precious individuality, we panic. We cannot bring ourselves to pay that price, even for awareness of God.

Nevertheless, assuming that we are sincerely anxious to stop thinking, how do we set about it? Most of the practices associated with yoga are aimed at the same end; control of breathing, concentration on a single point, repetition of a single word or syllable; but these are all practices which seem difficult to carry through and which may have undesirable physical side effects. I prefer to suggest the more direct methods of concentrating attention upon the question under consideration, and consciously heading off and eliminating every distracting and irrelevant thought. The chosen subject on which one concentrates may be in the form of trying to isolate, in the middle of one's physical and psychical entity, the universal; it may be the contemplation of Jesus as a living presence. It may even be possible simply to concentrate on the elimination of irrelevant thought, so as to leave the whole being open.

This process imposes a separated awareness of the mind and will; inside my head the thoughts fly up like kites in the wind, but I hold the string, I wind them in until they fall and flutter to the ground. Then up shoots another one, and I wind that in, and that too flutters and dies. But who or what is the 'I' that does this thought-stopping? That too is a thought and 'I' stop it. So one approaches, by efforts which call for the deepest resources of one's being, to the condition of true silence; not just of sitting still, not just of not speaking, but of a wide awake, fully aware non-thinking.

It is in this condition, found and held for a brief instant only, that I have experienced the existence of something other than 'myself'. The thinking me has vanished, and with it vanishes the sense of separation, of unique identity. One is not left naked and defenceless, as one is, for example, by the operations of the mind in self-analysis. One becomes instead aware, one is conscious of being a participant in the whole of existence, not limited to the body, or the moment. This sounds like a description of a hallucinated state, and certainly it is an alarming experience when first encountered. But it differs from what I understand to be the condition induced by hallucinogenic drugs such as LSD (conditions which I would recognize as an opening, but a limited opening, of the identical doors of perception) in that the condition acquired without drugs is under control; one can leave it at the ring of a telephone bell, however reluctantly; it does not restrict or inhibit action, it does not accentuate the pre-existent mood, lifting the optimist to heaven and plunging the depressive into hell, and, most important of all, it carries a conviction of its essential truth which persists and enriches life outside the brief experience.

It is in this condition that one understands the nature of the divine power, its essential identity with love, in the widest sense of that much misused word. And the experience rings true; once we have gone so far we are bound to recognize the nature of our experience and there is no hiding from its implications.

I feel apologetic about this chapter. To many of my readers it will probably seem an inadequate and inaccurate sketch of an experience infinitely profound and moving. To many more it will appear as a ludicrous description of how to practise the art of self-deception. The words, as words, will not convince anyone; they are not intended to. They are only the outline of an experimental method, in itself one of many but the only one I can describe from experience. The purpose is not to describe my own experience – for language is ill-adapted to the adventures of the non-material world, and any description can be no more than a well or badly chosen metaphor – but to describe the experimental set-up. Attempt the experiment open-mindedly and with humility; there can be no guarantee of any particular result, or indeed of any result at all; you must draw your own conclusions from such evidence, positive or negative, as you find.

PART III

Belief and Behaviour

CHAPTER I

The Moral Law

A BELIEF such as I have attempted to describe is an end in itself. It does not need to be justified by reference to its effect on the individual or on society. It is justified by inward experience, and its outward effects are subsidiary. Nevertheless, it is reasonable to ask what these effects are; does it lead men to violence and hatred or to love and compassion; does it make them utterly self-centred or utterly selfless; or, perhaps worst of all, does it leave them outwardly the same mixed bag of good and bad that it found them? Equally one may ask more specific questions. These are various moral issues on which our society is divided, questions such as the justification of war, the proper treatment of criminals, attitudes to homosexuality, and pre-marital sex, the right attitude to money. On all these matters one may with some justification ask, 'Where do the Quakers stand?'

The general question can be answered with a certain precision and assurance; with the assurance moreover that non-Quaker society will endorse the answer from its own observation. The effect of their beliefs on Friends is to make them better people than they would otherwise have been. Individually they have their faults; I know hot-tempered Friends, stubborn Friends, boring Friends, blundering Friends. There may be among us vicious Friends and dishonest Friends, even so I would guess that they are less vicious and less dishonest than they would have been without some glimpse of the God within them. As a Society we are rather earnest, lacking in dash and sparkle (though some of the newer and younger Friends are happily redressing the balance), quiet, peaceable, friendly, full of concern for others. Friends do not pass by on the other side of the road; Friends do not have one set of principles for Sunday and another set for weekdays.

As a comparatively new member of the Society I am able to write this eulogy without embarrassment. I do not feel myself included in it. In any case, to say that Friends are a good deal better as people than the average random group is not to say that they are perfect; only that their aim is high and they do make sincere efforts to reach it.

There is a delightful story from Colchester Meeting of a Friend who drove up to the Meeting House in her Mini, rather late for a language class at the Technical College, only to find the parking space in the forecourt completely blocked by a large Bentley, which stood in such a way as to leave very little room at either end. She was just going to surge on round the town looking for somewhere else to park when another member of the language class came by and, with skilful direction, enabled her to slip into the gap between the Bentley and the fence. As she got out of her car she thanked him, and said of the Bentley driver, 'He might at least have had the decency to put the thing up at one end and leave room for others. And in any case, he's got no right to be there, he isn't even a Quaker.'

'What,' said the gentleman who had helped her, 'are you a Quaker?'

'Yes.'

'Then if you are a Quaker you shouldn't get so angry.'

'It's because I get so angry that I *have* to be a Quaker.'

There speaks every one of us; it is because of our imperfections that we need the support and encouragement of belonging to the Society.

Now, having said that Quakers are by and large rather good people, and made the necessary modest disavowal of perfection, it would be convenient to go on to a clear statement of the Quaker line on various moral issues. Unfortunately for one attempting to make such a statement, the Quaker attitude in this is as in so much else is non-rigid. I discussed this problem once with a group of weighty Friends. This phrase meant what one might expect in the nineteenth century, but is now, I am happy to say, increasingly used in a gently teasing way to describe those perceptive experienced Friends to whom one turns for advice. To call them 'weighty Friends' makes sure they will not think too well of themselves.

I propounded to my weighty Friends the plan of this part of the book, and explained that I thought the reader was entitled to ask what is the Quaker attitude to this or that; to unmarried mothers and their children, to alcoholics, to juvenile delinquency. My weighty Friends said, and they were of course quite right, that you could not have an attitude to a problem in the abstract; there were no problems, only people. Every individual has to be approached with the love which came from knowing God in yourself and seeking to find, and answer to, that of God in others. Thus it is by striving always to come closer to God in oneself that one is able to respond to others, to find the Christian way with difficulties and problems, which is not a specified solution to any generalized problem but an individual solution for an individual.

And this is perhaps one of the most infuriating things about Quakers. More orthodox religions present a rigid code of beliefs and of consequent behaviour, and so enable us to identify the gap between profession and practice. The Quaker has only one fixed point, his direct experience of God's love within himself. It is to this that he turns like a magnet to the north, and in every situation this is his compass, by which he is guided. Thus it is almost impossible for anyone else to decide whether or not a Quaker is responding to a particular situation rightly, in accordance with his own inner light. The nearest one can get is to follow his path, to be as deeply concerned, and to consult one's own inner light. At that stage one tends to lose interest in checking up on other people's performance; the shortcomings of one's own behaviour are too apparent, and the divine imperative too insistent.

Nevertheless, while accepting that my weighty Friends are perfectly right, and that no formalized strictly Quaker attitude to any moral issue can be presented, I still feel that the inquirer is entitled to at least a discussion of the application of our beliefs to real-life situations. It will just have to be, like so much else in this book, undogmatic.

Religions tend to distinguish between the spiritual and the material world in a hard-and-fast way. Some provide special communities for the spiritual life; most provide for a class of people specially devoted to spiritual matters, in the form of a priesthood. It is usually clearly stated that the best thing one can do with one's life is to devote it entirely to the spiritual path to the exclusion of material concerns, and it is sometimes implied that this is best achieved by actual withdrawal from the affairs of the world. Now the first part of that statement is acceptable enough, but the second part is slightly more suspect. It may be that the easiest way to be devoted to the spiritual life is to withdraw into a contemplative community; I am not sure that it is the best way. I suspect that this is another example of man's inbuilt urge to distinguish. Perhaps it is something to do with the way our brains are constructed, the actual type of logic circuits employed; for whatever reason, we seem to have an irresistible urge to classify, to sort everything we come across into tidy separate packets.

The concept that has taken longest to worm its way into non-scientific thinking, indeed which still does not find ready acceptance in some scientific circles, is that of uncertainty and imprecision, that things cannot be divided up neatly as we would like. The truth is not in division and distinction but in the unity which embraces diversity. One thing modulates imperceptibly into another; light is both a wave motion and a stream of particles, there is no hard line between hominoids and true man, the more precisely you define something, the less likely it is that the definition is valid. So, in the same way, the attempt to separate the spiritual and the material diminishes both. We find the divine spirit in ourselves, and we know it to be in others. We also know it works through the world of men. Why then should we withdraw from the world? Looking at Jesus, the exemplar of God in man, we see that he withdrew from the world only briefly, to find his own way to God in solitude. Then he returned to the world, to demonstrate, as it seems to me, living by the spirit in the world. Here was a life devoted entirely to spiritual matters, completely detached from the cares of the material world, because to him they were not cares, and yet utterly concerned, concerned for everyone with the true concern that comes from an awareness of their divine inner nature. He lived in the everyday world, and took part in it, but his only concern in every action, however mundane it seemed, was to bring those with whom he came in contact to a realization of God.

There are sound and practical reasons why Quakers have had to be mystics with a regular job. England is no place for mendicants and hermits; the climate is unfavourable, they have Catholic and pre-Reformation associations and the Elizabethan poor-law and the rise of the Puritan ethic have both served to discourage them. As a new sect, Quakers had no invested capital to sustain separated communities; a few were men of substance but most were of modest means. Debarred from public office and the professions by their refusal to take oaths and their inability to subscribe to the Thirty-nine Articles, they could not command the sinecures in the gift of the Church and state, and so turned to business. On the whole, they did very well at it, attributing their success, with some reason, to their firm adherence to honesty and sound principles. Then again, the basic belief in God in every man was expressed in the rejection of a separated priesthood, and if there are no separated priests then everyone is a priest, and spiritual concern cannot so easily be limited to one day a week.

Thus Quakers have worked out a way of living, varying according to their social environment, but in essence the same everywhere, in which they are good citizens, good neighbours, good masters and good workers, but always aware that 'good' means to them 'in accordance with God's will'. This leads to one warning which is worth bearing in mind. You may rely on any Friend you encounter to deal honestly and considerately with you in any matter you please, and within the limits of human frailty your trust is not likely to be misplaced. But do not presume upon his loyalty. Do not think that, because he has been for many years a teacher in your school, a member of your committee, or a personal friend, that you can persuade him to do something, in the name of friendship or the good of the organization, which he conceives to be wrong. At this point he will refer to a higher loyalty, for which over three hundred years past Quakers have willingly and cheerfully gone to prison and, if need be, died.

Here, once again, is this firm centre of belief; the knowledge that God's will is the supreme law and that God's will can be known to the individual, not just in terms of generalized commandments and ethical rules, but in terms of every specific situation. There is always a right course and a wrong course, and we may know the right if we will be quiet and 'with diligence wait to feel the Lord God to arise, to scatter and expel all that which is the cause of leanness and barrenness upon any soul; for it is the Lord must do it, and he will be waited upon in sincerity and fervency of spirit . . .'[1]

1. Stephen Crisp, letter dated Amsterdam 10 February 1663 (old style), *Letters of Isaac Penington and Others*, ed. John Kendal, 1796, 'Christian Faith and Practice in the Experience of the Society of Friends', London Yearly Meeting of the Religious Society of Friends, 1960, § 236.

CHAPTER 2

Quakers as Peacemakers

IT is generally understood that Quakers are pacifists, and indeed many have first come into contact with the Society when, as conscientious objectors in time of war, they found themselves working with Friends, perhaps in a Friends Ambulance Unit. But while most Friends are opposed to the use of violence, some are absolute pacifists and all are concerned to reduce strife and conflict, it is not true to say that all Friends completely reject the use of armed force. As usual, the comprehensive generalization is too all-embracing.

The historical background is even somewhat equivocal. Fox himself refused a captaincy in the Civil War 'I told [the Commonwealth Commissioners] I lived in the virtue of that life and power that took away the occasion of all wars and I knew from whence all wars did rise, from the lust, according to James's doctrine ... I told them I was come into the covenant of peace which was before wars and strifes were.'[1] Yet there were Friends who fought or were civil magistrates. Nevertheless, the trend was towards not bearing arms, not fighting under any circumstances. There are of course precepts enough in the New Testament to have guided early Friends in this direction, and these were reinforced by the emphasis on 'that of God in every one'. Indeed, the theology is easy; there is no difficulty about enunciating a doctrine that eschews violence, recognizing other lives as of at least as much importance as one's own, although there may be great difficulty and suffering in following such a doctrine. The theological problems are on the other side, in creating a defensible argument for using force to defend your own possessions and person against others, and this is a difficulty which has never been adequately faced and overcome.

The Quaker standpoint was defined in 1661; there had been a rising of the extremist group known as the Fifth

1. George Fox, *Journal*, ed. J. L. Nickalls, C.U.P., 1952, p. 65.

Monarchy Men, and those sects who were suspected of being subversive, including of course the Quakers, were under pressure. Hence the 'Declaration from the harmless and innocent people of God called Quakers' which ran:

All bloody Principles and Practices we (as to our own particular) do utterly deny, with all outward wars and strife and fightings with outward Weapons, for any end, or under any pretext whatsoever. And this is our Testimony to the whole world . . . that Spirit of Christ, by which we are guided, is not changeable, so as once to command us from a thing as evil and again to move unto it: And we do certainly know, and so testify to the World, that the Spirit of Christ which leads us into all Truth, will never move us to fight and war against any man with outward Weapons, neither for the Kingdom of Christ, nor for the Kingdoms of this World.[2]

Whatever the motives behind this declaration, which could well have included a reasonable wish not to be persecuted for other people's risings, it has had a remarkable influence on Quaker attitudes. This is partly perhaps because it is beautifully written (and seventeenth-century English is so often irresistible), and partly because of that last lapidary phrase 'neither for the Kingdom of Christ, nor for the Kingdoms of this World'. Even if it was put in to counter the undoubted tendency of Fifth Monarchy Men and the like to tie their rebellions to religious aims and to justify them with evidence of divine instructions, it does establish a clear line counter to the most widely used argument for the Christian to take up arms; that generally wars are bad, but this particular war is a holy war, blessed by the Church, and against evil enemies. The harmless and innocent people of God came out firmly against the holy war.

As time went on, this rejection of violence became a 'testimony', that is to say it became a required Quaker attitude, and as the Society became more rigid the testimony became more of an absolute requirement. Yet even so, it had been carried through in the difficult conditions of the time of persecution, demonstrating that it was a remarkably strong

2. George Fox, op. cit., pp. 399–400.

weapon against bullying civic authorities. This of course is really irrelevant; non-violence is not proposed as a more effective weapon against your enemies, more powerful than gunpowder and less likely to get damp; the argument for non-violence is that it is right, and that one should do that which is right and take the consequences.

In later wars, Friends took their stand against the emotional current of patriotism and nationalism, and did something of great value in showing, in different times and places, that the non-violent attitude could be maintained. In so doing, such people as William Rotch of Nantucket, who threw a consignment of bayonets into the sea so that they should not be used in the American War of Independence, or John Bright, who resigned from the Cabinet rather than be a member of a Government which resorted to armed force, have created a pantheon of heroes who make it difficult for Quakers to look in a detached fashion at their peace testimony, for to modify it might imply that their attitudes, and hence their actions, were insecurely founded. Moreover there are with us still many Friends who have suffered for their beliefs in wars of our own time; are we to tell them they were misguided?

Some Friends would at least insist that the testimony cannot go unquestioned, that we cannot say categorically 'we do not believe the use of force can ever be justified in any circumstances'. They point out that Friends do not generally oppose the use of limited force by the police; they do not insist that criminals should be allowed to operate private armies unopposed: why then should nations be allowed to behave in a like manner? These Friends would argue for an international peacekeeping force, for a measure more realism than the absolute position implies.

I suspect that the difference of view is less significant than appears. For one thing, we Quakers do not rule countries, or command votes in the United Nations. We can only express our convictions in relatively limited ways, and when it comes to what we can do and say, the absolute question is of very little importance. The common ground, on the other hand, is wide; particularly in interpreting the peace testimony in the positive rather than the negative sense; in stressing not that we will not use force but that we will strive for peace, to remove the occasions of war; the political divisions, the misunderstandings, the unfair distribution of wealth, from which wars spring.

In this sense the Quakers have worked over the years. Obviously when war does break out our actions must be to alleviate suffering, and hence the Friends Ambulance Units founded by Philip Noel Baker at the outbreak of the First World War. But though this is the activity the world at large associates with Quakers in wartime, we would prefer that people should take a little more note of what we do between wars. Philip Noel Baker went on to work with Robert Cecil and Fridjof Nansen in the formative years of the League of Nations; Pierre Ceresole, a Swiss Quaker, ran a work camp for French and German young people at Verdun in 1920, and out of this grew the Service Civil International, with its British element, International Voluntary Service (originally 'for peace'); the Family Service Units were originally started by Friends in the Second World War as an alternative form of service for conscientious objectors.

There are also a number of Quaker organizations and institutions which are fairly directly aimed at increasing international understanding, many of them as part of Quaker Service, the 'foreign affairs' side of Quakerism. There is a Quaker team at the United Nations; and at UNESCO – as a non-governmental organization with consultative status – there are centres in London, Paris, Geneva, Vienna and Delhi, as well as Quaker Houses and William Penn Houses in other capitals. In Berlin a Quaker International Affairs Representative is concerned with East-West German rapprochement, while the Q.I.A.R. in Tokyo has a particular concern for China. There are a number of conference sequences: the International Dialogues in West Africa, in which about 300 West Africans from fourteen countries have participated in eleven seminars in four years; the International Conferences and Seminars Programme in South-East Asia; and the British and Soviet Philosophers Conference on aspects of moral philosophy.

There is also the series of more than fifty diplomats' conferences which have been held since 1952, attended by about 1,000 diplomats from eighty-three countries. These have as their purpose the bringing together, from as wide a range of countries as possible, of mid-career diplomats and professional people so that they may explore some of the basic factors of world affairs and probe more deeply into the social and cultural influences, the human aspirations and spiritual values of our time, in a way not feasible in ordinary official contacts. The friendships made at these conferences have often been of great help in other aspects of Quaker international work, at the United Nations and elsewhere. Moreover, meetings of diplomats, some of whom have taken part in Quaker conferences, are held at intervals at William Penn House in London and at the Paris, Vienna and Delhi centres and elsewhere. Such gatherings help to create a 'cell' of men of goodwill who are deeply concerned for right relationships in international affairs.

But the attempt to minimize strife cannot only be seen in terms of encouraging the development of mutual understanding in general terms. There are also specific situations, trouble spots which have to be dealt with. These are the places where the political answer is all too often that the talking has to stop, the only solution is force. There have been, on a number of occasions, successful Quaker initiatives in such conditions. Their success often depends on confidence and confidentiality, and so one cannot always say much about them. But there was, for example, a visit to India and Pakistan by three Friends just after the fighting in 1965, which provided a trusted channel of communication between governments when normal relations had broken down. There was also the contribution to the solution of the problem of the South Tyrol, which started from the concern of one man, Joseph Pickvance. His efforts were supported by a group of Friends in Birmingham, set up for the purpose by the Peace and International Relations Committee, and involving diplomatic initiatives in Vienna, Copenhagen and Rome by British, Danish and Italian Friends. There are, I know, Friends in various parts of the world today either engaged in, or laying the foundations of, similar activities. It is too late to try to establish yourself as a trusted go-between when the bullets are flying and the propaganda battle is at its height; the trust has to be generated by long years of patient honesty.

Friends are also concerned with peace research; indeed the subject itself is closely associated with the name of Lewis Fry Richardson, after whom the Richardson Institute for Conflict and Peace Research is named. Richardson published his *Mathematical Psychology of War* as early as 1919, and his achievement has been the basis of much of the work which has been done since. It is strange that the aspects of human activity which are most likely to have a radical influence on the future of the race are the last to be accepted as academically respectable. Indeed, this same thought leads on to the aspect of working for peace which Friends have still to take into their general thinking – why, if war is so terrible, is it so universal? The answer to this fundamental question is surely to be found in some deep need of the human personality, and it is in the study of ourselves that we may find some of the secrets of our passion for violence. There is a penetrating passage in the psychologist Alan McGlashan's book *The Savage and Beautiful Country* in which he points to the child, the poet and the madman as dwelling in the unconscious, and the loss of this contact as the malaise of mankind. He identifies three ways out of this condition, the symbolic living-out of unconscious aspects in ritual, the actual living-out of the unconscious drives in war or in ritualized equivalents such as Carnival and Saturnalia, and the direct experience of 'the timeless world of primordial images in whose depths the meaning of life is contained ... keep still, keep still and listen ... no other reality in the world of time and space ... compares with this "illusion" ... where the temporal touches the eternal'.[3] Now it is of course interesting to us that his third way is so close to our experience, but more important that he sees war as meeting an essential need of the human psyche, a possible

3. Alan McGlashan, *The Savage and Beautiful Country*, Chatto & Windus, 1966, p. 43.

way of establishing contact with the unconscious aspect. Not fortunately the only way, but unhappily all too accessible.

If it is necessary to look more deeply into our personal motivations, into the hidden desires for violence, even if only vicarious violence, that lurk within the most saintly of us, it is also very necessary to recognize the relationship between international affairs, which are normally thought of as the sources of war, and the internal patterns of society. Would Hitler have come to power without the economic disasters forced on Germany? How far has American belligerence in our own time been sustained by the fear that contraction of the arms industry might bring economic collapse?

How any individual will behave – whether one would be a conscientious objector in a future war, whether any future war would allow time for taking a stand – are questions which cannot be answered. We can say that in the past most Friends have been strongly pacifist, with a variation between those who would work with the Friends Ambulance Unit or a similar non-combatant organization in time of war, and those who insisted on having no connection, however tenuous, with the struggle and went to prison for their convictions. We can also say that Friends are active, on many fronts, to identify and eliminate causes of conflict. Inevitably, the pattern of our attack varies, as different aspects of the problem come to the fore. It may sometimes seem that our efforts cannot be significant, that we are so few, albeit a well-meaning few, while the big battalions are organized in the efficient (well, efficient-seeming) Service and Defence Departments of the great nations. And yet – as in so many fields, a few determined well-intentioned people, guided by the inward light, do have an influence. In any case, the question of influence or effect is secondary. As Neave Brayshaw put it:

The Quaker testimony concerning war does not set up as its standard of value the attainment of individual or national safety, neither is it based primarily on the iniquity of taking human life, profoundly important as that aspect of the question is. It is based ultimately on the conception of 'that of God in every man' to which the Christian in the presence of evil is called on to make appeal, following out a line of thought and conduct which, involving suffering as it may do, is, in the long run, the most likely to reach to the inward witness and so change the evil mind into the right mind. This result is not achieved by war.[4]

4. A. Neave Brayshaw, *The Quakers: Their Story and Message*, 1921, p. 45, 'Christian Faith and Practice in the Experience of the Society of Friends', London Yearly Meeting of the Religious Society of Friends, 1960, § 606.

CHAPTER 3

Materialism

THIS is going to be an uncomfortable chapter for me to write and for you to read; less high-minded than pacifism and less fascinating than sexual morality, materialism is the moral problem we would all prefer not to face.

The teaching of Jesus is quite explicit. There was the man who asked what he should do to gain the eternal life. Jesus told him to keep the Ten Commandments and then, 'If you wish to go the whole way, go, sell your possessions and give to the poor and then you will have riches in heaven; and come, follow me.' When the young man heard this, we are told, he went away with a heavy heart, for he was a man of great wealth. I can understand his feelings.

I am not a man of wealth, but I sit writing these words in my study in an Edwardian family house in Putney. From my window I see other familiar houses ringing their small but refreshing gardens, splashed now with the late leaves of autumn and lively with varieties of birds. Overhead, every minute or so, a million pounds of jet aeroplane roars across the sky to London Airport. The roads are lined with cars; between aeroplanes I can hear pop music, Beethoven violin sonatas, and the brisk encouragement of a television commercial, all overlaid on top of birdsong. Down the hill is Wandsworth, where in smaller houses housewives fight a continual battle with the dirt and grime blowing down from the gas works, factories and power stations along the river. Further on still, the houses round Brixton are packed with immigrants from India, Pakistan and the West Indies. They live eight or ten to a room, and a number of their children have died in tragic circumstances involving badly designed oil stoves. Up here on the hill we don't expose our children to that risk; we have a few hundred pounds worth of central heating.

But let us look beyond the shadow areas of our big cities,

where racial intolerance grows out of a pathetic struggle for living accommodation and jobs rejected by everyone who can aspire to something better. 'Why don't they stay in their own countries?' is a question often asked, and seldom honestly answered. They don't stay in their own countries because even a bus conductor's job – or National Assistance – and an overcrowded room in a rotting Birmingham or Brixton slum represents a higher standard of living than they could hope for in their own sun-warmed, starving countries.

We are all willing to talk jokingly of our poverty, and sometimes a group of well-paid professional men will leave for Canada, or Australia, because they are not, in their own opinion, well enough paid. Yet the plain fact is that the poorest of us is better off than millions of our fellows in other countries, and most of us are, by world standards, disgustingly rich. And the Society of Friends looks at itself and realizes that while it has very few rich members, it has very few of the very poor.

The tradition of Friends in this matter of money and the world's goods is admirably moderate. Friends were never given to extremes of giving away all their goods or to the piling-up of fortunes. Whether they had much or little, they viewed their possessions as held in trust, not for their own or their children's benefit but for the Lord's work. They therefore gave up all articles of luxury, living plain and simple lives in plain, simple surroundings, and wearing that plain simple mid-seventeenth-century costume which became the uniform 'Quaker dress'.

Inevitably this insistence on simplicity became formalized almost into affectation. The Quaker dress had been a simple serviceable suit in a plain hard-wearing colour; with the passage of time it became an elaborately archaic costume. The eschewing of luxury became the disregard of creative art, with unhappy consequences the Society is only just beginning to overcome; at one time in the nineteenth century the Quaker home contained no music and at most three pictures: engravings of Benjamin West's painting of Penn making a treaty with the Indians, a plan of Ackworth School

and the stowage plan of a slave ship. This rigidity, this making of formal restrictive rules, was alien to the Society's true meaning. We have seen that, as early as 1700, Margaret Fox had been anxious about the growth of a formula for plain living among Friends, and particularly the formalization of plain dress; happily, in the long run, her words have been heeded. Friends have long given over 'plain dress' and dress and live like everyone else. They are generally un-ostentatious, but if they have a peculiarity in this it is only that they do not dress up for Meeting on Sunday to the extent that Church-goers dress for Church. It is quite usual to see a family at Meeting dressed ready for a day in the country, in anoraks and boots, or in jeans and tee-shirts for the seaside. The Meeting I attend is remarkable for the variety of footwear it displays – I hope it will not make my Friends self-conscious if I say that week after week I note with interest and delight the suedes, the boots, the elderly Veldschoen, the sandals and the Chelseas, and never a respectable, polished black Oxford pair of Sunday-go-to-Meeting shoes among the lot of them.

All this is well enough it its way; we started with a concept of stewardship, we have weathered the excesses of sumptuary law and emerged with a tradition of moderation, and again the idea of stewardship, of using what we have of the world's goods for God's work. Unfortunately we cannot leave it there. Jesus did not say, 'Live a comfortable but un-ostentatious middle-class life, buy yourself a family house, furnish it discreetly and get yourself a medium-sized car, and then devote what you have left (after holidays and insurance) to the service of God.' He said in plain terms, 'Sell your possessions, and give to the poor.' What do we do about that phrase, accept it and act on it, accept it but do nothing about it, or explain it away as not for us?

Let us first try to explain it away. Of course, Christ spoke for his time, and what was practicable then is not so practicable today. In Palestine nineteen hundred years ago one could live more easily perhaps without wealth. Yet, when it comes to the point, Christ does not say 'give up working for your living'. He said to those who lived when he did, 'follow me' and meant the words literally; we who cannot follow his actual footsteps can still follow his way, his teaching. And this particular teaching is 'sell your possessions'; it is not earning a living and buying your bread that is the barrier to spiritual life, but possessions. Yet by the way we gather and hold possessions and base our whole society on them, one would think one could hardly open a sewing box without finding camels slipping through the eyes of all the needles.

My attempts at explaining away are not doing very well. Unfortunately, all the great teachers have stressed the need to be detached from the phenomenal world, to be centred on God and not attached to material things. Where others stress non-attachment, Christ emphasizes non-possession. To have possessions, but not to care whether you have them or not, is more difficult than not to have them and not to seek them. It is not impossible for a rich man to find his way to God, he has only for a start to be completely non-attached about his riches – and we are back with the camel again.

Great wealth is a burden which few of us have to bear, but possessions on a more moderate scale we all have. If we seek to be non-attached, we may find the idea of stewardship helpful. Let us look at it this way; our physical bodies are vehicles for the divine spirit within us; our physical bodies need warmth, food and shelter; a man can only begin to turn his attention to the immaterial when his basic material needs have been met. As I have suggested, the dominant ego is a force for physical survival but a barrier to spiritual development; therefore let us accept the easy satisfaction of our basic physical needs as a step towards freeing us for the desire and pursuit of the whole. We are children of a complex materialist society; a handful of rice and a length of cotton cloth would not free us of material desires, but our society gives us, relatively easily, a moderate abundance. Let us accept this as a crutch to walk with, lent to us to help us until we are strong enough to walk without it. We can see the idea of trusteeship in large fortunes, whose possessors often do turn them to the service of others. In the more modest and individual case it may be rather that we are allowed the use of the money and goods we possess so that we may offer instead our lives to the service of God and our fellows.

In the 'Advices and Queries' we are advised to pray

that spiritual energies in yourself and in others may be released for the furtherance of God's kingdom. Life brings many conflicting responsibilities and choices. To one, the summons may come to apply himself with fresh energy and vision to his present work; to another, to make a complete change, perhaps even to retire early or to limit his engagements so that he may be free for new service of God's appointing. When you have a choice of employment, choose that which gives the fullest opportunity for the use of your talents in the service of God and your fellow-men.

This may seem to be a pious platitude, not to be taken seriously, but in my experience it is widely and deeply considered. A number of Friends in middle life will give up their career and, for example, go to Woodbrooke, the Quaker college at Birmingham, for a term or so in order to look at themselves objectively and seek a new sphere of activity. I recall also, with admiration and respect, the Friend who was talking of his twenty-odd years of service in Africa and India. I asked how he had come to this. He explained that he had been a merchant banker until, at the outbreak of war, being a conscientious objector, he had first gone overseas under the auspices of the Friends Service Council 'and somehow', he added, 'there was always so much to do that I never found time to go back to merchant banking'.

But the 'Advices and Queries' are not a set of exhortations written by a set of superior beings for the guidance of lesser mortals; rather they are a distillation by Friends of the imperatives under which they find themselves. So, in choice of employment, we do tend to consider 'the service of God and your fellow-men' rather than simply career advancement or material well-being. This does not lead to every member of the Society being a social welfare worker. Each individual must find his own role and respond to the opportunities which open to him. So we pursue careers in, for example, teaching, the civil service, local government or commerce or industry; but when the decisions come to be taken, our Quakerism helps to decide which way we go.

But apart altogether from the question of how the individual uses his life and treats his possessions, there is a problem here for the Society of Friends as an organization. The Society as a whole has possessions; the property of the Meeting Houses, and also considerable invested wealth, large sums of money left under trust deeds by wealthy Friends. We do not compare with the great institutional churches; we have only, in round terms, about £2 million put by. However, after all that I have said about Quakers carrying their religion into practice, the reader is entitled to a description of the Society's use of its wealth, and to some indication of how far it carries the principle of Christian stewardship.

First, this wealth is split up into a great many separate funds, partly the consequence of the organization of the Society and partly because it has come largely from legacies or contributions given for specific purposes. Quakers first put money into a common pool, for the purpose of relieving distress caused by persecution, or to provide for the support of those who were called to be itinerant ministers. Later, sums were subscribed or bequeathed for foreign mission work, or to provide for the education of Friends' children or for the maintenance or construction of Meeting Houses. So much of the capital is tied up in trusts for specific objects, not all of which now correspond to the most urgent of needs.

Second, the capital is invested, largely in government and local authority stocks or in company stocks and shares. The trustees have avoided investing in undertakings uncongenial to Friends – that is to say they have avoided armaments firms and distilleries – but the government does use our money indifferently for hydrogen bombs and childrens' allowances; and when we lend money to the institutional investors such as banks and insurance companies we have no control over their investment policy. In general the Society has in the past acted like any other prudent trust management, accumulating capital and meeting expenditure from the interest.

If this thoroughly bourgeois attitude seems to accord ill with Friends' beliefs, I can only say that Friends are beginning to ask the questions themselves. Could not that part of the capital which is not under legal restraint be spent over a period of years; could not more of the capital which must be invested be invested in projects of direct social benefit – say housing projects for the most needful classes of society – even if the yield was much reduced? Could not capital be used to support ventures in co-partnership in industry which might demonstrate ways in which an advanced technological society could be structured with some regard for values other than maximizing profit?

Perhaps subsequently I will be able to record the outcome so far of this questioning; that London Yearly Meeting eventually decided on a more radical policy in regard to resources, that this attitude spread among other Yearly Meetings and influenced the churches, so that there seemed a real prospect of the Church being identified not so much by its wealth or its poverty as by its willingness to use resources instead of harbouring them. When that happens, when we are able to make ourselves give up all that we have collectively, we shall have to face the problem individually without evasion.

Financial conservatism is an aspect of our bourgeois heritage, and the fact cannot be overlooked; indeed at the present time there are a number of indications that we have to face the question squarely, of whether we can hold consistently the beliefs we do and also retain our respectable middle-class attitudes. It is not an intrinsic part of Quakerism; those rugged seventeenth-century individualists who founded the movement were not concerned with prudent investment or preserving the existing social order. But somehow with commercial success we became very respectable; we acquired too big a stake in commodity markets and the stable structure of capitalism. Our concern with the exploited and under-privileged was admirable, but did not extend to altering the system that ensured exploitation and lack of privilege. That is to say, as a Society we made no attack on the basic social organization; individuals were frequently drawn to experiments in communal living and have demonstrated over and over again the difficulties of operating a Christian communist enclave in a capitalist society. Nevertheless, we shall need to learn from these experiences if we respond to the present stirrings in our midst.

As I see it, the concept that we share, however implicit and undefined, of the interaction and interpenetration of the spiritual and the material, prevents us from solving our dilemma by the classical technique of withdrawal. We cannot say simply 'We disapprove of the ways of the world and will have no part in them.' But equally we cannot find any existing socio-political system which seems to us to reflect the inner light; we cannot point to any country, from Greece to Cuba, from South Africa to China, from the U.S.A. to the U.S.S.R., and say 'there is the model'. On the whole, Great Britain, with all its faults, seems as good a starting point as one can find; yet it can only be a starting point. What can we do to change the basic 'each for himself' mentality which is implicit in our whole economic structure; in the competitive nature of industry, the bargaining between industry and the unions, the power structure of the unions themselves?

This also is a problem which is currently concerning Friends. They incline towards the cooperative enterprise solution, but there are some uncomfortable and inescapable difficulties. We would like to see human relationships, the welfare of the community, put before the maximizing of profit. But the lynch-pin of free enterprise capitalism is that though individuals may suffer, the community as a whole benefits if the maximizing of profit is the main drive. Clearly we dispute this, and so there is a conflict between socially desirable policies and those which maximize profit. Hence our co-ownership enterprise, putting people before profit, will make less profit than it might. How can a firm making less profit than it might survive the competition of other firms not so inhibited? Its return on capital employed will be low, it will not attract risk capital for expansion, it will have unexploited potential (how appropriate that word 'unexploited' is!) and will be vulnerable to take-over.

These are some of the problems. How can one, in the

middle of a profit-motivated society, demonstrate that another way is possible; and this in itself is a microcosm of the larger problem of how could one build a country on the basis of love and caring in a world moved by greed and fear? There are no obvious solutions, but the fact that there are no obvious solutions does not make the problem go away.

CHAPTER 4

Towards a Quaker View of Sex

THE title of this chapter is the title of a pamphlet, first published in 1963, which achieved certain notice, almost amounting to notoriety, and probably did more to bring Friends into public view than any other activity of the last decade. The interest it aroused was partly due to its intrinsic value, its considered and concerned attitude to the problem of sexual behaviour and morality, its open-minded approach and its insistence on trying to present a viewpoint which was truly Christian and Quaker rather than orthodox, compromising or woolly. Partly too it had shock value; if people had ever thought of a Quaker view on this subject it was of a strictly Puritan ethic, a rigid morality which unhesitatingly condemned every deviation from the pattern of chastity before marriage and fidelity in marriage, the pattern which is preached but not lived.

Historically, Quakerism shared this view. Indeed, from the seventeenth to the nineteenth centuries, sex does not show as a major problem or preoccupation. Individual members had their difficulties, and fell short of the accepted standards, were visited by elders and on occasion disowned for laxity of conduct, but nobody suggested for a moment that any other standards could be considered. Throughout this period the Society held the commonly declared Christian ethic: that sexual relations were proper only within the bounds of matrimony. The Quakers had fought for the right to be married in their own way, without the intervention of a priest, but that established, Quaker marriage was no different from any other marriage, and the Quaker attitude to deviations from the established code was the same as that of any other noncomformist Christian. Perhaps the inherent optimism of Quakerism was apparent, if one looks deeply enough, in a slightly less Puritan attitude, a less than wholehearted acceptance that sex was basically sinful and marriage at best a palliative, but that was all.

The First World War brought far-reaching changes in society and started a process of questioning established attitudes which is still going on today. The Second World War accelerated the process. By the late fifties some Friends were becoming concerned as to the way they should respond to the problems of young people who came to them for advice on sexual difficulties, particularly those of young homosexual men. A group came together to discuss this; it contained four psychologists, four teachers, a housewife and a barrister.

They were not in any sense an official group, but as they talked together, they came more and more to feel that it was necessary to put down their conclusions and to make them public. They prepared their pamphlet, carefully entitling it 'Towards a Quaker View of Sex' (my italics) and doing their best to make it clear that they were trying to help the Society of Friends to formulate its views and not in any way claiming to express a view already accepted by the Society. The pamphlet was published under the auspices of the Home Service Committee in 1963.

Today, particularly in the current version, which has been revised to clarify some points which were misunderstood and to remove some phrases which caused un-needed offence, it does not seem a very radical document. For one thing, it is much concerned with the nature of the homosexual, with understanding his problems and providing a background of knowledge of sexual physiology and psychology against which his situation must be viewed. In the intervening years we have had the prolonged open debate around the Sexual Offences Act which legalized homosexual behaviour between consenting adults in private; the vindictive cruelty of the law has been modified and in the process the whole area has been openly discussed.

For all that, 'Towards a Quaker View of Sex' is still an interesting and valuable document, presenting an attitude towards sexual behaviour which is relevant in a wider context.

Its world is one of troubled, unhappy people; its appendices – 'Origins of Sexual Behaviour', 'Deviations Considered', 'Sources of Help' and an extensive glossary – indicate its concern with those for whom the question of premarital intercourse is the least of their problems.

The basic attitude is founded on the acceptance of the definition of sin *'as covering those actions that involve exploitation of the other person'* and of a *'...Christian standard of chastity...'* as not *'...measured by a physical act, but ... a standard of human relationship, applicable within marriage as well as outside it'*.

It is in the application of these principles to real situations that 'Towards a Quaker View of Sex' moved outside conventional attitudes and found it necessary to make statements and reservations which gained it a publicity amounting to notoriety, and caused discussion within the Society of Friends which was, for Quakers, almost violent. The authors saw 'Impersonal exploitation, the dangers of pregnancy, the disruptive effect of a series of love affairs involving intercourse ...' as 'heavy arguments in favour of continence in the young unmarried.' But they recognized that experience before marriage could have depth and integrity and contribute to the growth of personality, that some might feel it right to anticipate their marriage deliberately, that mature unmarried couples unable to marry might still build a permanent and lasting relationship. There are, they considered, no clear-cut answers to the questions they posed; in dealing with human relationships at their deepest rules are irrelevant.

They felt constrained to point out, however, that

if the traditional code seems now to be of little value, either in restraining us or in pointing out the way to generous living, then more than ever we need the presence of God in our judgements and decisions ... What now can we say to those who do not accept God in their lives and may indeed reject any religious influence? – to the numerous boys and girls who tumble into sexual intimacy when they are little more than children, who are confused by what it does to them and escape from confusion into toughness; to the young adults whose bottle parties are followed by indiscriminate sexual indulgence; to those whose marriages are unsatisfying and who seek distraction elsewhere; to the homosexuals living in a hell in which they are torn between a genuine impulse to tenderness and an overwhelming sense of lust? For those who are already involved we can do little, except insofar as we meet particular cases; and then our approach must be through compassion – the reverse of moral judgement.

Now, the Society of Friends contains many members who found 'Towards a Quaker View of Sex' refreshing in its sincerity and honesty, a direct and infinitely valuable attempt to examine a contemporary problem in the light of human behaviour and personality. But it also contains many members who have a deep conviction of the inherent moral rightness of the sexual code our civilization has adopted – or at least taught – and these members were disturbed at the inability of the authors to take a definite stand on the side of that code. To them, 'Towards a Quaker View of Sex' was too permissive; compassion could not allow them to escape from the duty of declaring their conviction that sexual intercourse belonged exclusively within marriage. Hence the outburst of dismay.

This particular dispute is now history, and the outcome was nothing very remarkable – the pamphlet's revision to which I referred at the outset, which did not greatly modify its content, but which did clarify a few passages. It is worth mentioning only because it is typical of a form of stress which must always exist within the Society, and which, in different contexts, will recur from time to time. If the Society was an authoritarian, dogmatic body this sort of issue would be easy to deal with; attitudes on contraception, marriage, and homosexuality could be set down and would remain as definitive statements until the Society as a whole agreed to change them. As it happens Friends are not like that, and the fact that authoritarianism makes life easier for the authority does not appeal to them. They are committed to the guidance of the light within them, and they have to accept the uncertainties which arise, thanks to human fallibility, from attempts to be guided by that light. There are, as I have shown, ways by which Friends seek to find common ground; by meeting together, by eschewing debate in the usual sense, by opening their hearts and minds to each other. But when the community is in a state of change, when the circumstances in which the working of the divine will is to be seen are being modified, there are no fixed rules, and Quakers must bear the burden of being changeable. Inevitably as they encounter experience which makes them more aware of the contemporary problems which they must bring into their thinking, some change more quickly than others; and the Society then develops stresses between those who are convinced that a change of attitude is necessary and those who are not so convinced. And there is no deciding by a majority vote that one group is right and the other wrong.

Despite the controversy it aroused, 'Towards a Quaker View of Sex' undoubtedly made explicit the basis of the Quaker view on sexual relations which is generally accepted. It is not a statement about behaviour but about attitudes; it is an insistence on the integrity of the person. It states quite plainly that the important issue is how one person considers another; the extent to which we see the other as an individual, equally deserving of respect and consideration.

There is in particular one further aspect of 'Towards a Quaker View of Sex' which I think should be stressed. It is a mine of straightforward factual information, with no differentiation between socially acceptable and unacceptable aspects. It does not cover some matters simply because they are not relevant to its main area of concern; for example, it does not give detailed information on the available methods of contraception and how they are available and to whom. And of course, it has in some areas been overtaken by events; while reference is made to the emergence of strains of venereal disease resistant to antibiotics, the rapid increase in sexual infection in recent years constitutes a new problem, directly rooted in changing patterns of sexual behaviour and the widespread rejection of conventional sexual morality.

The maintenance of a rigid sexual ethic has in the past been very largely based on ignorance and fear, particularly fear of conception and of venereal disease. Yet surely, this is not a sound basis; moreover it is not even a practicable basis, not practicable any more, at least. I do not think we would wish to recreate that ignorance if we could; rather I would suggest that our efforts to establish a sound sexual ethic require that we do all we can to dispel ignorance. We want to be able to talk freely about what we think to be the true foundation of good relationships, and this requires that we talk against a background of generally understood sound knowledge. If, after all, we cannot convince others that a certain pattern of behaviour is wrong and undesirable by sound arguments, whether they be founded on social utility or religious teaching, we surely do not want to induce them to adhere to given patterns of behaviour from ignorance.

I have quoted already the passage from 'Towards a Quaker View of Sex' in which the authors face the problem of those whom it is difficult to reach on the basis of a fundamentally religious approach, even one as undogmatic as Quakerism. Is there nothing one can offer, except compassion, insofar as we encounter particular cases? I feel certain that what we can offer is very much through our own lives and our contact with others. It is all to the good to restate, whenever possible, the fundamental concept of personal integrity, and perhaps to remember John MacMurray's comment, 'If you ask me "Will chastity" (which he defines as 'emotional sincerity', 'expressing what you feel') "prevent men and women from having sexual intercourse outside marriage?" I can only answer "I don't know." "But that is surely the really important point" you may urge. I answer "It is *not* the important point. Compared with the importance of personal reality, of chastity, it is a point of no significance." '[1]

Human relationships, human activities, do not come about as a result of a carefully planned course of reading, they are a consequence of the influences bearing on us continually, the influences of our upbringing and of our interaction with others. If now we are alive in a society where these influences have resulted in attitudes which are in direct conflict with what our own inner experience tells us to be right, what should we do about it? What do we say and do

1. John MacMurray, *Reason and Emotion*, Faber & Faber, 1935, p. 142.

about young people who tell us that everybody sleeps together if they want to, that it is an enjoyable and harmless activity, that it is better to gain sexual experience in this way than to launch into marriage in ignorance and to find that, in addition to all the other stresses, you have to face an unsuspected incompatibility, or even in the extreme case (and such cases are by no means rare) a complete incapacity for normal relations?

I think we should certainly resist the temptation to say that they are wrong. Insofar as they are expounding contemporary patterns of behaviour they are right; people do behave in this way – how many, what proportion, we do not really know. Sex is generally enjoyable and generally harmless; if it were not it would not be so popular. Marriages which start from no experience can move effortlessly to a full and happy relationship – so can marriages where both partners have experience with others and have had a trial run together. And both patterns can run into trouble. To talk in terms of 'You are wrong – and even if things are so they shouldn't be' is to apply to one field of human activity the authoritarian attitude we are so anxious to avoid. We should also note in all seriousness the truth of the comment in 'Towards a Quaker View of Sex' that 'Unfortunately it appears that those of low sexual drive are often pillars of respectability who find it easy to enjoin upon others (especially upon deviants) the sexual abstinence which comes naturally to them.'

Rather I would suggest that we approach all discussions of sexual ethics with a desire to deepen our understanding of ourselves and of others. If Freud may be accused of having made too much of sex as *the* fundamental motivation, there is no doubt that it is a tremendously strong force, and that it can be extremely dangerous when repressed. The health of a human society does depend profoundly on our finding acceptable ways of liberating the psychic energy associated with sex, and liberating it in a genuinely creative way. To this end I have stressed the importance of making knowledge widely available, and of redressing its inadequacies. Beyond that, we should emphasize that sexual relations are only important as an expression of deep interpersonal relationships. Our consideration, therefore, cannot be limited to sexual behaviour alone; this, as John MacMurray says, is incidental. Correspondingly, it is not our sexual behaviour, which is private and generally known only so far as we care to make it known, which will influence others, but our general behaviour. If we are given the opportunity to encourage young people to accept the concept of personal integrity and the inviolability of the human personality, it is not talking about our own attitudes to sex that will help them to accept what we say, but the example we set in our lives, in all relationships, whether or not they involve the sexual element.

As for rules – the old rules are gone, and there is no bringing them back. We have to go forward from where we are. As a starting point there are two rules which have been proposed and which can certainly be endorsed – never bring an unwanted child into the world; never exploit another person. Beyond this come the positive injunctions, 'Love the Lord your God with all your heart, with all your soul, with all your mind' and 'Love your neighbour as yourself'. These two rules say nothing about who should sleep with whom – which is perhaps not as important as we imagine – but they say everything about human relationships.

A Note on Race and Colour

THIS is a note and not a chapter; it should hardly be necessary to explain the tolerance of Quakers in questions of race and colour nor to detail the type of community relations activity in which they engage. Generally they will turn their hand to whatever seems the most helpful activity in their particular area.

The purpose of this note is to report a curiously illuminating piece of recent history. It occurred in 1968, when Kingston Monthly Meeting, feeling that 'the situation calls for a public statement ... to make the position of the Society unequivocally clear' brought forward to London Yearly Meeting a suggested draft on 'Race Relations in Britain'. Yearly Meeting gave general support to the draft but appointed a small group of Friends to revise it and bring it forward to Meeting for Sufferings.

The draft was slightly modified by Meeting for Sufferings when they accepted it at their meeting in November 1968. This is the published text:

In the present controversy about the place of immigrants in Britain we feel moved to make a public statement on fundamental principles which we hold.

Throughout history, groups of people of widely differing origins, religions and social customs have shown that they can become united into coherent national communities. In our own country Celts, Saxons, Normans, Huguenots, Jews and people of various cultures have been blended into our present nation, and have learned by experience that differences in innate ability and personal qualities are between individuals rather than between groups.

This diversity of individual endowment is a great asset to the community. The members of every new group of immigrants have brought their own contributions to the common national heritage. Differences of skin colour or of cultural background should not be allowed to prevent today's immigrants from doing the same.

There is a unity which goes beyond physical characteristics and deeper than personal endowment. We have found again and again that there is an inward spirit – that of God in every man. At the deepest level all members of the human race are one family.

It follows that all members of that family should be equal in the eyes of their fellows, and should not be denied their full rights, responsibilities and freedoms. We recognize that in the world as it is today what is considered politically and economically possible falls short of that principle and that there are often real difficulties of adjustment; but that is not a reason for abandoning the principle or for failing to work towards it by every means in our power.

We are concerned, therefore, that all people who come to live and work in Britain, and their children and children's children, should be able to feel at home here, as so many newcomers have done in the past. For our part, we are glad to welcome them as neighbours in our streets, as colleagues in our work, as friends in our homes and as relatives by marriage in just the same way as those who are already a part of the community.

So far, so good, and the statement is much what one would expect. So also was the first part of the discussion by Meeting for Sufferings; one Friend thought the statement 'one of the weakest and worst written' he had encountered, another thought it a 'paragon of lucidity'. But then Friends began to take objection to the final paragraph 'We are glad to welcome them ... as friends in our homes and as relatives by marriage ...' The objection was on grounds of honesty – that however desirable it was that we should welcome immigrants in our homes and as relatives by marriage there were many Friends who would not so welcome them. There was a suggestion that the word 'should' be inserted in the text – but in the end the sense of the Meeting was to let the wording stand.

Thus the Society has gone on record as answering the classic question 'would you let your daughter marry one?' with a firm 'Yes'. As a matter of fact, from what I can see from the Engagements and Marriages columns in the back of *The Friend,* some of our sons and daughters have had this tendency for some time. Nevertheless, there is, on this issue at least, a firm public statement; moreover it was decided on after full and serious consideration of its implications. I wonder sometimes whether Meeting for Sufferings was being a little too 'tender'; were the cautions uttered there the reflection of the feelings of those present or of their concern for less liberal Friends not there? It's very difficult to say, and often our concern for the feelings of others is a subconscious reflection of our own uneasiness. But at the end of the day the message was clear – roll on the multi-racial community.

CHAPTER 5

Crime and Punishment

It would be natural enough for Quakers to be concerned with penal reform from motives of enlightened self-interest; from the times of persecution in the seventeenth century until the present day there has usually been some issue between the Quaker and the civil power, and the consequence of such differences is usually that some Friends end up in prison. Not taking oaths, not paying tithes, not being prepared to serve as a soldier, assembling unlawfully, all these have led to the imprisonment of Friends; and if we are now exempted from oaths, and no longer persecuted simply for being Quakers, we still find ourselves at odds with the state over violence, war and oppression. Among Quakers, something well above the average for a respectable middle-class group have seen the inside of a prison from the prisoner's viewpoint, both in Britain and in America.

Yet, in fact, the Quaker interest in prisons and prisoners, in the whole way in which society treats those who do not keep its laws, has its roots more in the conscious application of Quaker beliefs to the world about them than in the effect of imprisonment in bringing conditions to their notice. The first Quaker to put forward a radical proposal in this field was probably John Bellers, a second-generation Friend who did not himself suffer imprisonment and was comfortably off. Over the first quarter of the eighteenth century he published a number of pamphlets on social questions which were far in advance of his time. He proposed schemes for the employment of the poor, for the setting up of hospitals for teaching and research, for the improvement of Parliamentary elections and for the reform of the criminal law.

Bellers was a man of deep spiritual insight, and it was from the depths of that insight that he drew his concern for the poor, the oppressed, even the criminal. But his mind was

essentially practical, he was that type of utilitarian phil-
anthropist whom one associates more with the nineteenth
century, for ever working out explanatory calculations to
show how those whom society neglects or punishes are themselves a potential source of wealth.

Bellers drew attention to the direct conflict between the
Christian teaching and a system which hanged a man or a
child for theft. He proposed that felons should be imprisoned and put to work, and so turned into honest citizens. It
isn't as easy as that, but at least it was a start, a better way
than hanging indiscriminately.

One of Bellers' last writings was a letter urging Friends to
visit prisons and to seek to lead the prisoners to the light. It
was in this spirit that Elizabeth Fry started her pioneer work
in visiting women in prison, but that was nearly a hundred
years after Bellers. Elizabeth Fry was also a well-to-do
Friend with no prior connection with prisons, and she too
started her work out of a concern for the prisoner, as a
human being like the rest of us.

Since Elizabeth Fry, concern with crime and the criminal
and penal reform, with first restricting the death penalty to
murder and then achieving its abolition, has been a major
Quaker interest. Direct experience of prison regimes has
been an important factor, in that Friends have been able to
speak with authority about the conditions they wish to
change – they represent perhaps the most articulate and responsible body of ex-prisoners – but this is incidental to their
concern, which is based on compassion and regard for the
unfortunate prisoner. This is indeed one of the less rational
aspects of this particular Quaker attitude; there is a tendency to extend compassion to the criminal at the expense of
his victim; and it was left to Margery Fry (who, though born
a Quaker, left the Society in despair at its smugness) to conduct the campaign which ultimately led to the Criminal Injuries Act. Perhaps this irrationality suggests the reason why
this particular aspect of social reform has attracted so much
interest, more indeed than it might justify on a rational
analysis. The criminal is an underdog, an outsider, a nonconformist. The Quaker identifies with him; to a deeply

Christian Quaker every criminal, however debased he may seem, is a reminder of Jesus consorting with social outcasts and himself given over to a criminal's death. To any Quaker the criminal is a symbol of man's inhumanity to man; too often the roots of crime are to be seen in the way we have treated the criminal, in bad homes, bad schools, the whole cyclic pattern of the rejected. The most important step in avoiding a life of crime is to be born in the right part of the town.

There is of course no definitive solution, no easy set of rules for the reform of society and the conversion of the criminal classes into right-thinking citizens. Instead there are a number of individuals with their own personal views as to which is the most important area of reform. The views of Quaker reformers are generally in line with those of professional and academic penologists; indeed the two groups interpenetrate. Apart from those Friends who undertake voluntary work with prisoners, there are Friends in the prison service itself. There are also Friends who have left the prison service, because they believe that as run at present it can do only harm. There are also many Friends in other services concerned with prisoners and their families, in the probation service and the welfare services. But between those who believe that the system can be improved from the inside and those who believe it to be beyond improvement, there is a large measure of common ground as to the nature of the problem.

The problem is, in broad terms, how to convince society that it must spend a great deal more on its most apparently worthless members, that having suffered one loss by their activities it must then pour good money after bad by spending on their care, education, treatment and study, and that such a course is both morally right and economically desirable.

The situation is complicated by the survival of several different ethical attitudes to criminals, some of them old and discredited, some newer but almost as suspect. There is the concept of revenge; while few people would consciously put this forward as a proper basis for our attitude to crime, nevertheless it is a deeply implanted attitude, and all attempts at reform, which seem to reduce the hardship inflicted on the criminal, come up against the general subconscious desire to exact retribution. Then again there is the idea of expiation. If all our criminals were Raskolnikovs there might be something in it; but they are not, and it is no good our feeling that a period in prison enables the prisoner to expiate his crime, if he doesn't share our view and possibly doesn't even recognize his act as a crime.

Yet even though we may recognize the ideas of vengeance and expiation as an adequate foundation for a penological theory, we have to face the over-simplified attitude of the criminal 'You're there because you earned your medicine and that's that.'[1] Faced with such a primitive response, one wonders how, from our present lack of understanding and lack of ability to communicate, we have the effrontery to think that we can devise a reformatory system at all.

A newer ethic which is also dubious is the vague conviction that all crime is the fault of someone other than the criminal, that by improving material conditions and education we can eliminate crime. The social history of the last century shows that this is not true; whatever we might do by building the Kingdom of Heaven on earth, that is, by a complete spiritual revolution, nothing short of that is going to eliminate crime, and even that might leave us with some marginal cases which would be difficult to assess.

The essence of the enlightened attitude to criminals is simply that we would be better off without them. Therefore, let us not concern ourselves with retribution or expiation or with apportionment of guilt between them and us. Rather let us try to understand why people take to crime, and how we can divert them from that path. Here then is the first need for more money. We spend at present, in Britain, some £340 million on the law enforcement services and probably considerably less than £1 million (nobody seems to know exactly) on research into criminal behaviour. The reason for this ratio is not that we know all the answers; such evidence

1. Peta Fordham, 'View from the Receiving End', *New Society*, 18 April 1968, p. 558.

as there is suggests that most of our efforts at constructive rehabilitation, at persuading the criminal that there is a better way of life, are misdirected simply because we do not understand the criminal's motivation. No, the difficulty is to bring public opinion and politicians to realize the high cost of the criminal to society and that more knowledge is the first prerequisite of reducing the incidence of crime.

Public opinion also needs to be brought to see that present expenditure on prisons is, in the current phrase, of low cost-effectiveness; that is to say, we are not getting much for our money. Without denigrating in any way the efforts being made by the prison service to use imprisonment as a means of rehabilitation, the fact is that the conditions of over-crowding and understaffing in mainly archaic buildings makes the prison regime little more than a restriction of freedom and an imposition of authority, often imposed as a last resort when the courts, having tried everything else, do not know what to do with an offender. This may well be very bad for many prisoners (we do not have enough research results to be categorical) in that a regime which restricts freedom may encourage the immature attitudes which can cause criminal behaviour. Many criminals in fact, those who are inadequate personalities and find the world too much for them, find some sort of protection in prison life; their treatment should be such as will fit them for more responsibility in the wider world, not a further dose of sheltering paternalism. Similarly, the authoritarianism of prison life is of dubious benefit. Most criminals need to be encouraged to take responsible decisions for themselves, not taught un-hesitating obedience. In particular the insistence on strict discipline in Detention Centres for young offenders may well help to train a young man to be an efficient member of a team, but this capacity might be employed in a safe-breaking team as well as elsewhere. Prison may act as a deterrent, but as such it is clearly not very effective. It does not serve the purpose of changing criminals into acceptable members of society, and if it does not do that we should ask ourselves whether it is worth the money.

Again it must be stressed that those in the prison service

know this very well, and know to a greater extent than the layman what type of treatment is likely to bring about the desired change. In the majority of cases the criminal is the product of a bad environment, an inadequate family background in the decaying areas of a big city, where the accepted ethic embraces a wide range of illegal activities, where being out of work or in prison is endemic and involves no social stigma, and where a law-abiding life offers little more in terms of comfort, in return for a great deal more hard work, than a spell inside. In such lives, the only colour is the excitement of crime and the indulgence of spending the proceeds. It will cost a great deal, in terms of effort and money, to reconstruct our system so that it offers these men an opportunity, by helping them to discover their own full personalities and capacities, and by giving them the training and education that will enable them to find themselves a worthwhile place in the world outside and will give them the desire to do so.

In rebuilding our prison system in this way, with better accommodation, better facilities, more opportunities for proper psychiatric guidance, training facilities and productive workshops doing real work under competitive conditions, we should not think only of the prisoners, but also of those who operate the service and of those who are the innocent victims. It does not need much imagination to see the value to the prison officer of changes which turn him from a warder into a teacher and helper; the changes which have already taken place have all depended on their willing cooperation. It is more difficult perhaps to envisage this sort of change as benefiting the victims, yet nothing in the way of retributive action helps the victim and any treatment which turns a man from crime reduces the number of victims of crime.

Obviously, any action affecting only existing criminals does not go to the root of the problem. The replenishment of the criminal population comes from the poorest and least privileged sectors of society, and Friends have repeatedly emphasized that redressing the balance and improving the environmental conditions of these parts of our society are a high priority. The aim must be to check and correct the conditions that give rise to crime, while at the same time we learn more about the nature of crime and the criminal and about ways of bringing criminals to acceptable behaviour.

So far, so good, but there is another aspect which must not be ignored. There is a type of criminal quite different from the inadequate personality who might be led to a better view of himself and his place in the world. In recent years it has become more and more apparent that there is a small but growing number of professional criminals, expert, intelligent men who have taken to crime because, if pursued single-mindedly enough, it pays. Perhaps also the ruthlessness and the violence for which they find scope meets some deep need in their personality. At all events they exist, and we have little idea what to do about them. Constructive rehabilitation is something of a laugh when one is thinking of the professional robber of banks, and organizers of protection rackets and the like, who use violence and intimidation as the tools of their trade. We talk – the judiciary often talk – in terms of the protection of society; since we do not know how to make them any more acceptable we keep them in custody because they are dangerous when loose.

It is important to keep the perspective, however. The great majority of the prison population are pathetically inadequate; a numerically small group are violent, dangerous men. The treatment appropriate to the first group would be useless with the second, and it is a simple waste of money to maintain for the whole population a system which, in its security arrangements and restraints on liberty, attempts to match the determined ingenuity of the truly professional criminal. Moreover, if we consider the probable motives of the two types (here again we lack evidence) it does suggest that while detection and imprisonment are not likely to deter the socially inadequate, and indeed clearly do not deter them, it is at least possible that a high detection rate, followed by a period of imprisonment, which corresponds to enforced unemployment, may deter the more intelligent professionals, if we are right in suspecting their prime motive to be a desire for material wealth, easily acquired with a lacing of thrills and risks. If so, then this class of crime can be contained by more effective detection and a deterrent sentencing policy. But if the motive is not easy money and cheap thrills, if there is a strong element of working out a grudge against society, then such a policy is likely to be counter-effective in terms of changing attitudes, and will indeed only operate as a way of protecting society.

Yet we have to recognize this for what it is, an admission of total failure. To have produced a criminal sub-group in society is one level of failure, to be forced to use deprivation of liberty as a sanction is another, to be driven to contemplate imprisonment for the protection of the community, so that anything short of a true life sentence is a calculated risk, is a failure so complete as to make one wonder whether this course is really so morally preferable to the eighteenth-century solution of hanging for everything. If we have to accept it, to accept the long-term maximum-security prisoners, then we must recognize the inhumanity to which these men have forced us, and redouble our efforts to find more civilized ways of dealing with the problem they represent. Above all we must never lock them up and forget them.

In all our discussion of Friends' concern with penal affairs there is one question which tends to obtrude itself. Those involved are intensely practical, unsentimental yet humane, and they form collectively one of the best regarded and best informed specialist authorities on their subject. For all that, and without in any way questioning the importance of their work, our bulging prisons contain 39,000 men and women. There is some dispute as to what constitutes homelessness in this country, but on any one night over 18,000 people are in welfare accommodation. Similarly we are not quite clear what constitutes poverty, but one estimate suggests that some 350,000 families are living in poverty, including about 1,000,000 children.

Of course, Quakers are concerned with both these problems, usually through association with other bodies, with housing associations, with all the welfare agencies which try to help the poor and the homeless. But the fact remains that we have a special position on penal reform, and we don't have the same special position on poverty and home-lessness.

The reasons may be partly historical; a respectable middle-class group in the habit of going to prison for its principles is in a particularly favoured position for commenting on the imperfections of the system; a group of professional men including magistrates, solicitors and Home Office civil servants is likely to find its social conscience concentrated on the unfortunates who come under their professional notice; a Society which has seen the impact of an outstanding personality like Elizabeth Fry on the prison system of her day is likely to take a particular interest in continuing her work.

Moreover, the criminal element in the population does represent, in a particularly acute form, the failure of the community, and for Friends the outcasts, the undeserving, must always be a particular challenge. And since, with limited numbers, we must to some extent concentrate our efforts, perhaps penal reform is a good choice. At all events, since being expert is a consequence of past experience, not of future intentions, whether or not statistical evidence or ethical considerations would lead us to rank penal affairs as the first priority in social welfare at home, we have the experience which makes us an authority, and so are likely to continue as one.

CHAPTER 6

Religion and Social Order

As I have written the preceding five chapters I have been uneasily aware of their inappropriateness, not to what I have to say but to what my reader might expect of me. The general title of this part is 'Belief and Behaviour'; its purpose is to set out what the effects of Quaker belief are on those that hold it and, through the individual Friends, on the society in which he lives. The reader may therefore expect a set of attitudes, at least some moral guide lines; instead of which each aspect of social behaviour, as I have started my discussion of it, seems to have led me into further inquiry, speculation, suggestions.

My suggestions and speculations may not be acceptable to all Friends, but I think the way in which they arise will be acceptable. Because, as it seems to me, this is how Quaker concern operates. Every time we are aware of a social problem, we are forced to consider it, not against a background of defined rules, but against the standards of our own inner light. We may read the best expert treatises, we may read our Bibles and our devotional works, but in the end, in George Fox's words, 'Christ saith this, and the apostles say this; but what canst thou say? Art thou a child of Light and hast walked in the Light, and what thou speakest is it inwardly from God?'[1] So, if it is an individual case, not a problem but a person, we will be driven to share in their difficulties, and to understand their predicament, and to do whatever we find to be right for them. Not necessarily to give them material help, though this is often what must be done, but to do whatever seems to us, from our inner source, to be right. However, if we are thinking of a generalized problem, rather than facing an individual person, it seems to

1. George Fox, *Journal*, 'Christian Faith and Practice in the Experience of the Society of Friends, London Yearly Meeting of the Religious Society of Friends', 1960, § 20.

me that the consequence of bringing the problem to this reference standard is a tendency to find fairly radical ways of attacking its root causes.

The inner light, after all, is little concerned with compromise and socially easy transitions. It is concerned with the right; it is concerned with man's pilgrimage towards God; and the material circumstances of this world are available as mere tools and pawns in that pilgrimage. Thus to be concerned about peace or sex or money or misfits in this way is to be concerned with how these things can be part of the path to God, and not at all with how they can be accommodated with the minimum disruption of the social order.

The range of acceptable policies, practical policies, as the politician calls them, is really the range from the minimum disruption of things as they are which will produce the changes in society on which the majority insist to the maximum disruption which the majority will tolerate. There is usually very little distance between these two measures, which is why we accept systems of government whereby large amounts of time and great numbers of our most intelligent legislators are busily engaged for most of their time on trivial or purely formal legislation. If they were to apply themselves to real issues all the time they would produce more social disruption than would be acceptable to the majority. Hence, wherever a democracy in any form is practised, the legislature can bring to fruition only a handful of significant reforms in a year. The rest of the time is preempted by the machinery of government, and by measures trivial, measures parochial or measures laughable.

Practical policies, in the true sense, are quite a different matter. One can bring about social revolutions just as fast as people, as individuals, can adapt to changes, and people can really adapt to changes very fast indeed, particularly if those changes are the right ones, in the sense of according with the divine will, with the light which is in every man. While most men do not want to know about that light there will always be a lot of noise about sectional interests, and economic principles, and national security. But the light is there, even in those most concerned with their own bank balance, and major social reforms do in fact go through, quite smoothly, despite the strong sectional interests opposed to them.

The Quaker assumption is that to God all things are possible, and that even if he does not apparently and immediately bring about the particular issue one is working for, there is no escaping from the imperatives imposed by the inner light. If, in the quiet centre, I know I must not take up arms, I must not take up arms. If, in the same way, I know I must work for freely available contraception for all who want it, or for the ending of racial discrimination, I must so work. If I am told that whatever you do there will always be housing problems, and if in the deepest centre of my being I know I must attack those problems even if they appear insoluble, then I must attack them.

This attitude has been with the Society from the earliest days. To know of a problem, a difficulty, something adrift in society, is to develop a concern to right it. One shares that concern with Friends, they endorse it, and participate in it. Then together the attack is launched. It does not matter greatly what the world says, whether Friends are accused of being impractical idealists or laughably out of touch with reality. We are used to these comments; we are quite prepared to be, as a non-Quaker newspaper study said, '... continually in and out of prison, always for opinions which were revolutionary then, but became thoroughly respectable later on.'[2]

Thus the quiet, grey, unobtrusive Quakers can be dangerously radical.

For this is the essence of the teaching of Jesus, and the essence of great religions everywhere; that the spiritual has supremacy over the mundane. This is why religion must be institutionalized, why the individual must be separated as far as possible from direct spiritual experience, for if this is not done men see God and know his will, and that is the end of political power and personal aggrandizement.

In a different context, R. D. Laing has written:

In the last fifty years we human beings have slaughtered by our own hands coming on for one hundred million of our

2. Ruth Adam, 'The Quakers', *Sunday Citizen*, 14 June 1964.

species. We all live under constant threat of our total annihil-
ation. We seem to seek death and destruction as much as life and
happiness. We are as driven to kill and be killed as we are to let
live and live. Only by the most outrageous violation of ourselves
have we achieved our capacity to live in relative adjustment to a
civilization apparently driven to its own destruction.

He goes on to a most significant discussion of the relationship of 'us' and 'them', of the way in which we are influenced
by what others think and what we think they think and
what we think they think we think and so on 'in a logically
vertiginous spiral to infinity'.[3]

This all rings true and leaves us asking perhaps, 'But
what world would it be if we did not take account of others,
and their experience, their ideas?' Laing – and history is
with him – implies that the alternative could hardly be
worse than the situation we have been brought to by our
present attitude. Those of us who are aware of the spiritual
alternative see there the standard and guide which replaces
concern with what others think, with what 'they' will say. It
is an alternative which meets Laing's requirements that
'perhaps men and women were born to love one another,
simply and genuinely, rather than to this travesty that we
can call love. If we can stop destroying ourselves we may stop
destroying others.'[4]

From this rather abnormal (in the sense of 'not average')
viewpoint, the way this part of my book has developed is not
surprising. As one considers social and ethical problems one
cannot, if one is any sort of a Quaker, any sort of Christian,
any sort of human being, be unconcerned. To be concerned
is to think deeply, to think deeply, in the Quaker context, is a
reference to the inner light, and out of this comes, most
probably, ideas about action. So it seems to me inevitable
that each chapter should lead to a speculation and hence to
suggestions of change.

I wonder now if I have considered the right issues, for
surely there are other aspects of society as much in need of

3. R. D. Laing, *The Politics of Experience*, Penguin Books, 1967, pp.
64 and 66.
4. ibid., p. 64.

an overhaul as those I have picked on. Perhaps not in one sense, because our physical survival depends on the avoidance of physical violence and our individual mental survival on the avoidance of psychical violence, and both are only possible if there is individual acceptance of the possibility and actuality of love. My five chapters are about this thesis, and will serve as examples. Writing about these things is after all not very important – what matters is feeling about them.

One conclusion, which I have touched on above, is worth emphasizing. Quakers are a threat to the established order of society. They are not all of one political persuasion; there is no danger of their selling your country to the Russians, the Chinese, the Americans, the socialists or the capitalists. The trouble is, and I cannot stress this too strongly, that they put the will of God first – even before the safety and well-being of their native land, even (writing for the English reader particularly) before the maintenance of their own class in society. These quiet committees working in modest surroundings at Friends House in the Euston Road, London, are dangerous to society because there is no knowing when they will hear the still, small voice counselling them to a course which may have far-reaching consequences.

Do not misunderstand me. The Friends are not themselves great innovators; in their own affairs they are cautiously conservative. Nor would they wildly and wantonly force change on others. It is simply that by their whole practice of worship and manner of proceeding they are prepared to wait on the Lord. If you do this, you are much more likely to know his will than if you spend your whole time thinking, scheming and planning. Given you know that will, and work towards it, you will find yourself the subject of a 'push from without and a pull from within' – the momentum builds up, and in time (Quakerism encourages patience without resignation; all that sitting quietly in Meeting!) the concerned Friends find society going their way. By that time we are a minority tailing along with the big battalions; and somewhere, in some quiet corner, a Friend is conscious of a new concern.

Nor do I claim any uniqueness for Friends in their insight

into what needs doing in our world. After all, there is nothing unique about a Quaker except that he is a member of the Religious Society of Friends; from every other viewpoint he is just a human being. And awareness of the divine will is not conditional on membership of a particular society; it depends simply on the subjugation of the ego, the suspension of thought, the open-ness of the mind and heart. This can happen to those of any religious persuasion or none – though in the latter case they should be urged to find a religious belief to rationalize their experience lest it prove too much for them to live with.

It is indeed a fact that those of whatever belief and background, who allow themselves to be the willing instruments of God's purpose, find that the purpose is everywhere the same. This is shown in the curious coming together of such people in a variety of groupings and organizations. They are of course all human and fallible. They tend to have disagreements about tactics and organization, to take offence at each other and so on. But over the years they keep on coming together, for this purpose and for that, because the inner light shows them the way.

If I, as an outsider and non-participant in most of these activities may be allowed a comment, which is most sincerely meant, it would be that the effect of these groupings which work for the betterment of humanity would be infinitely enhanced if they could spare a part of their energy for inquiring into their spiritual situation and building up their awareness of their essentially non-material guidance and direction. I know the Friends involved in such activities share this view and operate in this way; I am not suggesting that all their colleagues should join Friends, but only that in their common enterprise they should follow Penington in 'performing their own peculiar service'.

Quakers are not perfect; they are essentially human and weak and inept and stupid like everyone else. But their being Quakers does make a difference to their attitude and their behaviour and it is to this that their influence in history and society, which is out of all proportion to their numbers, is attributable. There is a tendency to put the cart before the horse, to say that they are people who find happiness in serving others and who seek to find religious belief through such service. This is quite the wrong way round, apart from having a concealed and unjustified implication that Quakers are simply those who have a particular psychological quirk which drives them to service and sacrifice as a means of self-gratification. What comes first is the religious experience which leads to religious belief. Out of this comes a compulsion to work for others in some way or other. For many it is in practical matters, for some it is a drive towards a contemplative and mystical life – for this too serves others, bringing us all closer to true awareness of God through its actual being.

A Friend once remarked in Meeting that, 'One of the wonderful things about the working of the Holy Spirit is that it makes us want to do what we have to do' and it is I think from this that the Quaker draws much of his energy and enthusiasm. Conscience or duty, in the ordinary sense, knowing rationally that what you are attempting is right, cannot quite provide the motivation one so often sees in Friends, something beyond zeal, a positive self-indulgent relish of their chosen activity. Little wonder the quietist element in the early nineteenth century shook their heads over social welfare work as 'creaturely activity'!

As a consequence I have noticed the evidence of an intense and sincere gratitude in those Friends who have spent their lives in service. I remember one at a conference on service overseas describing with zest the primitive conditions in which he had lived in parts of Africa, the almost intolerable difficulties, the never-ending problems – and expressing his most heartfelt thanks to those at home whose contributions had enabled him to spend his life in this way, just as those of us in his audience were feeling very glad that we had not ourselves had to bear what he had borne. And yet, even then, one was conscious of a slight unease; could it be envy that he had lived right through his knowledge of God in such exotic surroundings? It is neither easier nor more difficult to go to the end of the earth in answer to the moving of the spirit than it is to answer the same spirit when

it calls you to stay where you are and to do nothing outwardly. What is infinitely difficult and infinitely rewarding
is to hear and to obey.

Implicit in this whole attitude is a grave danger, which has
been used by the organized churches in earlier times as a
decisive argument for a separated priesthood and a hierarchical structure. How are we to know that we are indeed hark-
ening to the will of God? In knowing God within us we are
also made aware of the Devil; will we not be likely to mistake
the voice of self-will for the voice of God, to persuade ourselves not that we want to do what we have to do, but that we
have to do what we want to do? Surely it is best that the
dangerous power of deciding what is right and what is
wrong should be reserved to those specially selected and
trained for the task, and that they should be organized and
controlled by those of greater insight and wisdom who have
risen to high ecclesiastical office?

Yet if one selects a priesthood primarily on a sense of vocation, or hearing the call, it is difficult to see why personal
awareness of God's will should be limited to this one group
of people and then mainly to their selection and segregation.
How can one know that a priest has a genuine call to priesthood and yet not accept that others may be genuinely instructed of God in other matters?

Quakers recognize the vocation of service to God, but in
our experience the call comes to us all, men and women
alike, if we will but hear it. Hence there can be no separated
priesthood, only a priesthood of all, reconciling the demands
of the material world with the imperatives of the spiritual.

However, there is still the question of how one ensures
that one is not led astray. There is a plentiful history of sects
which have been led by what they considered the will of God
to immorality (usually of a sexual nature) and to anti-social
behaviour, and there are many cases of individuals who have
seen visions and heard voices, which have told them to kill
and destroy.

Well, against such risks I can only point to the history of
the Friends, and to their general avoidance of such disastrous
confusions. The story of James Nayler is however a demon-

stration that the risk is there, and for the reason why the risk is in practice slight and the Nayler story effectively unique, I can only point to the three rules for handling a 'concern' which were first established in the seventeenth century and which still, generally, keep us to the right courses.

First, a true prompting that is from God will never require that you act with violence or so as to bring manifest harm or hurt to others. Second, if you will sit quiet with your concern a long while, if it be truly from God, it will strengthen continually, but the devil – that is the ego – is in no wise patient, and if your concern is in truth come from your own will and desires it becomes, as you sit, first restive and then faltering. But God is not so changeable. Third, carry your concern to a group of Friends, open your mind to them, and then wait quietly upon the Lord together, and hearken what he says to each one of you, for if all are plainly of one mind, that is God's will, but if one says one thing, and one another, then that is not from God but from your own thoughts and wills.

Today we are not as disposed as we might be to bring our every problem to a group of Friends, though we still use very freely the first two rules. There is much to be said for the revival of the third; it often happens that a Friend will voice a concern with some social injustice at Meeting, and will be strengthened and supported by the Meeting's response. But we do not, generally, use the group to help us with personal problems, with simple decision taking. We are too shy, too careful of others' time, too proud. And yet it seems to me that here we have a valuable and profound resource which could well be of great benefit to us, and which we ignore. Of course, most of our decisions do not matter greatly one way or another; simply by sitting quietly by ourselves with our problem we can generally decide whether to go to central Wales or the New Forest for a holiday. But there are problems which leave us baffled, the question whether to move to another district, to the benefit of one member of the family and the disadvantage of another, problems of emotional relationships – if we do not encounter them from time to time we are not properly alive. It is pride that keeps us from asking others to help us in these matters; if we once admitted that we could not manage our lives without God's help and that even then we need the loving care and support of our Friends, how many more would admit their parallel need and ask for our help?

Once again I have been led into comment and speculation, and perhaps I have followed these themes far enough. Yet it is important to show that this alternative to imposed discipline, this inner-directed life, does have direction and control, and is not a cloak for anarchy, or inaction. But in the end the proof is not in words but in experience.

PART IV

Organization and Practices

The Organization of the Religious Society of Friends

THERE is a myth that George Fox, seeing the need for some organization among his followers, decreed the structure which has lasted practically unchanged to the present day. The truth is not quite so Mosaic; the outlines and principles have lasted unaltered for three hundred years, and so to our infinite confusion has the terminology, but the functions and operations have been modified, to suit changing circumstances. Meeting for Sufferings still exists, and is still a representative committee, but it is no longer concerned with making a record of those Friends who are suffering persecution and with lobbying against persecution; it would, in fact, be better, if more prosaically, entitled 'the Executive Committee'.

However, certain principles have stood. The Society is composed of its individual members, and these are grouped in Meetings. A Meeting is a gathering; at the absolute minimum one person waiting on the Lord is a Meeting, and Meetings have survived before now with only one member. But generally, a Meeting is where two or three are gathered together. There remain some awkward matters of terminology before we can go any further. A Meeting, without qualification, is a Meeting for Worship, whether on Sunday or any other day. It is strictly an occasion. 'Meeting for Worship will be held here at eleven.' 'Put your coat on, it's time to go to Meeting.'

Here we begin to become involved in the structure of the Society, for the individual Meeting for Worship is also generally the lowest level in the organization for the management of the Society's business. There is one exception to this, for certain small Meetings function only as Meetings for Worship, their business functions being exercised through a larger neighbouring Meeting which is a 'Preparative Meeting'. A number of Preparative Meetings in a larger area constitute a 'Monthly Meeting', several Monthly Meetings may together be a 'General Meeting', but all the Monthly Meetings in Great Britain collectively form 'London Yearly Meeting'.

Looking outside London Yearly Meeting, we see that it is numerically only a small element in the world family:

World Membership by Continents

North America	122,000
Africa	42,000
Europe	24,000
South and Central America	6,000
Asia	2,000
Australia and New Zealand	1,500
	197,500

That is to say, in round figures, 200,000, of whom London Yearly Meeting accounts for some 20,000.

In considering these figures, however, it must be remembered that of the North American membership some 60,000 belong to Meetings affiliated to the Friends United Meeting (that is, the meetings which followed Gurney in the nineteenth-century divisions) and 24,000 to the Evangelical Friends Alliance, based on those who found the Friends United Meeting insufficiently credal, Christocentric and scriptural. These groups have been actively proselytizing missionaries; as a consequence East Africa Yearly Meeting, associated with Friends United Meeting, accounts for 32,000 of the Friends in Africa; and the work of the Evangelical Friends Alliance, particularly of Oregon Yearly Meeting, associated with the National Friends Church of Bolivia, is the reason for the relatively large numbers in Central and South America. If we subtract these and the 8,000 Friends in Madagascar who are now integrated into the United Church of Madagascar from the World membership, we are left with 38,000 in North America, 20,000 in London Yearly Meeting, 2,000 in Ireland, where a single Yearly Meeting unites North and South, 1,500 in Australia and New Zealand and small groups scattered over the rest of the world (excluding the Russian and Chinese spheres of influence), all keeping generally to the ways of London Yeary Meeting. Thus the unprogrammed silent meeting found in Britain and parts of the U.S.A. (particularly of course Philadelphia) will also be found wherever Quakers are scattered and few. Where Friends have emerged as a numerically significant group, and particularly where a Friends' Church has been established or where Friends have become incorporated in a church, there is generally a programmed service, a paid pastor, and a strong evangelical and scriptural emphasis.

Now as if it were not enough to call every element of this world-wide organization a Meeting, distinguishing them only by geographical and periodic adjectives, there are also other Meetings within London Yearly Meeting (and doubtless elsewhere) which are no more than committees. I have already mentioned Meeting for Sufferings which acts as the Society's general purposes or executive committee; there is also a 'Six Weeks Meeting' of long standing, which administers certain funds collectively for Meetings in the London area. Its main concern is with buildings and premises.

This insistent use of the word 'Meeting' has a particular significance, for it stresses the links between all the organizational levels of the Society. All these Meetings are Meetings for Worship as well as for business; all start and finish with a period of silence, all may wait in silence at any point in their proceedings, seeking to discover God's will; there will be no votes taken, no overriding of the minority by the majority. Significant it may be, confusing it certainly is; sufficiently so as to justify a worked example, as the mathematics textbook would call it.

I attend Richmond upon Thames Meeting. This was started about twenty years ago. Our numbers most Sundays are between twenty and thirty, representing a fairly substantial growth since I came to the area some five years

back, when it was something of an event to reach double
figures. Until recently, although a recognized Meeting, we
were part of the Preparative Meeting of Kingston upon
Thames, some three miles away, from which our founders
came.

With the growth in our numbers, we felt able to take on
responsibility for our own affairs, and now we are a Preparative Meeting in our own right. A Preparative Meeting,
as its name implies, prepares business; we meet (usually on a
weekday evening) once a month, to agree our view on
matters arising at Monthly Meeting and to decide on any
issues we want to put forward to that meeting. Our Monthly
Meeting is called Kingston and Wandsworth Monthly
Meeting and consists of five Preparative Meetings, Esher,
Kingston, Richmond, Wandsworth and Wimbledon. It
meets, as might be expected, once a month.

It is in the Monthly Meeting that the power of the Society
resides, for it is Monthly Meeting that decides who shall be
admitted to membership, what matters shall go forward to
Yearly Meeting, and what should be referred to Preparative
Meetings for their consideration. Above Monthly Meeting
there is the London and Middlesex General Meeting which
meets occasionally for 'conference and inspiration, and for a
broad oversight of the life and witness of the Society within
its area'.

In the book of members of the London and Middlesex
General Meeting I am recorded as a member of Richmond
Preparative Meeting in the Kingston and Wandsworth
Monthly Meeting of London and Middlesex General Meet-
ing. And the whole local organization is a constituent part of
London Yearly Meeting, the final constitutional authority
of the Religious Society of Friends in Great Britain.

Every Sunday, then, I go to Richmond for worship, and
once a month I attend Preparative Meeting one evening.
This naturally is the opportunity for dealing with business
relating strictly to our own Meeting – with the question
(which has occupied us much over the last few years but has
now had a successful outcome) of getting our own Meeting
House, or with our participation in some local activity, or the

planning of our winter series of discussion evenings. We, in common with most Meetings, do not restrict the attendance to our formal membership, but are happy to have with us anybody who attends Meeting for Worship and feels sufficient concern with what we are doing to want to come to our business Meeting. Those who are wondering whether to apply for membership often find it very valuable to come to Preparative Meeting and see how we deal with practical affairs. Some days after Preparative Meeting, Monthly Meeting takes place. This is rather like an Elizabethan 'progress'. It often takes place at each constituent Meeting House in turn. It is a meeting of all who can attend, though limited to members; and to ensure a minimum representation each Preparative Meeting is asked to collect and forward to the Clerk of Monthly Meeting the names of a few Friends who undertake to be present. Friends who are not members of the Monthly Meeting should notify the Clerk of their presence, and attenders may be present only by permission of the Clerk. General Meetings were until recently Quarterly Meetings, but they now occur as necessary. They are of marginal importance organizationally, but offer an opportunity for Friends from a wide area to meet and discuss matters of common interest.

Yearly Meeting occupies five days once a year. It is mostly held in London, but every few years it takes place in a provincial centre. Any member of the Society may attend, though once again names are sent forward by Monthly Meetings of those who undertake to attend, thus ensuring a balanced minimum representation. Non-members may only attend by special permission.

The standing executive of the Society, Meeting for Sufferings, is made up of representatives of every Monthly Meeting and sets up (and on occasion demolishes) the other committees of the Society. While Meeting for Sufferings has a general remit, the other committees take particular fields as their concern.

The Friends Service Council (not strictly a committee of London Yearly Meeting, since it is supported jointly by

London and Ireland Yearly Meetings) takes responsibility for activities alongside, and for the benefit of, those not Friends, particularly in overseas countries. We have already seen one aspect of their work in the field of promoting good-will and seeking solutions to causes of tension in the world; their main activity is in combating the effect of natural and man-made calamity, and in assistance to developing countries, including educational assistance. Quaker Service – to use a wider term to cover the work of F.S.C. and its analogues in other Yearly Meetings, for they work very closely together – started from the mission activity of the mid nineteenth century. It has come to be concerned, however, more with identifying, and helping to meet, the needs of those with whom we work. Much of the activity is dictated by world conditions; if there is less to do in North Africa there is more in Nigeria and Bangladesh; and as well as the depressingly familiar problems of famine and sickness in the wake of disasters, occasionally natural but usually man-made, there is also the steady unspectacular work in education and development of food production and health services. F.S.C. work does not look so much like missionary activity these days; the vigorously nationalistic countries of the developing world would not accept it if it did, and besides, as William Sewell, after long years in China, told those at home who wanted to put spreading the Gospel, old style, before assisting others in their own search for a valid way of life, 'I have lived too long in China to think that there is anything I can teach my Chinese friends half so valuable as what they have taught me.'[1] Quaker Service is a two-way traffic; we receive as much as we give, and if we seek to

1. I cannot forbear to quote from a letter I had recently from William Sewell. 'I left China with an amateurish philosophy of strengthened belief in that of God in all men (whatever one might mean by God – Inner Light – Christ?). I felt strongly that revelation (or our apprehension of it) is continuous and always being unfolded; that the institutionalized vested interests of the Christian Church ... made it almost impossible for the will of God to be heard through the Church, and that 'God' was speaking through all sorts of people, through Mao Tse-tung for example (although this does not make Mao a Quaker – far from it!).'

answer the needs of those we go to serve, they also, by allowing us to serve, answer a need in us.

Perhaps the Committee most likely to affect the non-Friend in Britain is the Home Service Committee. Its function is to encourage and deepen the spiritual life of the Society and to make its message known to those not in membership. It is Home Service Committee that planted those eye-catching little advertisements in the papers – 'You mean to say Quakers get married without a priest?' or some such provocative headline – that had many an unwary reader devouring the small print and writing to George Gorman at Friends House, Euston Road, London, N.W.1, for further information. Indeed, it had some part in my own progress to Quakerism. I missed out, for some reason, on the excellent conferences for inquirers which they run; if this book has raised a continuing interest in any reader's mind, I suggest writing to George and getting invited. I need hardly add that you will not be plagued by Friends from your local Meeting ringing your doorbell; it is the inviolable rule that no local Meeting is ever informed of inquiries directed to Friends House unless the inquirer specifically asks for this to be done.

Of the remaining committees directly responsible to Meeting for Sufferings, some special explanation is required in respect of the Friends Education Council. The Council does not run the Friends Schools, that group of distinctive, mainly boarding, schools which occupy a middle position between the orthodox 'public' schools and the 'progressive' schools in the Bedales/Summerhill tradition. The Friends Schools (their pupils are now more non-Friend than Friend) are autonomous, each with its own governing body; and though Friends play a dominant part in their direction, the Friends Education Council is not the controlling power. The F.E.C. is concerned to foster and support individuals and institutions engaged in educational endeavour, to seek the right lines of development in education and to interpret these to Friends, and to help young people to understand the meaning of Quakerism and to find spiritual meaning in their lives. It produces material to help those who run children's Meetings and classes; and is also concerned to present educational developments to the Society, and, conversely, to put the Society's views on education before the government and other bodies when appropriate. For a first-class survey of Friends Schools (and a model of how evidence should be prepared and submitted) I recommend the informative and readable evidence the Council put to the Public Schools Commission.

The other principal Committees – the Committee on Christian Relationships; the Peace and International Relations Committee; the Social Responsibility Council (incorporating the former Penal Affairs, Race Relations and Social and Economic Affairs Committees); the Quaker World Relations Committee, which keeps in touch with the linking body between different Yearly Meetings, Friends World Committee for Consultation – operate in the fields their titles describe. They work with minimal and devoted full-time staffs, and their activities are conducted largely through their own members, or through the links they have with individual Meetings. In some cases there is a single 'correspondent'; in other cases Meetings have a corresponding committee. Indeed there are Friends who feel that the Society proliferates committees until its members are so involved that they have no energy for anything beyond keeping the machinery moving.

The structure is not really so complicated as it seems, though the terminology and some of the customs are both curious and archaic. It is decidedly upsetting to new members to find, for example, that if a person who intended to attend Monthly Meeting is not there when the Clerk recites 'Kingston Preparative Meeting nominated the following members to attend: Mary Jones . . .' one says, not 'she can't come, she's got 'flu,' but simply 'Prevented'. And if someone is inaudible, instead of 'Speak up', a firm voice is likely to observe that 'Our Friend is not heard.' It is all rather formal and late eighteenth century, and helps to fossilize us in our past. If, as seems to be the case at present, the membership is maintained by convincement, there will soon be a majority who do not know the correct Quaker ways, and more direct, twentieth-century utterance will take over. Some gain, at some loss.

If we look past these minor curiosities at the actual organization, however, there is nothing so unusual in it. It is hierarchical, in the sense of moving up from local level to national level through several stages. It has certain oddities which are only explicable historically, but then few organizations avoid that. The odd thing about the Society is its complete democracy, the extent to which the executive business Meetings are open to all, hence avoiding all such problems as the difference between a representative and a delegate. In theory – theory of management, that is – such a system is unworkable. The potential attendance at London Yearly Meeting is 22,000; what if even a quarter turned up? The actual attendance is between 400 and 500; there are appointed by each Monthly Meeting a 'sufficient number of Friends who will undertake to be present', but they attend as individuals, neither representatives nor delegates. What if they are outnumbered by a few coach-loads of Friends from one district or of one view? Surely such a Meeting is infinitely susceptible to organized pressure groups? And how can one operate committees like Meeting for Sufferings, F.S.C. and Home Service, with nominal membership running into hundreds?

The answer is to be found in the way in which the Meetings operate, which is not at all a question of procedure in the usual sense. However, before we go on to consider how these Meetings operate, and what actually happens at them, some further general points need to be made. The first is that there is no discrimination against women in the Society. At all points and for all purposes men and women are equal members (you will notice a shudder run through the Meeting if you call the women 'ladies'). There are many organizations which claim to work like this, but the distinguishing feature of the Quakers is that it is true in practice and has been so since George Fox convinced Elizabeth Hooton. Women are equally eligible with men for all offices in the Society, and do in fact hold them, and in spite of Dr Johnson's comment ('Sir, a woman's preaching is like a dog's walking on his hind legs, it is not done well but you are surprised to find it done at all.')[2] women have ever taken their due share in ministry.

The second point is that the Society has no separated priesthood; we are all equally responsible for the conduct of our worship. Some, it is true, have distinguishing titles, our clerks, elders and overseers, but these are posts of responsibility, not posts of authority. The authority the society recognizes is the authority of God, sought through the working of our Meetings and recognized and accepted by the individual.

Thirdly, let it be understood that Meetings for Worship are open to all; and all are welcome, whether they are members of the Society, or regular attenders who are not in membership, or sincere seekers after God, or those who have found God in another way and come to broaden their experience of other faiths – or even the plain curious.

2. J. Boswell, *Life of Johnson*, entry for 31 July 1763.

CHAPTER 2

Meeting for Worship

MEETING for Worship is the Society's most vital and creative activity. The difficulty in giving an adequate description of it to anyone who has not experienced it is that practically nothing happens; nothing, that is, in terms of outward activity. Nevertheless, we had better start with a description of the outward appearance. The following account is based on British Meetings. It applies fairly well to Meetings in many other parts of the world; but it does not describe the Meetings of parts of America and of Africa. Some Yearly Meetings – e.g. in parts of the U.S.A. and those in South America, Madagascar and some in other parts of Africa – have developed a programmed Meeting, led by a pastor and incorporating hymns, prayers predetermined and extempore and an address. These Meetings may or may not include opportunities for silent worship.

Meeting may take place at any time, in any suitable place. All that is necessary is a room, some chairs and the assurance of being undisturbed. Customarily, Meeting is held on Sunday morning, at 10.30 or 11.00 a.m.; but there are also mid-week Meetings, at lunch-time or just after work; and some Sunday Meetings are held in the evening. Many Meetings have their own Meeting Houses, but others meet in hired rooms or private houses.

The room has chairs or benches set round in a square or a circle, perhaps two or three ranks deep. There is a table in the centre, on which there is usually a vase of flowers; and a few copies of the Bible (both the King James and New English translations) and 'Christian Faith and Practice in the Experience of the Society of Friends'. One bench or row of chairs may be distinguished by being placed on a slight platform if the Meeting House is fairly old; or perhaps the sensitive eye will notice a group of four or five chairs in the front row just a little separated from the others. These are

for the elders, of whom more anon. The decorative scheme
in Meeting Houses proper is calm and restrained, and there
is nothing to distract either eye or ear. Perhaps a wall clock
is quietly ticking, or the brush of a branch can be heard
against a window if the shrubs in the Meeting House garden
need trimming – but nothing more.

A little before the set time of Meeting, the first comers
arrive and sit down. As always, people get into habits, and
tend to sit in the same place from week to week, but except
for the elders' bench there is no distinction between one
place and another. It is said that one weighty Friend kept an
isolated Meeting going for years by himself attending worship every Sunday, though there were no other Friends to
worship with him. He became accustomed to a certain seat,
and when by chance a visiting Friend arrived one Sunday
and sat in that one seat, out of all those in the empty Meeting House, the old gentleman went up to him with the
words, 'Welcome Friend, thou art in my place.' I have said 'a
little before the set time of Meeting' because Meeting starts,
not at the time on the notice board, but when the first worshipper arrives. 'The first that arrives in your place of meeting ... turn in thy mind to the light, and wait upon God
singly, as if none were present but the Lord; and here thou
art strong. Then the next that comes in, let them in simplicity of heart sit down and turn in to the same light and
wait in the spirit, and so all the rest coming in, in fear of the
Lord, sit down in pure stillness and silence of all flesh and
wait in the light ...'[1]

In fact, the first five or ten minutes of Meeting is the set-
tling-in period. People come in, and sit down, and settle
themselves in their places. Then someone else comes in, and
sits down and so on. We all try to be on time for Meeting,
but there are all the accidents and delays of ordinary life to
make sure we are not. So it is only after about ten minutes

---

1. Alexander Parker, letter to Friends dated 14 November 1659, (old
style), *Letters, etc., of Early Friends*, ed. Abram Rawlinson Barclay,
1841, 'Christian Faith and Practice in the Experience of the Society of
Friends', London Yearly Meeting of the Religious Society of Friends,
1960, § 262.

that the Meeting begins to 'centre down', that is, that the real stillness develops, and the silence deepens.

Now, there is no programme at all for a Quaker Meeting, and so there is no guarantee that anything at all will happen. What usually happens, and this is purely a statistical observation, is that the silence remains unbroken for some fifteen or twenty minutes. Then someone – anyone, for this is unarranged and unpremeditated – stands and speaks for a few minutes, and then sits down. The silence continues. After another ten minutes or so another person may stand and speak, and so on. An hour's Meeting without any ministry is unusual, but not unknown; an hour's Meeting in which more than about six people offer ministry for a total time of more than fifteen minutes is also unusual but not unknown.

Of what does the ministry consist? It consists of whatever people are moved to offer, and I think those who have read this far will understand why it does not consist of the random garbage of the subconscious. Meetings are advised to arrange for the reading of the 'Advices and Queries' over a specified period, but not within too limited a time, so that every month or so the Meeting is likely to be given direction by the reading of a brief but insistent passage from this source. Readings from the Bible are fairly common; certain passages from the poets recur, particularly in the ministry of Friends who grew up when learning by heart was part of education. I am getting to know quite well certain favoured passages from John Greenleaf Whittier (the only Quaker poet of anything approaching First Division status). Otherwise, much of the ministry has a somewhat personal and anecdotal point of origin. That is to say, though it is concerned with man and God, it tends to take as a starting point an everyday incident, the book by the fireside, the talk on the radio, the word spoken or overheard in the High Street. From this comes a commentary on God's relationship to man and man's relationship to the world around him. Since it is unprepared, unpremeditated, it is not and cannot be profoundly intellectual; any quotations are those which the memory holds, any felicities of phrasing are accidental, or so it would seem, and the argument can be only as taut as the speaker can assemble without prior consideration and the aid of notes.

We shall revert to the question of spoken ministry, and explore the more difficult subject of unspoken or silent ministry, when we are considering the inward content of Meeting for Worship. For the present I am only attempting an explanation of what happens outwardly, and spoken ministry fills a small part of the hour. Time passes, the bees hum against the windows, or perhaps the steady rain beats down. Outside, the clocks of the churches begin to strike the hour, first one distant chime, then another, and another. Now, the significance of the elders' bench is apparent. One elder turns to another, they smile and shake hands. There is rustling around the room; everywhere smiles of greeting and handshakes. The clerk stands, welcomes visitors, reads the notices – of Meetings, fund-raising activities, conferences, study groups and so on, both Quaker and other – and says for whom the day's collection is being taken. The Meeting breaks up, sometimes just exchanging a few words before dispersing, sometimes having a cup of coffee together. Generally speaking, Quakers are very anxious to give a personal welcome to visitors, so much so that newer members of the Meeting often extend the visitor-treatment to older members returned after absence, but this, though mildly embarrassing, is better than letting the stranger slip in and out without a word said.

If the Meeting is large enough to produce a fair crop of children there may be a delightful variation on this pattern. Meetings vary in their treatment of children, but it is accepted that few children can sit through an hour without becoming restive and also that there is a need for them to be advised and helped towards understanding, since most schools do not provide very inspired or coherent guidance. There is therefore a children's class conducted by one or two Friends with the aid of lesson notes and pamphlets provided by the Friends Education Council. The age range is often considerable, perhaps from three or four years old (or even a baby in a carry-cot in the corner) up to say twelve, and the methods are as varied as the Friends themselves. One will thump out hymns on the piano, another encourages the making of drawings on themes from the Bible and Quaker history, another will take a chance remark and lead the group on to a discussion of fundamentals, at whatever level they can compass. The educative effect is liberal, since there is a rota of Friends who undertake this service and thus the children get a different view each week.

In certain Meetings this goes on for about three quarters of an hour, and then to those in the main Meeting comes a sound as of mice in the wainscot, growing to a clattering like a herd of young heifers on the stairs, then subsiding to a shuffling and giggling at the door. The door opens, the children stream in and fan out to find their parents and sit by them. The Meeting goes on as before, perhaps including spoken ministry, perhaps in silence. Even the youngest can usually manage to sit quiet, if not, strictly speaking, still, for ten minutes or so. In other Meetings the children come into the main Meeting at the beginning and withdraw after the first quarter of an hour.[2] Whichever way round it goes, in my experience the Meeting usually has an introspective phase every few years in which it wonders if it wouldn't be better if the children came in at the end – or the beginning – of Meeting.

This is what happens, in outward appearance, at Meeting for Worship. The theory of it is simple enough; it is, in Alexander Parker's advice quoted earlier, to 'turn in thy mind to the light and wait upon God singly'; in the words of Jesus, 'For where two or three have met together in my name I am there among them.' The intention is to wait in patient quietness, knowing ourselves to be ever in the presence of God, but by our quietness making ourselves open to him, so that we can know his will. Thus, in spoken ministry we do not speak ourselves, but from the guidance of God within us.

2. I cannot resist telling a delightful story from Oxford Meeting. In the gathering silence a small clear voice asked 'Mummy, why are they all so quiet?' The embarrassed mother hushed the child, but shortly after, an elderly Friend rose to his feet and started his ministry 'The last Minister raised a very important point . . .'

This simple theory is liable to one objection, that what guides us, what we find in the silence, may not be God. The orthodox Christian might suggest that we receive promptings from the devil, that a properly ordained priest is needed to distinguish between the divine and the diabolical. The down-to-earth man of the world may explain it all as sheer imagination. The psychologist may propose the subconscious as the source.

On the need for a properly ordained priest as arbiter of good and evil, one can only point to the comparative success of the two methods in holding people to the right paths, even in the limited and perhaps misleading sense of moral behaviour. It is also significant, though we have no wish to make points at the expense of other churches, that there is a great diversity of belief as to what constitutes a properly ordained priest. The Apostolic Succession has had its moments of aberration through the centuries. We find in fact that there is truth in the words, 'Be still and know that I am God'; to be still is to know, without the need for any system of distinguishing good from evil, God from devil. A priest cannot tell us more clearly or more unequivocally what we inwardly know.

The man of the world's objection is in a way the same as that of the psychologist. I am afraid the only way to convince a severely practical man is to persuade him to expose himself to the experience. It is something of a shock therapy if it works; on the other hand, it is, of course, the easiest thing in the world for a person to attend without participation, to refuse to make the first move towards opening himself to any influence, imaginary or not. This is true of both plain man and psychologist; to the latter one can say we do not dispute that what we find within ourselves is the subconscious. But also we find the unconscious – Jung's collective unconscious, the 'deep unconscious', and in our experience this can properly be equated with the individual's awareness of God.

But all objections, the whole body of that unwritten book *Objections to Quaker Belief*, are irrelevant in a sense because the belief itself is secondary to the experience, and the reality to the individual is his own individual experience. So it is important, not to pursue the ramifications of belief and the interactions of different religious and psychological theories, but to plot, as plainly and as far as we can, some of the varied paths that lead to the experience of God.

As I have said before, there is no claim by the Society of Friends that they alone hold the key, that only through the Christian Church, and their Society within the Christian Church, can one come to God. An inquirer said to me after a recent Meeting, 'This is all very well, but what you have been talking about is what I have been doing by myself for thirty years past. There's nothing new in it.' I was tempted to reply that novelty was suspect in statements about man's relationship with the divine; it was more than likely that the study which had ever been the concern of profound people should have yielded up its secrets long ago. Here, above all, that which is true is not new, and that which is new is not true! But I did not say this. Instead I suggested that as ours was already his way he should join us in our collective worship. For we see ourselves as part of a greater unity: '... no variety of practices, which is of God, can make a breach in the true unity'[3] and our practice is only one of many ways to God. True, most ways are very similar in essence; true also that the method varies widely among Friends. But this is only to be expected. To seek God one must unstop the channel between man and the deep unconscious; for this one must curb the dominating ego, and stop the incessant noise of thinking. How this can be attempted varies from individual to individual, because in each case the form of obstruction varies. But the aim is always the same.

When I first attended Meeting I had behind me nearly forty years of continuous thinking. I could grasp the concept of inner quiet, for I knew enough to realize that the tape recorder in my head was running every conscious minute, and I knew that the actual thinking required to programme my activities was only a fraction of the total. The rest was spent on reliving the past, 'scripting' imminent situations, or

3. Isaac Penington, *Works*, 1681, Part I, pp. 240–42, 'Christian Faith and Practice', § 222.

building fantasies. The first two activities are perhaps more widespread than the third; by 'scripting' I mean imagining how situations might develop, under the mistaken impression that this will help one through them. In fact they always go wrong, and one usually finds oneself floundering through the prepared script, with the other character using a completely different text. How much this is common experience I do not know; at least, there I was, in a Meeting, invited to be still, with this well-established merry-go-round in possession of me.

My first method of breaking loose from thought was through music. I knew that music at least induced complete surrender; I suppose I knew without being conscious of it, that various of my musical experiences were in fact deeply spiritual. So I started, since there was no outward music, to play over music to myself in my head. I chose chamber music, late Beethoven quartets, music which is at all times near to the barriers of consciousness. As time went on, at that Meeting and others, I heard what I can only describe as unwritten music, music which shared the reality of the music I knew but which came from some other source than memory. That was one way towards stillness; the music expelled all sequences of ideas, all rational thought, all concept of the time past, present and future, and sometimes, in its heart, there was silence.

It is in these moments that one may be driven to spoken ministry, or one may receive intuitive knowledge about some matter which does not demand to be shared. The nature of the difference between intuitive knowledge coming from the deep unconscious, from the divine and universal centre that is God, and a random thought, a projection of one's own psychic twists and repressed impulses, is so profound as to be inexplicable. This knowledge is not always comfortable or comforting; it may go counter to strongly-held conscious views; it is often counter to subconscious attitudes of which one is not aware. In this way it leads directly to an inner confrontation which is never easy. But one is none the less convinced. The voice is a still, small voice; yet once heard it cannot be ignored.

Yet another way to the heart of silence is through expanding the awareness, and reaching out from your own self to those around you, trying to encourage your feelings to encompass those of your fellow-worshippers and ultimately of the unknown others. This is an enlargement of perception which in purely human terms cannot be attained; our emotions are ours, not other people's. Yet it is possible; not by human effort but by surrender, by submitting to a power not of oneself that is yet in oneself.

This same essential submission comes to others through meditation, through holding the mind still upon the nature of the divine, upon whatever aspect of God or his manifest presence in the world is most true to them. This is prayer in the sense, not of petitionary prayer, but of devotion. I suppose my music, since it led me in the same direction, was all I could manage by way of prayer.

To seek for the true silence, in which God may be heard, is an intensely personal but not a lonely quest. One is not conscious in the usual sense of other people in Meeting. Their breathing, the odd cough, the rustling in a handbag for a handkerchief, the turning of the pages of a book; these are not noises which disturb. Somehow, as the Meeting centres down, the silence becomes more palpable, so that noises make little impact on it. It is stronger than they are.

The *silence* of a religious and spiritual worship is not a drowsy unthinking state of the mind, but a sequestring or withdrawing of it from all visible objects and vain imaginations, unto a fervent praying to, or praising of the Invisible Omni-present God, in his Light and Love; his Light gives wisdom and knowledge, and his Love gives power and strength, to run the ways of his commandments with delight. But except all excess of the body and passions of the mind are avoided (through watchfulness) the *Soul* does not attain *True Silence*.[4]

In our life as a religious society we have found it true that the spirit of man can come into direct contact with the Spirit of God, and can thereby learn from God. A man who has experienced the sense of contact with the Spirit will not only wish to listen for himself to what God may say, and in the secret of his own heart

4. John Bellers, 'Epistle to the Quarterly Meeting of London and Middlesex', 1718, p. 14, 'Christian Faith and Practice', § 243.

speak with God, but he will become conscious that fellowship with other human beings, especially if they be seekers like himself, will strengthen and deepen the sense of communion. The way of worship through silent communion, in which there is freedom for spoken prayer or ministry, springs from the fundamental experience of the Society of Friends, and is a constant expression and working out of its central principle.[5]

I have tried to explain what the seated silent company are attempting to do, and I have suggested that one is being driven to spoken ministry. Most of us are agreed that the spoken contribution comes best from resistance overcome; one tries to stay silent but fails. Nevertheless, all ministry is not unprepared – it might seem incompatible with the concept I have outlined to come to Meeting with a book in one's hand and a marker between its pages, but this is done, and wisely done. The point is that one should not come with a determination to reveal this passage or minister on this theme, but rather that if the thought of such ministry has arisen one goes prepared to offer it. If in Meeting the spirit moves you further, go with it. If in Meeting the ministry of others and the power of the Meeting goes in another direction, put your book to one side, and go home with it unread.

As to being driven to speak, that is difficult to describe to anyone who has not experienced it, particularly since in most circumstances we are all clearly divided into those who speak at every opportunity and those who do not speak publicly at all. Yet at Meeting for Worship, though indeed some speak more often than others, who speaks, and when, is not decided by any thought of frequency of utterance, neither the idea of 'I spoke last week, I mustn't speak this week', nor 'If I don't say something soon I shall lose my status as the Meeting's principal theologian.'

Sitting quietly, working inwardly to find the centre, the stillness, listening for the voice of God, which may bring a concept into your consciousness either as a thought, a word or a visual symbol, one does not want to speak. Then the idea

5. Berks and Oxon Quarterly Meeting, 'A Message to Seekers', 1919, 'Christian Faith and Practice', § 233.

comes, and grows. One has something to say, it must be said. One stands, and starts talking. The words seem to arrange themselves; not me, but God in me for a brief while. Then suddenly the idea is expressed, the words stop, one becomes conscious of oneself again and sits down. That is as near as I can get to describing it; the following description by Elizabeth Salisbury, first published anonymously in *Quaker Monthly* for July 1968, parallels my own experience and describes what must always be an intensely personal experience with outstanding honesty and clarity.

ON FIRST RISING TO MINISTER

When I became a fully paid up member of the Society of Friends two years ago, I brought with me a fashionably open mind on most topics and a willingness to enter fully into the life of the meeting, except in one sphere. I could not and would not minister in meeting for worship. Strange really when I reflected that one of the many things that had driven me from the established church was the low status of women, symbolized in the stubborn refusal to allow their voices to be heard in the worship of the church. Why was I not then eager to stand up and be heard after all those years of sitting mute and inwardly protesting?

It was not just a question of disliking the sound of my own voice. I was quite prepared to give out notices for the clerk, to speak in support of an appeal which concerned me, or to join in discussion groups on almost any topic. I even reported back to monthly meeting after my first experience of Yearly Meeting; and though my heart was thumping wildly as I did it and I was very glad when it was all over, I never thought of refusing to do it. I accepted that reporting back was one of those things one did; the price one paid for the privilege of being a 'Friend appointed to attend'.

But ministering in meeting – that was quite different and not for me.

After more than three years' attendance at a variety of different meetings I had collected quite a gallery of speakers. There was the Friend who leapt to his feet as if shot from a gun, spoke rapidly and then as abruptly sat down again; the Friend who rose weightily in his place and delivered a well-prepared sermon, with introduction, exposition, recapitulation and epilogue, and containing at least one funny story; the Friend whose ministry rambled all round the houses and, just as you were beginning to wonder what it was all about, made you ashamed of your uncharitable thoughts by drawing all the strands together in an illuminating way; the Friend who drew his inspiration from the Bible and came with his passage already marked; the inaudible Friend, the incoherent Friend, the inspired Friend, and, dare I say it, the tedious Friend.

I had firm views about the ministry and they tended to be diametrically opposed to the views of weighty Friends who wrote to *The Friend* from time to time bewailing 'the quality of our ministry'. I thought a pennyworth of inspiration was worth a deal of Bible study. I had listened to sermons on the Bible and theology for years, and now looked to Friends for that illumination which comes direct from another's personal and deeply felt experience. I was truly impressed by the fact that so often the topic round which the thoughts and prayers of the meeting crystallized chimed in with what I had been thinking about all the week and frequently extended and broadened my own speculations. And I was grateful to those Friends whose sharing of their own experience illuminated mine. But I knew I should never speak.

One of the few things I 'knew' about Friends before I attended my first meeting for worship was that they all sat around in silence until the spirit moved one of them to speak; whereupon he got up, literally quaking, and testified. As a demythologized Christian I was a little embarrassed by that word *spirit*, and as a nicely brought up young lady I couldn't see myself either quaking or testifying. I frequently wondered about those who spoke in meeting and I longed to ask 'What does it feel like? Did you really "quake"? Did you really feel that the spirit was moving you? How did you know it was the spirit and not, say, a desire to cap the last speaker or a feeling that it was your duty to add to the ministry of a rather dull meeting?' Of course I never did ask any of these questions but for the sake of others who may have longed to ask them, here are some answers from my own experience.

For in spite of my intentions, the time came when, as I should have foreseen, I made my first halting contribution to the ministry. It was an experience quite unlike any other I have known, totally different from any public speaking in which I have engaged. For some weeks before this particular Sunday I had been puzzling over and questioning in my mind various problems connected with my work. It was one of those episodes of spiritual upheaval which most of us go through from time to time when we seem to question our normal certainties, poke around the foundations of our daily life and discover to our alarm that some of them are very shaky. I had been in this highly charged state for several weeks.

On this Sunday morning, though, I went quietly to meeting with the family, my recent preoccupations submerged by the business of getting us all dressed and breakfasted and to the meeting house on time. But as the minutes ticked by and I sat in the healing peace I began to be aware that something inside me was formulating a question which urgently needed to be asked. I say 'something inside me', because it seemed at the same time to be both me and not me. I discovered to my horror that this something was urging me to get up and ask my question. My heart was pounding uncomfortably and I began to shiver (I don't know whether this was obvious to those around me; I was certainly aware of this shivering, but shyness prevents one from asking afterwards whether these physical symptoms are visible to others). To start with I resisted this prompting. I looked round the room and noticed several Friends before whom I was reluctant to make a fool of myself. I could not get up and speak in front of them. I would rather die first. The shaking and pounding diminished a little as I decided this. But not for long. Soon it started up again, insistent, not to be denied. This time I told myself, 'I'll count twenty and then if no one else has spoken I shall have to'. Again a slight abatement of the symptoms. But to no avail. I counted twenty and then fifty and still no one spoke. Now I sat conscious only of this overpowering force which was pushing me to my feet until finally I had to give in to it.

Afterwards I found it difficult to believe that I had spoken. It was all over so quickly. Had I really stood up in front of all these people and testified? Well, hardly testified; but yes, I had been driven by some inner prompting which, for want of a more precise word, one might well call spirit; and yes, I had quaked, most fearfully, with something which was more than just the fear of making a fool of myself before family and friends.[6]

The sequence of contributions to a Meeting develops, usually in a fairly logical and associative manner, from one speaker to another. I think that I am not alone in feeling

6. Elizabeth Salisbury, 'On First Rising to Minister', *Quaker Monthly*, Volume XLVII, No. 7, July 1968.

that it would be wrong to set down a record of ministry from an actual Meeting, or to try to create a synthetic example. Ministry is of God; it exists in its proper context, of words before and after and of ready hearers, and should not be transplanted out of that context. However, there is what could be considered a book of ministry, prepared in the true spirit of devotion, and any sequence from 'Christian Faith and Practice in the Experience of the Society of Friends' can be taken as a pattern for ministry.

One phenomenon of ministry is sufficiently often encountered to be worth recording. This is the extraordinary answering of one person's perplexity by another person's ministry. I have myself been the instrument of this process, most memorably when I was leaving London shortly after I first started attending Meeting. On the last occasion on which I would be attending Friends' House, Euston Road, I thought that I would get along early and mention to the clerk that I would not be there in future, and express my thanks for the help the Meeting had given me. I was not early, I was late, so then I thought I would tell the clerk after the Meeting. Half-way through I was impelled, against my will, to stand and tell the Meeting I was going, to speak of how much the Meeting had meant to me, and to express the conviction which I already had that I would be applying for membership. I sat down convinced that I had made a fool of myself, that what I had said was wildly inappropriate for that time and place. After Meeting, one of the Friends wishing me good-bye said, 'I am so glad you spoke as you did. There are a very few of us here who carry the Meeting from week to week, and most of those who attend are unknown to us, people travelling through London, students, the curious, the drifters who come one week and are gone the next. We sometimes wonder if we ever do anything for anybody, and it was a great encouragement to us to hear your ministry.' And I realized that I had been the vehicle for giving support where it was needed.

It is the essence of the Meeting for Worship that the distinction between spoken ministry and silence is not significant, that the two elements are understood as variations on the same theme, so that we even speak of silent ministry. Every member of a Meeting, whatever his formal status, whether elder or attender or casual visitor, contributes to the Meeting. Sometimes this contribution is spoken; generally it is silent. All who sincerely seek God, whether or not that is the name we (or they) would put to their search, give something of themselves to the Meeting in which they are joined. This giving is not a conscious act of will, but a conscious act of surrender. The worshipper gives himself up to God; the more complete his submission the more he becomes open to the Holy Spirit, and the more, through his openness, he contributes to the filling of the Meeting with the power and the grace of God. It is the silent ministry of others which helps those in spiritual difficulties, those who are torn between one side of the personality which wants to find God and another which rejects him. It is through the interaction of those who cry out for help and those who wait patiently on the Lord in humble submission that one person is driven to stand and speak, not knowing why or for whom, and so to answer the cry.

P. W. Martin, in *Experiment in Depth* draws attention to the Meeting for Worship as a practising form of what he calls the experiment in depth; and describes the Meeting in the following terms:

In form, the Meeting consists of a handful of men and women, often less than a score, rarely exceeding fifty or a hundred, who sit together for about an hour, for the most part in silence, in an ordinary room or hall. The silence is broken only if someone feels 'called to the ministry'. When this happens, the one so stirred normally speaks, for some few minutes perhaps, often less, of something that has come to him out of the silence. He may be followed by one or two others, equally brief, typically taking up the same thread and continuing it.

When it is successful (which, needless to say, is not always) the Quaker Meeting for Worship is indubitably a method by which the deep centre is experienced and the experience transmitted. How this comes about is at present a matter of surmise rather than knowledge. Partly, no doubt, it is due to the concerted seeking in silence. Since there is little to distract attention, the libido is free for inward exploration, for the discovery of the Kingdom.

Partly it is attributable to the fact that in such Meetings there may be at least one or two present – possibly a number – who in their lives have gone over to the deep centre. These, as it were, can help to 'take the Meeting down'. It is not only in speech, but also in silence, that Plato's 'light from the leaping flame' can pass. Partly it may derive from the fellowship-in-depth of a 'gathered' Meeting. This sense of togetherness is a characteristic feature. In a Meeting that has 'centred down' there is simultaneously the feeling of the most complete unity and the most complete individuality. Equally characteristic is the ministry itself. The call that comes to speak in the Meeting for Worship is experienced (at least by some) as wholly different in kind from ordinary speaking, being marked by a trepidation, a pounding of the heart, a feeling akin to dread, even to people thoroughly habituated to public address. At its best, as in George Fox's day, the ministry has the character of the transforming symbol, bringing to the common fund words and images which make possible a new direction of energy. The fact that, whether or not he speaks, everyone in a Quaker Meeting has responsibility for the ministry, is perhaps the most potent factor of all. In a Meeting where no word is said there is still this silent concentration of responsibilities, which in the end may be more effective than any form of speech.[7]

This is Meeting from the psychological viewpoint, yet it is also close to the religious viewpoint. What one is talking about is the same; it is just a question of what adjective is used. Perhaps the time is ripe for overcoming our remaining repressions and taboos and bringing back into use the simple, old-fashioned three-letter words like 'God' that have fallen out of polite usage.

7. P. W. Martin, *Experiment in Depth*, Routledge & Kegan Paul, 1955, pp. 239–40.

CHAPTER 3

Other Meetings, Other Worship

A LITTLE while ago my Meeting held an 'Open Forum' for
the general public. It was just like any other public meeting;
people sat in rows on chairs facing a platform on which were
a chairman and two speakers. Apart from the subject matter
of the talks and the subsequent questioning it could have
been a meeting of the local civic society. This type of Meeting is unusual with Friends; we adopt it only for occasions
where we expect many people not used to our practices.
Otherwise Friends' Meetings, large and small, whatever
their immediate purpose, are always concerned also with
worship.

This sounds enormously pompous and self-satisfied, like a
Victorian business man larding his conversation with texts
while refusing to reduce the hours of work of small children.
How can one combine property management – and we own
and let quite a lot of property – with worship? Let us start by
looking at the working method of a Monthly Meeting,
which has, among other things, to do just that.

At business Meetings, whether Preparative, Monthly or
Yearly, there is no chairman. At a table, where one would
normally expect the chairman to be, sit the Clerk and the
Assistant Clerk, referred to collectively and impersonally on
occasion as 'the table'. Meetings start with silence for a few
minutes, silence which is the silence of worship. This Meeting is not one in which human beings are going to argue
their divergent opinions, until one or the other gives way or
a middle-of-the-road compromise is reached. This is a Meeting whose intention is to find and follow the will of God.

The Meeting then goes on – for it starts with the silence,
not when the talking begins – to hear the minutes of the
previous Meeting and to discuss whatever affairs are before
it. The items are usually introduced by someone – perhaps
the Clerk or the Assistant Clerk, perhaps another member of

the Meeting – and the discussion is much like any discussion, except that it is generally calm, and slow moving, with none of the cut and thrust of a political debate. If the emotional temperature begins to rise, someone will usually ask for a period of worship, and in the silence harmony is restored. As the discussion continues, the Clerk will be sensing the feeling of the Meeting. When he feels that a consensus has been reached he drafts a minute and reads it to the Meeting, which will either accept it or discuss it further. Sooner or later a minute is acceptable to the Meeting, even if it is a minute which says, 'We found this subject one of great difficulty, and could not clearly see God's will; we therefore agreed that the matter should be brought forward on another occasion.' When an acceptable minute is before the Meeting there is no voting; the Clerk asks whether it is acceptable, the Meeting replies 'yes' (or in the case of very scrupulous Friends 'I hope so', since they can only speak for themselves) and the Clerk moves on to the next item. At the end of the agenda there will be a further short period of worship, though this perhaps needs to be qualified; it is a further period of silent worship, the whole Meeting being a period of worship.

This pattern of conducting a business Meeting applies to the smallest Preparative Meeting, or even to two or three Friends gathered to settle an issue *ad hoc*, and equally to the conduct of Yearly Meetings. It raises two questions particularly; first, how is it possible to conduct business at all in this way, and second, is it effective, and equally effective, on all types of business?

On the first question I can best comment as a professional administrator and, to a limited extent at least, as a student of business methods. In my experience, the reaching of conclusions in committee is closely related to the degree of community of interest. If every member of the committee has the same ultimate aim in view and the same basic motives, then the committee is likely to reach useful conclusions quickly. Those members with relevant experience will present it, the others will assess it against their common aim, and the practicable courses of action will soon be apparent.

From there it is a short and simple step to choosing the most desirable of the practicable courses.

But committees do not generally operate in this way. Each member is usually differently motivated; either by self-interest or, at best, by concern for the well-being of the organization he represents. The overt aim of the committee (to which all members overtly subscribe) is seldom allowed to take precedence over the interests of the individual members. What is laughingly called a 'theory of games' comes into force; the committee is a battlefield where victory is to the psychologically strong. The demonstration of victory is the vote; if there is no vote it is only because no demonstration is needed, the enemy has capitulated. To foresee the outcome it is seldom helpful to know the facts of the case or the force of the arguments; far more significant are the personalities of the committee members and their group relationships.

It follows, of course, that committee government as usually practised is surprisingly ineffectual. Most committee discussions involve the humiliation of some of the participants, since there are winners and losers, and to lose is to be humiliated. The losers will give unconvincing support to the policy of the winners at the best, and will be constantly looking for a new battlefield of their own choosing, on which they may get their revenge. So policy is made and unmade, at meeting after meeting. swinging one way and another and making very little actual progress.

In Quaker business Meetings there is a much closer approach to a common aim and common motives:

Being orderly come together, [you are] not to spend time with needless, unnecessary and fruitless discourses; but to proceed in the wisdom of God not in the way of the world, as a worldly assembly of men, by hot contests, by seeking to outspeak and over-reach one another in discourse as if it were controversy between party and party of men, or two sides violently striving for dominion, not deciding affairs by the greater vote. But in the wisdom, love and fellowship of God, in gravity, patience, meekness, in unity and concord, submitting one to another in lowliness of heart, and in the holy Spirit of truth and righteousness, all things [are] to be carried on; by hearing and determining every matter coming before you, in love, coolness, gentleness and dear unity; – I say, as one only party, all for the truth of Christ, and for the carrying on the work of the Lord, and assisting one another in whatsoever ability God hath given; and to determine things by a general mutual concord, in assenting together as one man in the spirit of truth and equity, and by the authority thereof. In this way and spirit all things are to be amongst you, and without perverseness, in any self-separation, in discord and partiality; this way and spirit is wholly excepted, as not worthy to enter into the assembly of God's servants, in any case pertaining to the service of the Church of Christ; in which his Spirit of love and unity must rule.[1]

This, I think, gives the answer to the first question. It is possible to conduct any business by the Quaker method where those concerned show a common aim and motive; in the Society that aim and motive is provided by the religious basis of the Society. To the second question, as to its effectiveness, my answer would be that the method works best on the issues of most moment. That is to say, on any question of deep importance, whether spiritual or material, my experience has been that of the Minute of the Yearly Meeting of 1936 – guidance has come and light been given us, and we have become finders of God's purpose. The same has not always been true of Meetings concerned with lesser matters, questions of no great importance to God or man such as the adjustment of boundaries. Here I have been very glad that the Meeting was open to members only, and that nobody else was there to see us floundering about making heavy weather of a very trivial question. 'Needless, unnecessary and fruitless discourse' perhaps.

Friends of greater experience often speak with some impatience of the ineffectuality of the Society, of the great time it takes to make necessary changes in procedure and so on. A very few worthy wordy Friends are enough to prevent a

1. Edward Borrough, 'A testimony concerning the beginning of the work of the Lord', 1662. *Letters, etc., of Early Friends*, ed. Abram Rawlinson Barclay, 1841, 'Christian Faith and Practice in the Experience of the Society of Friends', London Yearly Meeting of the Religious Society of Friends, 1960, § 354.

Meeting coming to a conclusion, and somehow it is often those who are most opposed to change who seem to have the time to spare for business meetings. I can understand this view of the Society, yet I think it is somewhat out of perspective. In the things that really matter, the Society seems to move fast enough, often almost without discussion at all. In other matters, where the drag seems to be on, change may not be as important as we imagine. And those same worthy wordy friends have often saved us from stupidities.

It is hardly necessary to say that the various standing committees of the Society conduct their Meetings in the same way as other business meetings. The course taken by business through the organization, the distinctions between a matter which should go to Yearly Meeting, one to be considered by the Meeting for Sufferings, or something to be disposed of by the Home Service Committee or the Friends Education Council, need not concern us in any detail; the lines of demarcation are determined largely by the cross-representation of Friends on different committees, which enables them to see fairly objectively how the business would best be handled. Nor do we need to study in detail the way in which questions are referred from one level of Meeting to another except to say that there is a fair amount of reference, perhaps too much, but that a 'concern' – the appropriate Quaker word for a personal interest, amounting to a compulsion to act – may be raised by any member with his own Meeting and so may start on the route which leads to Yearly Meeting, to adoption by the Society as a whole and hence to the membership of the Society applying itself to that concern. To define the working of the machinery more precisely would be to exceed the precision of 'Church Government', the Society's very general guide to these matters, which 'is seen not as a code of regulations to meet every conceivable contingency, but as an embodiment of the corporate experience and wisdom of the Society'.

I have said that Friends conduct public Meetings, where numbers unacquainted with our practices are likely to be present, much like other public meetings. There is one private occasion on which the Quaker usage may come as something of a surprise to those who meet it unexpectedly. If you share a meal with a Quaker family, it may be preceded by a few moments of silent grace. Grace before meals, except on very formal occasions is now so unusual as to be something of a surprise; when in addition it is as silent grace it can be distinctly unnerving. I mention it here for the encouragement of Friends and the forewarning of their visitors.

In a Society so sparing of rules, so scrupulous in the avoidance of regimentation, inevitably there are few officials. There are the Clerks and the Assistant Clerks who form the table; but their function, whether at the smallest of Preparative Meetings or at Yearly Meetings, is to guide the Meeting in the conduct of its business and to present a minute which reflects the feeling of the Meeting. There are certain officers who are entrusted with specific duties of keeping lists of members or looking after funds, or making the returns and certificates required by law in respect of marriages and burials according to Friends' usage. Then there are Elders and Overseers, and they constitute the only approximation to an hierarchically separate class in the Society. Elders and Overseers will protest at my putting it even as strongly as that; they will insist that all they have is special responsibilities, and they are right in that they have no privileges. In lists of members they may get a little 'e' or 'o' against their names, just as attenders who are not members of the Society may get a little 'a'; that is all. At Meeting for Worship it is two of the Elders who signify the end of the Meeting by the smile and the handshake. But what else are they responsible for?

Apart from certain specific responsibilities such as 'the right holding of meetings for worship on special occasions such as marriages and funerals' their general remit is to nurture the spiritual life of the Meeting, guiding all who share in it toward a deeper experience of worship. This requires them to take a particular care for the quality of the ministry – both silent and vocal – and also to be concerned with extending the Meeting's understanding of its own potential and with sharing the Quaker experience with others; for example through discussion Meetings and study groups. Of these duties that of 'restraining where necessary that [vocal ministry] which is unsuitable' is the most dramatic; there are stories of the 'eldering' of those whose ministry has gone on too long either by means of some crisp phrase such as, 'Our Friend has spoken long enough', or through the gentler, 'Our Friend has given us much to consider, and it would be well for us to have a time of quiet in which to consider it.' But such interventions, and the situations requiring them, are rare. In the main the work of the Elder is unobtrusive support for the Meeting and its members, and continuing concern for the spiritual health of the Meeting.

The responsibilities of Overseers are to encourage attendance at Meetings for Worship and for business, to exercise a care over younger members and children and those in need of assistance, to welcome strangers and to cultivate sympathetic relationships with members and attenders, to encourage members and attenders to undertake service for which they are fitted and 'to deal in due time and in a spirit of Christian love and tenderness with any whose behaviour or manner of life is contrary to Christian witness, and to endeavour to restore such Friends to the fellowship of the church'. Their functions are thus more practical; as Yearly Meeting put it in 1871, 'to bind up that which is broken; to bring home the wanderers, to visit the sick and the afflicted; and to extend a loving care over the young and inexperienced'. Again, as with Eldering, the best of Oversight is that which goes unnoticed.

The whole concept of Elders and Overseers is that the functions of spiritual and material caring which would elsewhere devolve on a professional pastor should be carried by lay members. The degree of effectiveness of these arrangements varies from Meeting to Meeting; it depends very largely on the individuals. But at least there is an organization which provides for caring; and at least it involves a number of people and does not put an impossible burden on one man. The way in which it operates also varies from

Meeting to Meeting. Sometimes, all the Elders and Overseers as a group will share the responsibility for the whole
Meeting; sometimes there will be an allocation, with each
Overseer accepting responsibility for a certain number of
people. This can work very well indeed, if the Overseers dis-
charge their responsibility with skill and delicacy. I was once
under the caring eye of a particular Overseer; I only de-
duced who it was in the Meeting who had me on their list
when, in a time of domestic stress, help suddenly came to
hand. That is an example of the system working well, but it
also indicates how difficult it is to judge how well it works
overall. There is no way of measuring the effectiveness of the
Oversight of those who need neither help nor guidance, and
no way of measuring the extent of the unrecognized need.

My own guess would be that little material need goes unrecognized, and little obvious suffering. When someone is ill
or a member of a family dies, the help is certainly there.
More difficult is the question of mental stress, the incipient
neurosis. This is not simply a problem for Friends, but a
problem for western society; yet I feel that Friends should
consider it with particular care because they can perhaps do
something about it. Some at least of these troubles stem
from a fundamental lack of conviction about the purpose of
life, a sense of insecurity and worthlessness. To offer religion
as a cure, in crude terms, is worse than useless, yet in the end
it is a sense of values, based on a non-material experience,
which is often needed.

As against the unobtrusive best of pastoral care, there
is the other extreme, the interfering busybodying type
who cannot resist having a finger in everyone else's spiritual and material affairs, I think it is fair to say that few
Meetings are so blind to this danger as to appoint such
people as Elders and Overseers. The more common problem
is that of worthy and weighty Friends who continue in their
appointment though they are no longer by reason of age or
attitude suited to the task. Appointments are for three years
and Monthly Meetings 'should enter upon this as upon a
new appointment and not merely a revision of a more or less
permanent membership'. But who is going to tell Alfred B or

Christine D that they are not re-appointed? Besides, it is not
that they are positively unsuitable, it is just that Christine,
who is wonderful for her age, cannot really do very much
now, and that Alfred, since his business expanded so rapidly,
is really too heavily pressed and has become a little impatient
of the muddles and perplexities of people less well organized
than himself. But they are neither of them positively unsuitable, so we re-appoint them to spare trouble and their
feelings.

There are also many Meetings where even though the appointments are made with prayerful thought, there is no
doubt that the average age of Elders and Overseers is high
and many younger people feel that they exercise a restraint
over the Meeting and are out of sympathy with new ideas.
The same criticism is sometimes heard of Quaker committees. In reverse, however, I have heard worthy Friends
lament that they and their contemporaries, all getting on in
years now, were still so firmly in the saddle and could not
apparently find any younger people to take over from them.
To some extent this difficulty, insofar as it is real, stems also
from our not having a professional pastorate. If the work is
all to be done by the laity, inevitably it will be very much in
the hands of those who have the time to spare, those whose
main working life is over. Nor am I convinced that this need
be the disadvantage it sometimes appears to be. Older
Friends are, I suspect, much more anxious to understand the
viewpoint of the young than the young often credit, and I
believe they are also much readier to share the responsibility
with the young than is often admitted.

Those of us who are younger, or who have not been long
in membership, often feel that we should not push ourselves
forward, particularly if we cannot, because of other responsibilities, offer much time to the service of the Society.
But I think we would be better advised to recognize that our
retired Friends, having time on their hands, are happy to
work for the Society, but do need the benefit of our views
and ideas which are in closer contact with contemporary
thoughts and attitudes. This is not to say that my generation
cannot give any service – but that part of our service is in

giving our views, our comments, our ideas, even when we cannot back them with further action.

In suggesting this slight change in relations between the age groups I am not only concerned with increasing the influence of younger members of the Society. I am also concerned with the well-being of older Friends. By and large we are a long-lived Society, and retired Friends often have many years of active life before them. (This is not folklore; it is only to be expected that a Society which puts an emphasis on quiet, temperate living and relaxed silence should tend to be long-lived.) If those years are to be truly active, a necessary condition is that the mind should be open to new ideas, freshly stimulated and kept flexible by new concepts. I think younger people are sometimes unwittingly hard on their elders, denying them the needed stimulus of new ideas out of a misplaced consideration. Too often we keep silent lest we should shock, when if we spoke the comment might be, 'How very interesting!'

This chapter has gone far enough, from business Meetings to relations between age groups. It is, I suspect, a characteristic of the Society of Friends that the organization as such does not take much time to describe; but that an account of it quickly leads one on to discussion of relationship, and the consideration of how the organization may better serve the true ends of the Society as a company of seekers after truth. This has been with us from the beginning. 'Let all your affairs be managed in your meeting in the peaceable wisdom and spirit of our Lord Jesus Christ; not striving but bearing one with and for another; that the power of Christ may rest upon you, and rule in your assemblies.'[2]

2. Yearly Meeting Epistle, 1696.

CHAPTER 4

Entrances and Exits

UNTIL very recently the most usual way of becoming a Quaker was by the simple expedient of being born to Quaker parents. But this is no longer possible – and in future every new member will have taken a conscious decision himself, or, if under the age of sixteen, will have been the subject of a conscious decision on his behalf by his parents or guardians.

One becomes a Quaker, then, by convincement. Not, that is, by becoming convinced of any particular stated belief, but simply by becoming convinced that one should be a Quaker and by convincing a Monthly Meeting of this. To say how this comes about, in the earlier stages at least, is difficult; it is different for everyone. Perhaps it is as a result of local 'extension work' (one Quaker name for efforts to bring the Society to other people and other people to the Society), or perhaps it is a Home Service Committee advertisement in a newspaper, or a poster on a station, that leads to contact with Friends. Very often the first move is a letter to Friends' House, followed in due course by an unannounced appearance at a Meeting for Worship. Often, inquirers prefer to attend a Meeting away from their own area; they are, after all, taking the first tentative steps towards a sense of commitment and they naturally prefer to preserve their anonymity and independence, keeping their escape route open so that they can give up going to Meeting without ever being embarrassed by chance encounters with Friends who might ask why they have stopped.

In one way or another the inquirer attends his first Meeting for Worship, and despite all efforts to keep the escape route open he goes on attending. From this to being a recognized attender is only a matter of time, though what constitutes a recognized attender it is not easy to say. Some lists of members record them, distinguished with a small 'a';

many of those so marked are the non-member husbands and wives, or sometimes adult children, of members. They come to Meeting quite often, but they do not wish or intend to come into membership. Other attenders are less easily defined; some attend, certainly, but are, so to speak, permanent attenders; they derive benefit from Meeting, have much in common with Friends but yet find themselves unable to accept certain aspects of Quakerism and so will not apply for membership. Some again are attenders for the time being, who, given a clear leading, are likely in due course to apply for membership.

It is not the habit of Friends to try to win converts by persuasion nor to preach the merits of their ways against those of others. Nevertheless, attenders who appear to be ready for membership are given a little judicious encouragement. There is a moral tale of an attender who moved to another district after twenty years of regular worship. A Friend who commented that the Meeting had always been sorry that he had not felt able to apply for membership received the shattering reply, 'Nobody ever asked me.' So now we occasionally deliver a well-directed push, and its administration in cases of 'a sense of unworthiness or through shyness' or those who '. . . become habitual attenders through not realizing the importance of membership' is entrusted to the Overseers.

There are no conditions of membership. Such guidance as there is, is contained in 'Church Government', the second[1] part of the *Book of Christian Discipline of London Yearly Meeting of the Religious Society of Friends*, which, under its awesome and off-putting title contains the gathered wisdom and insight of Quakerism today. The introductory paragraph of Chapter 23 runs:

'George Fox and his early followers,' wrote Rufus Jones, 'went forth with unbounded faith and enthusiasm to discover in all lands those who were true fellow-members with them in this great household of God, and who were the hidden seed of God'.

1. 'Christian Faith and Practice in the Experience of the Society of Friends', London Yearly Meeting of the Religious Society of Friends, 1960, is the first part.

Our Society thus arose from a series of mutual discoveries of men and women who found that they were making the same spiritual pilgrimage. This is still our experience today. Even at times of great difference of opinion, we have known a sense of living unity, because we have recognized one another as followers of Jesus. We are at different stages along the way. We use different language to speak of him and to express our discipleship. The insistent questioning of the seeker, the fire of the rebel, the reflective contribution of the more cautious thinker – all have a place among us. This does not always make life easy. But we have found that we have learned to listen to one another, to respect the sincerity of one another's opinions, to love and to care for one another. We are enabled to do this because God first loved us. The gospels tell us of the life and teaching of Jesus. The light of Christ, a universal light and known inwardly is our guide. It is the grace of God which gives us the strength to follow. It is his forgiveness which restores us when we are oppressed by the sense of falling short. These things we know, not as glib phrases, but out of the depths of sometimes agonizing experience.

Membership, therefore, we see primarily in terms of discipleship, and so impose no clear-cut tests of doctrine or outward observance. Nevertheless those wishing to join the Society should realise its Christian basis. Words often seem inadequate to convey our deepest experiences, yet words – however imperfect – are necessary if we are to share with one another what we have learned. In *Christian faith and practice* and in the *Advices and queries* we have tried to express those broad principles of belief and conduct on which unity is essential. These find expression in our testimonies, which reflect the Society's corporate insights, and a loyal recognition of this is to be expected, even though precise agreement on every point is not required. We are aware of continual failures in our discipleship, and no one should hesitate, from a sense of unworthiness, to apply for membership.

Membership implies acceptance of responsibility and a sense of commitment. It implies a willingness to be used by God, however imperfect we may feel ourselves to be as his messengers. He will not miraculously deliver us from trials of temper and temptation, pettiness and pride, which are a part of human nature. In our worship together, and as we learn together in a Christian community, he will help us to overcome the limitations of our nature, to become more fully the people he intends us to be. 'Not as though we had already attained, either were already perfect, but we follow after . . . forgetting those things which are behind, and reaching forth unto those things which are before, we press towards the mark for the prize of the high calling of God in Christ Jesus.'

Now, this statement is not a creed or a doctrinal form-ulation, and indeed, it specifically rejects any such formulation. Yet it is a statement which attempts to say what is the agreed basis of membership, and as such it de-serves the same rigorous and critical examination as Friends on occasion apply when somebody tries to persuade them to a creed. In fact, Friends avoid this process in regard to these particular paragraphs of 'Church Government', especially those Friends who remember the stress of the Yearly Meet-ing session at which they were agreed. Enough that they were agreed; why stir up old controversies?

I think this controversy has got to come out into the open if this book is to be of any value; if it is to be able to speak to those for whom it is intended. It is not meant for hypocrites, or for those who would rather overlook insincerity or double-talk than have their sensibilities upset or their calm dis-turbed. Consequently it cannot be of value if anyone can see that there is a conflict inherent in the Society of Friends as I have represented it, and if it is clear that I have deliberately skirted round that problem.

The problem is in the reconciliation of the chapters I have written on fundamental beliefs, particularly Chapter 2 of Part II, with the passage quoted above. It all centres on a few phrases:

... because we have recognized one another as followers of Jesus ... the gospels tell us of the life and teaching of Jesus. The light of Christ, a universal light, and known inwardly, is our guide ... Nevertheless, those wishing to join the Society should realize its Christian basis ... As we learn together in a Christian com-munity ... 'we press towards the mark for the prize of the high calling of God in Jesus Christ'.

Apart from these phrases the whole of the quoted passage is, I think, in accord with what I have written elsewhere in this book; it emphasizes experience, not doctrine; and the unity that is based on shared experience – 'mutual discoveries of men and women who found that they were making the same spiritual pilgrimage'. And even among the 'Christian' phrases one can detect differences of degree and subtleties of expression. 'Followers of Jesus' – certainly. I cannot think that any Friend would be able to say that he did not recognize the truth of the teaching of Jesus as it has come to us, and wish with all his heart to follow it to the best of his capacity. As a statement of fact there is nothing exceptional about: '... the gospels tell us of the life and teaching of Jesus' – it does not even make any disputable assertions about the Gospels' truthfulness or historicity.

The next phrase is more difficult. 'The light of Christ, a universal light and known inwardly, is our guide ...' By saying it is a universal light and known inwardly we imply that it has no direct connection with historical events of nearly two thousand years ago. We also imply that it is available to everyone, and in fact we know many of our members to be aware of and guided by the light within, and yet to have no awareness of any presence they could identify with Christ.

So we come to the crux. What is the nature of the Christian basis of the Society of Friends, which those who seek membership should realize? It is a basis so circumscribed that it has kept us from full membership of the British Council of Churches; it is so delicately metaphysical that, from the evidence of the text of 'Church Government', it cannot be put into precise words. It is a perennial source of dispute; a short while ago, a reader seeing *The Friend* again after a lapse of twenty years protested that the correspondence columns seemed unchanged; still the unending dispute about whether or not we are a Christian Society.

This, I think, is the point at which I must take full advantage of (and carry full responsibility for) the fact that I am writing this book for the publishers and for my readers, and not at the request or command, or for the purposes of, the Society of Friends. I must step outside the picture, and comment as best I can as a detached observer.

Historically there can be no question but that the Society began as a Society of Christians, and for the most part of its life the Christian basis was accepted without demur by its members. The first publishers of truth, and Fox above all, devoted much effort to refuting suggestions that Quakers were not Christians, and to aligning their particular spiritual insights with the Christian tradition and with the words of the New Testament. However, a Society lives in its members and not in its history. Any discussion of what the early Quakers believed is interesting, and may well be illuminating; yet the important question is what Quakers believe now, not what they believed fifty or two hundred and fifty years ago.

The Society's statements, such as the passage of 'Church Government' just considered and other passages both in that book and elsewhere, represent a compromise between those to whom Christ is the only mediator between God and man, and those whose awareness of God is not essentially and exclusively through Christ. I have attempted in Chapter 2, Part II, to show how these views may arise and how they may be reconciled; especially how, in practice, I believe they are often reconciled in the working of the Society. But there is not always a reconciliation; there is often a compromise; and then we get these passages which swing uneasily between the language of the depth psychologist and that of the evangelical Christian.

Such compromises are harmful. They dissipate energy in controversy which is essentially unresolvable, because neither party can be converted to the view of the other. A belief is what you believe, and beliefs are founded on experiences, outward and inward. No amount of talking about the early history of Quakerism and no amount of sincere declarations of experience of the Living Christ will bring someone who has not that experience to be an exclusive Christian, just as no amount of talk about depth psychology, or discussion of parallels with other spiritual traditions, will take away their belief in the Living Christ from those of our Friends who possess it. Nor in either case should this be so. Beliefs are validated by one's own experience, not by the incommunicable and unshared experience of others. So what can the controversy do? It can raise doubts as to whether we should all be members of a single organization; doubts which are ridiculous in the light of our worshipping and working together. It can raise questions in the minds of those who might otherwise find God through worshipping with us as to whether they can join with us, or whether a body so apparently indecisive about its beliefs has any validity.

Let me go further. Every round of this controversy shows the participants losing sight of the essentials of Quakerism (of either type). They should not concern themselves with questions such as 'What are your beliefs, my beliefs, the Society's collective beliefs about Jesus Christ?', for such questions lead on to judgements of others, and the sorting of humanity into Christians and non-Christians.

It would be more productive and more Quakerly if the questions we asked ourselves were:

(*a*) Why do I have to have beliefs?
(*b*) Does it matter to me what other people believe?
(*c*) Is it important to me if those with whom I worship and work are exclusive Christians or not?
(*d*) If it matters to me, why does it matter?

This last question is, I suggest, the critical issue to which we should address ourselves. It is not a question implying a particular answer; I am not trying to suggest that it should not matter or that the reasons why it might matter are in some way suspect or discreditable. But it is surely very important to know why the convictions of others in this respect should matter so much to us. And it is worth remembering that one reason for attaching importance to uniformity of belief is not being quite sure oneself.

The early Quakers spoke of primitive Christianity revived. I feel fairly sure that Jesus himself would have been supremely indifferent as to whether we called ourselves Christians or not. I imagine, too, that he would have been quick to recognize and applaud other teachers whose teachings were similar to his. We need the teachings too badly to split hairs about the differences between them, or to worry about the names we give them.

I have said what I must say; it is directed to Friends in their divisions rather than to my non-Friend readers. In addition to being a matter of conviction on which I must speak plainly, it may help non-Friends to understand the differences they will meet with among Friends, and also to appreciate hidden differences which they may encounter. Having said so much, let us return to the matter of membership, defined by the three-paragraph statement which contains the references to the Society's Christian basis. Assuming one wishes to become a member, what is to be done?

All that is needed from the potential member by way of formal application is a simple letter, 'no more than a plain request', to the Clerk of the appropriate Monthly Meeting. The Monthly Meeting then appoints two Friends to visit the applicant, and on their report decides whether or not to accept the application.

'Being visited' can be an unnerving prospect; it should be and often is a heart-warming experience on which frequently close personal friendships are founded. Visitors are not looking for evidences of weakness of character, undue love of luxury, scrofulous French novels or ill-concealed bottles of sherry. Nor are they an examining board in theology and Quaker history, or inquisitors of a Quaker Holy Office. They are concerned to help the applicant towards a full understanding of the implications of membership and to understand him, his point of view and his attitude so that they may report informatively to Monthly Meeting. The visitation itself has the nature of an act of worship – it will probably start and finish with a short period of silence – in that it is aimed at discovering the will of God in regard to the matter in hand. To one who has slowly been driven into a closer relationship with the Society until he brought himself to apply for membership, who even then probably considers that he is quite unsuitable for membership, has an undue idea of his own imperfections and is in consequence suffering from acute nervous tension, the idea that the incident can be a matter of moment to God is probably the final push needed to topple him into an outburst of hysterical laughter. Yet this is the truth of sincere visitation. The visitors are not out to weigh up and judge the applicant. They offer their services in the process of seeking the divine will.

'Church Government' contains the following 'Advice to Friends appointed to visit applicants for membership' which could, I think, be usefully made known to the applicant as well:

> The visit should provide opportunity for a sensitive exchange of thought between the applicant and the Friends appointed, and should result in mutual understanding and enrichment, making it an occasion to be remembered joyfully. Though stiffness and formality should be avoided, visitors may well feel it right to start with a short period of silent recollection in God's presence. The visit should be a sharing of experience and should not be undertaken in a spirit of examination. The visitor should seek to help the applicant towards a fuller understanding of Quakerism and the implications of membership . . .
>
> Moral and spiritual achievement in an applicant is not asked for; sincerity of purpose is. The chief conditions to be looked for are that he is a humble learner in the school of Christ; that his face is set towards the light; and that our way of worship helps him forward in his spiritual pilgrimage. Visitors may need to make it clear that the Society is essentially Christian in its inspiration, even though it asks for no specific affirmation of faith and understands Christianity primarily in terms of discipleship . . . make sure that the applicant realizes why we dispense with outward forms and has considered seriously whether worship without them will meet his needs; also that he is aware that the pastoral care, which in other churches is given by a separated ministry, is in our Society a responsibility shared by all members.
>
> Though complete agreement with all our testimonies is not essential, care should nevertheless be taken to ascertain how far the applicant unites with the views and practices of Friends, and whether he realizes the intimate association between our practice and our faith . . .
>
> Many applicants have too lofty an idea of the Society as a Christian community, and of the quality of the lives of its members. They should be warned of possible disappointments . . .

Lest it should be thought that despite all the protestations to the contrary, 'visiting' is still a frightening experience, I should like to put on record how one meeting dealt with an ex-agnostic who put in an application. They chose as visitors a young married woman who, with her husband, was known to be already close friends of the applicant and his wife, and a weighty Friend considerably older in years with whom the applicant was not so well acquainted.

When the visitors arrived, they found that the applicant's wife had gone out for the evening, in order to leave them undisturbed, but had by oversight locked her husband out. He was hard at work picking out the putty from round the glass in the back door with a penknife. The young lady was debarred from too much activity by a fairly advanced pregnancy, but the weighty Friend demonstrated the effect of a lifetime of service to others by a masterly piece of house-breaking, using a hacksaw blade on the catch of a storm light. After such a beginning how could the visitation be other than mutually enjoyable and memorable?

There is some discussion within the Society as to whether membership is still a valid concept, and whether it ought not to be offered to all who ask for it.

The need for membership, as a formal category, is to a great extent connected with the need for people and money to run the Society's affairs. Membership offers few privileges – principally the right to attend Monthly, General and Yearly Meetings; and even these privileges are more rightly seen as responsibilities. Members finance the Society through their contributions, which are voluntary and of such amount as they think fit.

Seen in this light, membership is not a matter of joining an in-group or of being registered as a fully paid-up member of the spiritual élite: it is rather a matter of declaring a commitment.

If this concept of membership is accepted, it is reasonable to ask whether membership ought not to be automatically granted to all who ask for it, on the grounds that the decisive action is that of the applicant who declares his commitment in applying. Certainly the applicant takes a major step towards membership in applying, but I think there are strong arguments for keeping the granting of membership in the hands of the Meeting. First, it must be recognized that membership is not necessary to salvation, or an essential to spiritual progress. Man comes close to God by no man's aid, only by the help of God, and our Society, like every other church, is not of itself and in itself a way. It is an organization, neither good nor bad in itself but only as God works through it. Therefore, if we conclude that membership is not the right way for one person, but is for another, then if our conclusions are truly illuminated by the inner light, that is the way it should be.

Moreover, we must recognize that there are people for whom membership may not be right, because they do not fully understand the Society, or think it offers them something which in fact it does not, or because they are on their way to another path, perhaps returning slowly to a church they have long since left. We may think we see why they may not join us; we may not see the reason at all, and yet be clear that they should not join us. The essential is that we, with the applicant, should try to find God's will and should not be concerned either to preserve the quality of the club or to expand the membership.

The former concern was once a marked characteristic of the Society: up to 1859, for example, the normal consequence of 'marrying out' – that is to say being so unwise as to fall in love with and marry a person who was not a Quaker – was disownment. More recently, Meetings have had to decide whether or not to admit to membership divorced persons, and people whose lives in other ways deviated from the norm.

There is no established standard or code of practice, and in consequence different Meetings may vary in their treatment of apparently similar cases. Nevertheless the guidance of the Regulations – 'Moral and spiritual achievement is not asked for' and 'Many applicants have too lofty an idea ... of the quality of the lives of its members' makes it clear that Meetings would be completely out of harmony with the intention of the Society as a whole if they attached a great deal of importance to the applicant's degree of conformity with socially acceptable morality. Nor must we slip into the easy mistake of saying that it is not how people have behaved in the past but how they intend to behave in the future that counts, for this is really irrelevant. What matters is recognition of the need for God, commitment to the way to God, and, in the particular case of those who wish to join the Society of Friends, a true and general sympathy between the Society and the applicant over the method of worship and the relationship of the spiritual and the material life. Given that degree of unity, we may hope that the result of bringing a person into the fellowship of membership may be an improvement in the quality of their life, and this may be apparent in 'better' behaviour; but we should not expect this as an inevitable result. What we should expect is that if we are right in our decision to admit, membership should have a catalyzing effect, bringing about or accelerating changes in attitude and outlook which may be of a far-reaching nature. They will be rightly motivated; they will be the effect of the working of the Holy Spirit; but they will not necessarily be in accordance with society's tidy code of rules for polite behaviour.

The only alternative method of acquiring membership is by application by the parents or guardians on behalf of children under the age of sixteen whom they intend to bring up in accordance with the religious principles of the Society. Since the old concept of birthright membership was replaced by this provision, the number of children in formal membership has declined steadily, and the number associated with Meetings but not in formal membership has increased. Clearly, most parents these days prefer to leave the question open until their children are sixteen and can decide for themselves.

I have mentioned that marrying the wrong person was once a short cut to 'disownment' or expulsion from the Society. The reason for this was that early Quakers had carried their disapproval of 'hireling priests' to the extent of refusing to be married by them, and had been successful in establishing at law the validity of a Quaker marriage. However, when this was enshrined in the statute – the exception from Lord Hardwick's Act against Clandestine Marriages of 1753 of both Quaker and Jewish weddings – the provision applied only if both parties were in membership. Hence if one wanted to marry a non-Friend, one could not marry according to the Quaker usage, and if one married at a steeple house one was disowned.

From 1859 onwards, the way was clear for non-members to marry members by Friends' usage; from 1873 Quaker marriage was open to any who wished to adopt it. The form of a Quaker marriage is to my mind deeply satisfying, though in terms of ceremonial there is nothing much to describe. It is simply a special Meeting for Worship, in the course of which the couple take each other by the hand and make a declaration, in the form: 'Friends, I take this my Friend A. B. to be my husband/wife, promising, through divine assistance, to be unto him/her a faithful wife/husband, so long as we both on earth shall live.'

Alternatively the phrase 'through divine assistance' may be replaced by the words 'with God's help' and the phrase 'so long as we both on earth shall live' may be replaced by 'until it shall please the Lord by death to separate us'.

The certificate declaring where and when the marriage took place, and repeating the declaration, is then signed by the parties and two witnesses, and read out by some suitable person. At the end of the Meeting it may be signed by others; it is usually signed by everybody present.

Since Quakers are no longer doomed to marry other Quakers or else be disowned, we now rejoice in a great many marriages where one partner is a member and the other is not. I do not think it is reasonable to call these 'mixed marriages' – they are no more mixed than those between blondes and men with dark hair. If there is a major difference in basic outlook, then of course the marriage is likely to be under stress anyway; but given agreement on essentials, there is no cause of stress in the marriage and hence there is a tendency for the couple to move closer together in their viewpoints. Sometimes this means the Quaker resigns his membership, sometimes the non-Quaker applies for membership: this happens often enough to raise hopes that we are progressing from the formal exclusivity of 'marrying-out' to the inclusivity of 'marrying-in'.

As to leaving the Society, this may occur through resignation, termination or death. Termination of membership by the Monthly Meeting occurs either because the Friend has ceased to show any interest in the life of the Society and there seems no reasonable likelihood of his doing so, or because all trace of him has been lost, or because his conduct or publicly expressed opinions are so at variance with the known principles of the Society that the spiritual bond of membership has been broken. Such an event is rare, however, Meetings are urged to beware of undue haste and unwarranted assumptions in proposals for termination of membership.

Resignation is more common. We lose some 200 members a year, as against some 300 deaths and some 350 convincements. (Children coming into full membership keep the total membership just about constant at present, though over the longer term there has been a steady increase, from a total of 19,000 in the late thirties to about 21,000 today.) I do not myself think that we take this figure seriously enough. Resignations are roughly sixty per cent of convincements; without them the rate of growth of the Society would have been about doubled over the last thirty years. Obviously numbers are not a matter of prime importance, but it is a matter of some importance that the future of a Society which means so much to its members depends on a narrow balance of stability between those attracted to it and those who find themselves unable to stay in it.

Now all these figures are small percentages of the total, which means that the average Quaker joins the Society early in life and stays in it for a very long time, usually until he dies. The average length of membership, after all, is forty-two years, though we must expect this to fall as the present trend against child membership has more effect. Perhaps this is why, to my mind, we do not take the figure of resignations seriously enough. In any given Meeting there will not be very many, and they will all be for very good reasons. Indeed, I am sure particular Meetings take particular resignations seriously; what I wonder is whether we think enough about resignations as a whole, about the reasons for them.

If members leave us because they have found greater spiritual support from another church or organization, we may watch their going with regretful understanding. But if they leave because the Society has not given them what they expected when they became members, if our failing them means a life without a spiritual centre; then I think we should be very concerned, concerned to re-examine our own attitudes, concerned that we do not wittingly or otherwise encourage hopes that we cannot fulfil.

Nevertheless, despite the prevalence of resignation, the natural and normal end of membership is death, even if the normality rests on a rather slender arithmetical foundation. For those that die in membership or, as attenders, express a wish for Quaker last rites, the choice is between burial in a Quaker burial ground or cremation. In either case the service is in the form of a Meeting for Worship; a Memorial Meeting may also be held on some later occasion.

Seek out, if you have a liking for the quiet acre, a Quaker burial ground. The older ones are difficult to identify since there was a strong objection, established in course of time as a 'testimony', against marking graves with headstones. In Wandsworth Meeting House today (and doubtless in many others) there is a chart on the wall showing by precise measurements where the various graves are in the burial ground, and in the older part of the burial ground at Jordans, only the graves of Mary and Thomas Ellwood, Mary and Isaac Penington and William Penn and his family are marked with stones. These were erected in the latter part of the nineteenth century, when the practice was so far modified as to allow a memorial, provided it stated no more than the name and age of the deceased and the dates of birth and death. Moreover, a modest uniformity was preserved to guard against distinction between the rich and the poor.

So there they lie, those worthy old Friends, with their unassuming, uninformative stones, usually thick-shaded by trees and shrubs. Few new graves are added; most Friends today prefer cremation. But from the seventeenth century onward, the Quaker would always try to die in the way he had tried to live, according to his own inner light. No hireling priest should mumble set words over him, and if to escape the priest he had to eschew consecrated ground, that was no hardship. A piece of land could be bought, and graves dug and men and women buried there as well as elsewhere. Over the years, as it seems to me, a Quaker burial ground acquires its own especial air of peace.

CHAPTER 5

Debits and Credits

WE have reached the final chapter, the summing-up, the point at which, after taking careful account of assets and liabilities, a balance must be struck. I am all too well aware that many Friends will be ready with fairly substantial lists of shortcomings on my part – hardly a mention of Woodbrooke, the unique Quaker college in Birmingham; so little reference to the range and variety of Quaker activity on behalf of the less privileged, both at home and abroad; so scant a commentary on Quaker schools; such a casual glance at the American scene, and so on.

All this is deliberate. This is not the book in which you will find detailed descriptions of all the many aspects of Quakerism, this is a book about the beliefs and attitudes that I have found in the Society of Friends, in London Yearly Meeting particularly, but reflected whenever I have met Friends from other Yearly Meetings; the beliefs and attitudes which called me, a card-carrying agnostic humanist, in out of the cold and made me a Quaker by convincement. In a way, the other book would have been easier to write, a large and crowded canvas, a sort of Frith's *Derby Day* of foreign missions, schools, homes for the elderly, societies for sufferers from disabling diseases, holiday camps for retarded children, campaigns against intolerance and inhumanity; a collage of Quaker organizations, partly Quaker organizations, and Quaker participation in non-Quaker organizations, so involved that the proliferation of detail would conceal any basic design or lack of it.

I commented in the Preface that if Quakerism was only a historical survival it would be best left to historians; the justification for the inclusion of the brief historical sketch is not its importance in itself, but that I believe Quakerism to be important in what it is today, in the attitudes, beliefs and actions of members and attenders; and the history can help to illuminate the present. Part of this illumination shows the origins of attitudes in the Society which have a long and revered tradition, but which are sometimes to be seen in apparent conflict, where a traditional attitude and a contemporary expression of its underlying principle seem to be at odds. Another way in which the history is of value is in giving us an insight into the origin of some of the inconsistencies and defects we find. For the Society of Friends, let us admit it, is not perfect.

I believe the fundamentals of Quakerism to be as sound now as ever they were, and I believe that those fundamentals can be reinterpreted, along the lines of the second part of this book, to make a valid and valuable contribution to our time. But if I am not to be accused of starry-eyed idealism and an obstinate refusal to face unpleasant facts, I must admit that the Society of Friends has some substantial defects.

I feel, however, that the setting out of these defects is likely to give rise to more controversy and dispute than everything else I have written. Friends are well used to diversity of belief, and can accept with great patience and understanding the exposition of views which they do not share. Yet, when it comes to criticism of the Society, this is a matter in which we each feel more personally involved. Every criticism is likely to be taken personally and also every Friend has a private list of shortcomings of the Society quite different from those I shall categorize. I shall be blamed for saying too much and too little, for spoiling the Society's image and for lily-livered hypocrisy. But one thing does not worry me at all. In any other organization I should expect an operation like this to lose me most of my friends. I am quite seriously not in the least worried about that aspect; I am far more worried at the dear, over-conscientious Friends who will read this chapter and go hunting in themselves for vices of which they are completely innocent. I would like to include a Warning Notice to them – 'This does not mean you!' – but I am afraid they would assume it was directed at other Friends. All I can do is to disclaim responsibility for the consequences to any Friend of swallowing a criticism which has not been prescribed for him.

The Society as a whole suffers undoubtedly from being middle class. We have a disproportionate membership of teachers and middle-grade executives. Our advertisements attract response in the *Guardian* and the *Observer* but not in the *Daily Mirror* (though we also do rather well from the better-class women's magazines – including a lot of inquiries from men!). The good side of this is readily seen, in the admirably reasonable nature of a gathering of Friends; the weakness is in our failure to make contact with a wider society, and in a mild intellectualism that is seldom rigorous. We are, for example, determinedly non-dogmatic, yet we argue interminably about our own rather amateurish theology. Even so, the argument must never develop too sharp an edge; consideration for the sensibilities of others is ingeniously employed as an excuse to avoid challenging discussion. As against this, the tradition of plain speech is often used as a justification for statements which cannot be justified in any way. Thus, a Quaker theological discussion often ends in a ringing declaration of an indefensible belief. At that point what can one do? The very fervency of the declaration makes it quite clear that the speaker's sensibilities will be affronted if the brutalities of criticism are employed on him, and so he holds the field. These same techniques are often seen to great disadvantage in business Meetings, but despite the frequent concern of Preparative Meetings and Monthly Meetings with tedious detail, I still feel that the essential God-seeking nature of Quaker business Meetings more than offsets their defects.

I have also referred earlier[1] to the inconsistency of the Quaker attitude to material goods, the failure to carry through in this respect the consistency so evident in other matters. Not only are we as individuals quite orthodox in respect of money, and not only do the 'Advice and Queries' recommend a practical bourgeois attitude to accounts and wills, but we as a Society own a lot of property and have a tidy sum put by. Now I am not sure what our attitude to money and goods should be; I am clear enough that it should not be defined and laid down, but may vary from one

1. Part III, Chapter 3, pp. 136–41.

person to another. What I am not happy about is our tendency to turn a blind eye to this problem, to pretend that it is all somehow satisfactorily brought into focus by the reassuring example of the seventeenth-century Friends who showed that plain dealing could bring satisfactory profits. John Woolman thought the matter through, and limited his business to what would keep him, but then John Woolman was an exceptional Friend, and the Society, in England at least, found him an uncomfortable one.

The separatedness and oddness of Quakers is perhaps dying out. We do not dress differently and we no longer make a practice of using the second person singular. There are still a number of curiosities of practice, such as opening a letter 'Dear Charles Lamb' whether he be Mr Lamb, Doctor Lamb, Sir Charles Lamb, Lord Lamb, Prince Lamb or even Pope Lamb, and shaking hands rather more than is customary in England. There is a tendency to use standardized Quaker phrases, particularly in business Meetings.[2]

The worst aspect of separatedness is not, however, in these minor eccentricities, but in the sense so many Quakers have of belonging to a minority group. So we do, but surely if our religion really has meaning we should expect, as the early Christians and the early Quakers did, that it should spread throughout the nations. We may perhaps take a realistic view of how fast this is likely to happen, but we should at least want it to happen and see it as conceivable. Yet some parts of the Society do see its role as essentially a minority one, a little oasis of calm in the middle of a harsh and alien desert. Despite all the efforts of those who engage in extension work and outreach (Quaker terminology for trying to get across to the rest of the world), there are a proportion of Quakers and a few Meetings who really do not want to expand, who prefer to keep the Society as a club with a select and mutually acceptable membership. Yet it is probably unfair to say there are whole Meetings which have this attitude; they may appear to have it, but before concluding that

2. See the article 'A Quaker Phrase Book' in *The Friend* of 21 July 1967, for a delicious glossary – ' "while recognizing that" – "we disagree entirely" ', and so on.

this is the sense of the Meeting I would recommend a little judicious kite-flying. Often, even in the most stolid Meeting, there is a hidden fifth column, usually in the form of a demure old lady or a patriarchal old gentleman.

One way in which the Society as a whole perpetuates its historical separateness is by having its own organizations. For almost every type of activity – and all of them are wholly admirable – there is a special Quaker organization. Apart from the far-reaching issue of whether the Friends Service Council should coexist with and work with organizations with similar basic aims such as Oxfam and War on Want, or whether Friends would do better to give their funds and their energies to whichever of the non-Quaker organizations is closest to their particular concern (and there are strong arguments on both sides of that question), is it really necessary or beneficial to have a separate Friends Temperance and Moral Welfare Union, a Friends Guild of Teachers, a Friends Historical Society, a Guild of Friends Social Workers, a Quaker Fellowship of the Arts, a Quaker Medical Society, and associations of Friends interested in anti-vivisection, spiritual healing, and vegetarianism? When it comes to the point we would each make an exception for our own pet hobby-horse, but can we really justify the collective maintenance of such a numerous and diverse stable?

When one turns from the Society of Friends as an organization to the consideration of Friends as individuals, it does seem both rude and unkind to suggest that they have failings. Of course, Friends are human and have human failings; but to suggest that *as Friends* they are particularly subject to certain frailties – but then, as Friends they are marked out by their honesty, their consistency, their consideration; so there must be another side to the coin.

For example, there is a weakness for moral blackmail. You are a Friend, or an attender. Some Friend in the Meeting is very concerned with the well-being of unmarried mothers, or discharged prisoners. He himself is active in this matter, he has two or three particular problem children to whom he devotes himself, he runs a group or society in their interest, but there are still others that he cannot manage. Beware!

You will be cornered after Meeting, told the sad story, and asked point blank whether you could not keep an eye on 'A' until she has had her baby, or offer a room to 'B' when he comes out of prison. And if you do not develop a hide like a rhinoceros, and stoutly defend your right to be directed by your own inward light and not by that of other people you will soon find your house filled with other people's lame dogs and your time filled with other people's concerns.

The Friend who wants to commandeer you as an auxiliary to his own efforts is probably trying hard to avoid himself, to be so deeply involved in good works that he has a valid excuse for not coming to terms with himself. But no excuse is valid. The most insistent task is to come nearer to God, and it is on this that service to others is founded.

A fair warning should also be given about the prevalence of rigid attitudes. This book may have given the impression that all Friends are liberal in their thought, considerate of others, having a willingness to understand attitudes they cannot accept. This is not always the case. There are some Friends who have an authoritative outlook, either generally or in certain respects. As examples, you may well find in any Meeting:

a Friend who is rigidly Christocentric and finds it difficult to accept that other Friends' non-Christocentric views may be valid;
a Friend who is a strict total abstainer and considers all non-abstaining Friends to be failing in their testimony;
a Friend who considers that Friends should bring up their children after the manner of Friends, e.g. by making them attend Meeting whether they wish to or not.

This is not, I hope, simply a subjective list of opinions which I do not happen to share. It is rather a list of more commonly surviving Puritan attitudes, and the common factor between them is that they are authoritarian. In each case there are many who hold the same views on Christ, on drink, on bringing up children, but who accept that their own firmly-held opinions apply only to themselves, and cannot be extended to others. The particular Friends I am referring to are dogmatic about their own specific King Charles's head. As such they differ from the common attitudes of Friends, but one or more of them will be found in most Meetings.

Then there is another Friendly weakness. Their ideas of fun are generally unsophisticated, their sense of humour rather undeveloped. I use the word undeveloped advisedly, because I have found rich veins of unexploited satire in certain reprehensible Friends. When it comes to taking the mickey out of the Society there is no need to look beyond our own ranks; yet our affairs are generally conducted in a somewhat sober vein, and the parties we throw are usually more distinguished for the quality and variety of home-baked fare than the scintillation of their wit.

However, the most disturbing Friendly failing is visible both in Meetings and in individuals. It is difficult to name precisely but it is something like smugness yet not quite, something like lack of vision yet different. It is a sort of breadth of concern with completely unnoticed blank spots, a concept of service that has somehow become fossilized. It is flexible and adaptable thinking that is beginning to go arthritic, a following of the inward light that finds the glare too strong, a tendency to wish the still small voice would speak out rather more clearly, but preferably saying something more acceptable.

This draws a picture of old age, and in some ways the Society does show signs of ageing. There is no real willingness to reconsider the values of our various concerns, and particularly not to consider what is the most useful thing that a few thousand inner-directed people could do in this world.

The symptom of being middle class and middle aged is an acceptance of the world as it is. We are out to correct abuses, to succour the weak, to cherish the poor, but we are not, when it comes to the point, really anxious to build the Kingdom of Heaven. This would be a disruptive, disturbing operation which might upset some Friends, so instead of questioning the basic values of our society we accept them and try to ameliorate the worst features. Anything else would be too uncomfortable.

This is, in some ways, a vicious criticism and is obviously not true of the whole of Quakerism. But it is, I think, a fair exposition of the heart of the malaise, the reason why we are still a minority body, highly respected but limited in influence. We work in certain historically sanctified fields; our weight is behind work for peace, help for the developing countries, penal reform and so on. These are respectable Quaker activities, but there is no urge, in the body of the membership, to branch out into investigating the twentieth-century dilemma, into asking whether our world is nearer the Christian ideal than the other world in the East, into looking at the scale of the change needed and asking where the power can be found to bring about the change. We are in an ecumenical dialogue with the other Christian churches, whose outlook generally is probably narrower than ours; our dialogue with the non-Christian churches is more hesitant. We lament the misdirection of youth, and we do not make contact with the youthful elements, misdirected or not, that are on to something.

Another aspect of this is the lack of spiritual growth in the Society. By this I mean that there is a great deal of argument about whether we are Christians or not, a great deal of dredging-up of Quaker history to show what was or was not the attitude in the seventeenth century, and a great deal of mulling over of the new theology. But all this is backward-looking. It is relevant to the sifting-out of the difference between the Methodists and ourselves, or to the study of how we got some of our present attitudes, but it does not help us to talk to the world outside. When we talk of extension work, of trying to get our message across, the first difficulty is that we can hardly find a way of expressing the message. Partly because it is inexpressible, yes; but partly also because we do not apply ourselves to trying to relate our experience, what we have to offer, to the world outside.

This is not a matter of compromise. I am not asking that Friends should do the equivalent of the services with jazz which some churches have tried, nor am I asking that we should water down our beliefs until they are universally acceptable, a sort of weak spiritual gruel. What I do ask for is a thorough-going consideration of what the outside world is interested in, what we can offer it, and what terms have to be used to make it intelligible.

Thus if there are three aspects of human thought which have had a shattering effect on the orthodox religious and moral patterns of western civilization, they are psychology, anthropology and the development of the scientific method. Together they constitute the core of modern thought, yet it is precisely their terms and concepts that are least applied to matters of faith.

In fact, psychology, anthropology (and particularly its subdivision, comparative religion) and the scientific method will play havoc with belief if belief is not founded on and maintained by a constant welling-up of experience. If we are to construct this dialogue with our own time, we need to develop our understanding of these subjects, to apply their methods to our spiritual life, our faith and our belief. We must be prepared for the possibility that the exercise will destroy our faith, but a faith that can be destroyed so is not worth much, and we are better off without it. But if faith or spiritual insight is founded on experience, then to consider it in this light can only lead to deepened understanding and to a growing ability to explain our own understanding to contemporary man in terms of concepts he recognizes and appreciates.

At this point it is reasonable to ask why. Why making oneself a channel for the Spirit, and establishing a capacity to expound the essence of the religious message to an uninterested world is important, particularly at a time when that world at last shows signs of getting on very well, or at least no worse than usual, without religion.

For this it is necessary to look first at some of the characteristics of the world in which we live. It is no longer the world of history; a change has taken place which affects the fundamental relationship of man and his environment. The dropping of the Hiroshima and Nagasaki atom bombs were symbolic of this change, they were a declaration that man had the power to destroy his world completely and that he had achieved that power far in advance of attaining the wisdom to use it properly. In effect the timeless balance has been overset, man is no longer one animal among many, subject to checks and balances, dependent for his survival on his capacity to adapt to his environment. Now it is the environment that adapts, that is shaped by our actions, and in the quarter of a century since those symbolic mushrooms first grew, we have begun to see how fatally ill-equipped we are to have such power. We realized in time the malignant power of the atom, and even politicians were persuaded to limit the testing of weapons and the release of radiation. Today that seems one of the more controllable aspects of the general degradation of the biosphere, as we begin to face the grim truth that the arch-pollutant is man himself, and that the planned parenthood of the comfortably-off industrially developed community, with implied insatiable demands for water, cheap food, energy and manufactured goods is more of a menace than those countless mouths in other parts of the world which, despite themselves, consume so little.

I know, of course, that prophecies of doom are a staple feature of human existence. Some of the earlier ones – that all the coal would be used up before the end of the twentieth century, for example – were wide of the mark; and the optimist deduces from this that all such prophecies will be disproved, that there will always be a technological miracle to save us from the consequences of our profligate folly. This optimism ignores the deadly implications of the most recent warnings; that those same technological miracles that save us from immediate disasters may be making ultimate disaster more certain. In effect, it is irrelevant whether the particular ecological collapse which is predicated comes about, we are up against something on the scale of Browning's 'great text in Galatians . . . twenty-nine distinct damnations, one sure if another fails'.[3] It is really as simple as that; if we are damnably stupid we shall blow ourselves up with atom bombs. If we escape that, we shall be stricken with famine

3. Robert Browning, 'Soliloquy in a Spanish Cloister', *Browning*, Penguin Books, 1954.

and disease as a result of over-population. Increase the food supply and we shall be poisoned by organo-metallic chemicals. Limit the population and the growing wealth per head will exhaust our mineral resources – unless the growing industrial activity destroys the biosphere first.

Unless ... unless our basic assumptions are wrong. In particular, unless man can do something about himself, about his self-centredness, his destructiveness, his misdirected ingenuity. The whole history of mankind is of the dominance of these traits, these characteristics which ensure the survival of the individual in a largely hostile environment. The evidence is that man cannot change his own nature; evidence from history and evidence from our own examination of ourselves. There is only one tradition which offers an alternative; the sequence of great spiritual teachers who through the ages have taught that the indwelling presence of God in man can change him. This is not a secret or esoteric doctrine, not the private property of the Quakers, of the Christian churches even. It is a mystery, not because of what is claimed, but because the effect is incredible to those who have not experienced it. But it is a universal mystery. Christ taught the love of God for all men, the presence of God in all men; Christianity has made his message exclusive, by making it dependent on the episodic Christ, but the true teaching of Christ is inclusive. To be truly a Christian is to say 'yes' to every manifestation of the divine which is in this life, and that includes all those other teachings which incorporate the light of God.

Now, any man can sacrifice his ego, can crucify that which is nearer to him than his own flesh, and give himself to the divine will. That is one of the levels of meaning of the Crucifixion. It is not enough to look back to the physical death of another man's body; we are required to submit to a psychological death ourselves, to live on 'in the flesh' after the death of the ego, filled with the divine presence. That is one level of meaning of the Resurrection. Nor does this happen once, on one day of our lives, after which we are in God. Once it happens, it goes on happening continually, as we fight towards full awareness of God and slip back again and again. The dreadful battle between the light and the dark is continual, once it is joined.

Such is the spiritual teaching, in terms of mid-twentieth-century pop psychology. The terms are not important; beneath the elaborate myth imagery of the religions of the world lies always the same message. The religion itself may be dualistic or non-dualistic, the legends wholly or partially incredible, but underlying all we find the same essential teaching. The closer we move to the teaching of Christ the more the accretions of the Christian Church are cleared away, and the more we realize that his teaching is this, and that his concern was not that we should recognize a distinctive status in him, but that we should recognize the distinctive nature of his teachings. It is distinct from the standards and attitudes of the world around him and around us, but is not unique, being linked with earlier and subsequent bearers of the message.

But the essential teaching of God in man, and of the giving up of self-will, the surrender to the divine, is one thing. It has been available to mankind for thousands of years. It has not had a very obvious beneficial effect; it does not have much impact; in fact, by and large, it is ignored and the usual reaction to it is one of bored incredulity. Organized theological religion, based on a separated omniscient, omnipotent, exclusive and usually punitive deity, has had a much greater effect (even if on the whole the effects have been questionable). What then is the justification of the other teaching, the doctrine of the indwelling presence?

Perhaps justification is the wrong word. The justification of this teaching is in its truth, its validity. But to say *that*, in a mechanistic world, is to be asked for proof, and the wholly valid proof is inward experience. So it is the individual who must set about finding the inner light, seeking the presence of God within himself for only so can he become convinced of the reality of that presence.

So far one has been talking of the individual. The importance of the Society of Friends, it seems to me, lies in their presenting to the world a substantial number of people who accept this teaching and who stand up to be counted. They also demonstrate, fallibly perhaps, but more consistently than most such groups, a determined application of their beliefs in practice. Their methods of doing business show an alternative to the rule of force and the rule of the majority alike. Their opposition to the state on issues they consider essential shows that the state is not all-powerful. They are a model which shows that man can live by obedience to the divine will, without being completely inactive. They show that against the Oriental model of passive acceptance there is another way – a way that enables men to live better in the world and excites their endeavours to mend it.

Yet simply to be an example of a better way of living would be of little value if that was only available to a limited group. Sometimes Quakers look at themselves, shake their heads and say that they fear Quakerism will never have a wide appeal; it is too intellectual. To the extent that it is intellectual it is deviating from its proper way. The first Quakers were not notably selected from the intelligentsia, though some of them were very intelligent. Surely the truth is that in this matter, intelligence is not very important one way or the other. To the extent that you have it, it is a talent like any other to be used according to the promptings of the inner light. If the Society looks like a preserve of intellectuals (and I don't myself think it does; I think it is far more differentiated by social class than by intelligence) it is because Friends use what they have, not because they have that much more than others. And of course everything for Friends is related to their faith, so that such intelligence as there is available is applied to that. We do not recommend people to leave their brains at the door when they come to consider Quakerism, but on the other hand the understanding of our beliefs can be undertaken at many different levels of intellectual acuteness, all of which are relatively unimportant compared with the intuitive awareness which comes from experience.

No, Friends have become middle class for historical reasons, and their capacity to speak to the world at large has been sadly restricted. This was not always so; early Friends spoke to all manner of men and their words were heard. In the developing countries today Friends speak – by their actions and their silences – and are heard and understood. In Britain, there are difficulties, most of them within the Society, difficulties of attitudes, uncertainties about methods of communication. Nevertheless, this is to me the other major reason why Friends matter. Putting on one side for the moment these difficulties within, Friends are more than a model Society. They could, and should, become a growing point for a new society. I must be specific. I do not believe that we can change the world by organizational activity, by old-style men trying to plan and build organizations which will contain and control their violence and their stupidity. I do believe that each man can find within himself the presence of God and through that presence can be changed. And the Kingdom of Heaven is to be created, here, on this earth, and if we so desire, in this day, by individual violent, stupid men finding the presence of God in themselves and becoming citizens of the Kingdom of Heaven.

To some extent, then, I see the Society of Friends as important not only for what it is but also for what it could be. It is a model of the spiritually directed society; it could be the growing point from which an explosive outburst of spiritual awareness could start. And only such an outburst, only a radical change in our values and a corresponding change in the whole pattern of our society, can save our perilous civilization.

This is an idealistic concept which is easily brushed aside – the problems of the world are not to be solved by a few individuals sitting quietly together and changing their attitudes; it is all very well for the few but it won't change the masses; such movements only flourish in calm, stable societies where they are protected by law and order of a non-Quaker variety. Such are the counter-arguments of the reasonable man. But, in fact, history is against him. Great changes have been brought about by just such groups; Quakers have been particularly effective in this way. Quakerism did speak to the ordinary man in the seventeenth century and can do so again today if we can only reach him. At all events, if this will not speak to him, if we cannot change the world this way, it is abundantly clear that we cannot change it any other way.

To put it bluntly, the only way of escape from the problems of our desperate age is through the redemption (if that is not too loaded a word) of man, of individual men. Idealistic this may be, but the alternatives have been tried and give little hope of success. There are as many ways to God as there are men to seek him, and we need them all. The particular merits of Quakerism are simply that it is blessedly free from dogmatic accretions which are utterly irrelevant to today's problems, and it is non-exclusive; it does not claim to be the only repository of truth.

Quakers can therefore talk to all-comers, in terms of their own experience, and they do not have to couch the expression of that experience in particular symbolic terms. Nor do they feel bound to deny the validity of experience which is expressed in different terms or which is seen against a different religious or cultural background. This is not a facile eclecticism; it is not that we really do not care very much; it is not, as so many critics inside and outside the Society suggest, that we are too woolly-minded, too vague in our thinking, or too little concerned with the essence of religious thought to take a defined position. It is rather that the Quaker position is fully defined, but not capable of being put into so many words. Every Quaker defines his position fully and clearly by his life, and particularly by that central part of his life, his participation in Meeting for Worship. And it is here particularly that we can speak to others, of any religion or none. For those who come to our Meetings and sit quietly with us, our message is there. It is a message of hope, because it speaks of the available and continual presence and love of God, in each one of us.

Suggested Additional Reading

WHERE no publisher is mentioned, the books listed here are published by the Society of Friends or by one of its Committees. All of the books given which are in print can be obtained from the Friends Book Centre, Euston Road, London N.W.1., or through any bookseller.

First of all, without any question, comes the first part of the *Book of Christian Discipline of London Yearly Meeting of the Religious Society of Friends,* which is called 'Christian Faith and Practice in the Experience of the Society of Friends'. This is the literary testament of the Society and one of the best of bedside anthologies. The second half of *The Book of Discipline,* 'Church Government', is necessarily more mandatory, but not excessively so and mainly where obligations under the law have to be met; its tone and approach to regulatory matters is in itself an interesting insight; it contains the 'Advices and Queries' which are also available as a separate leaflet.

George Gorman's *Introducing Quakers* (1969) is a general book covering much the same ground as this volume but having the advantage of being shorter. Another invaluable and delightful book, *The Quaker Bedside Book* (Hulton Press, 1952), edited by the late Bernard Canter, is now out of print, but well worth looking for, as is *The Quakers* by John Sykes (Allan Wingate, 1958), who takes in some respects a critical, but a very perceptive viewpoint.

For history, three works in the Rowntree series deserve special mention: *The Beginnings of Quakerism* by W. C. Braithwaite, 2nd ed., revised by H. J. Cadbury (Cambridge University Press, 1955), *The Second Period of Quakerism* (1660–1725), by W. C. Braithwaite, 2nd ed., prepared by H. J. Cadbury (Cambridge University Press, 1961); and *The Later Periods of Quakerism* by Rufus M. Jones, two volumes (Macmillan, 1919). A. Neave Brayshaw's readable and re-

liable *The Quakers, Their Story and Message*, is now reprinted in paperback. Other good general studies are: *The
Story of Quakerism Through Three Centuries*, by Elfrida
Vipont, 2nd ed., revised (Bannisdale Press, 1960); *Approach
to Quakerism*, by Edgar B. Castle (Bannisdale Press, 1961);
and *Discovery of Quakerism*, by Harold Loukes (1970).

Many early Quakers were fascinating writers; it is a
matter of taste and stamina whether one can manage the
originals or whether a judicious selection is preferable.
George Fox's *Journal* is available in modern editions and
Friends Home Service Committee will supply on request a
list of books and pamphlets which includes selections from
most of the major Quaker authors. Penn, Penington, Nayler
and Woolman are the best ones to move on to after Fox, in
my personal view.

Two studies in specialized history are particularly worthy
of note: Arthur Raistrick's *Quakers in Science and Industry*
(reprinted David and Charles, 1968) and Fred Nicholson's
Quakers and the Arts (1968).

The series of annual Swarthmore Lectures represents an
interesting variety of personal commentaries on varied
issues, for example, from Kathleen Slack's fascinating statistical study, *Constancy and Change in the Society of
Friends* (1967), to such explorations in contemporary Quaker
thinking as L. Hugh Doncaster's *God in Every Man* (1963),
Maurice Creasey's *Bearings* (1969), Charles Carter's *On Having a Sense of All Conditions* (1971) or George Gorman's
The Amazing Fact of Quaker Worship (1973). These are
also mentioned in the Friends Home Service Committee list.

Index

Abel, Richard of Mancetter, 18
Ackworth School, plan of, 136
Adam, Ruth, 166
Adult schools, 61
'Advices and Queries', 139,
    231, 245
Alcott, Michael J., 95
Aldam, Mary and Thomas, 26
*Amazing Fact of Quaker
    Worship, The*, 246
Ambulance Unit, Friends, 130
Anabaptists, 23
Andrews, C. F., 99
Anger, Quakerism necessitated
    by, 122
Apology, 22, 106
Application for membership,
    see Membership,
    application for
Approach to Quakerism, 246
Arthur, King, 42
Arts, Quaker Fellowship of the,
    233
Assistant Clerks, 203, 208
Attender, 213–14
Attitudes, specifically Quaker,
    85
Audland, Camm and, 22

Babes and sucklings, out of
    the mouths of, 191n
Banks, Quaker, 42
Baptists, Particular, 23
Barclay, Robert, 22, 105–6
Bearings, 96, 110, 246
Beginnings of Quakerism, The,
    245

Belief validated by experience,
    218
Bellers, John, 43, 155, 195
Benson, Lewis, 110
Berks and Oxon Quarterly
    Meeting, *see* Meeting,
    Berks and Oxon Quarterly
Birthright membership, 213
Bishop, George, 84
Blackmail, moral, *see* Moral
    blackmail, weakness for
Bolivia, National Friends
    Church of, 178
Bonhoeffer, Dietrich, 108
Book Centre, Friends, 246
Boswell, James, 186n
Bourgeois attitude to accounts,
    231
Braithwaite, W. C., 245
Brayshaw, A. Neave, 63, 133,
    245
Bright, John, 129
Browning, Robert, 238
Burial ground, Quaker, 227
Burrough, Edward, 205–6
Business, conduct of, 204–7

Cadbury, H. J., 245
Camels, adept at slipping
    through needles, 138
Camm, *see* Audland, Camm
    and
Campbell, Joseph, 98
Canter, Bernard, 245
Career, choice of, 139
Carter, Charles, 246

Castle, Edgar B., 246
Catholic Quakerism, 110
Cecil, Robert, 130
Ceresole, Pierre, 130
Chardin, Teilhard de, 108
Charles II, King, 30
Charm against the Toothache, A, 104
Children, entry into meeting of, 191
Children, membership of, 224
Children's Class, 190
Christ, *see* Jesus Christ
Christian and brotherly advices, 41, 46
Christian Discipline, Book of, 214, 245
Christian Faith and Practice, 90, 187, 214n, 245
Christian society, Friends a, 75
Christian Relationships, Committee on, 184
Christianity, Quakerism as primitive, 32
Church Government, 90, 207, 216, 245
  advice to Visitors, 221
  on membership, 214
Churches, British Council of, *see* Council of Churches, British
Churches, World Council of, *see* Council of Churches, World
Clandestine Marriages, Act against, 225
Clarkson, Thomas, 44, 49–54
Clerk, 190, 203, 208
Colchester Meeting, *see* Meeting, Colchester
Commitment, 215, 222
Committees,

of London Yearly Meeting, 182–4
  often ineffectual, 205
Concern, 207
Conferences and Seminars, International, 130
Conferences, British and Soviet Philosophers, 130
Conflict and Peace Research, 132
Conservatism, financial, of Society of Friends, *see* Financial conservatism of Society of Friends
'Conservative' Friends, 56, 62
Constancy and Change in the Society of Friends, 246
Conventicle Act, Second, of 1670, 33
Convincement, 10, 45, 48, 74, 213, 229
Council of Churches, British, 107–8, 217
Council of Churches, World, 107–8
Cradock, Dr, 18
Creasey, Maurice A., 96, 110, 246
  quotation from G. Bishop, 84
  quotation from G. Fox, 32
Creed, rejection of, 8, 67, 78, 92
Criminal behaviour, research into, 158
Criminal Injuries Act, 156
Crisp, Stephen, 22, 126
Cromwell, Oliver, 28

Daily Mirror, 231
Darbys of Coalbrookdale, 43 45
Darwin, Charles, 62
Dewsbury, William, 26

Dialogues, International, 130
Discipleship, 215
Discourse, needless, unnecessary and fruitless, 206
Discovery of Quakerism, 246
Disownment, 45, 51, 60, 224
Divine purpose, 98
Dominance of destructive traits, 239
Doncaster, L. Hugh, 87, 91, 99, 246
Drinking, excessive, 48
Drugs, hallucinogenic, 117
Durham, J. B. Lightfoot, Bishop of, 93
Dyer, Mary, 30

Earnestness of Quakers, 121
East Africa Yearly Meeting, *see* Meeting, East Africa Yearly
Education Council, Friends, 183, 190
'Eldering', 209
Elders, 188, 190, 208–11
Epistle, Yearly Meeting, 212
Equality of women, *see* Women, equality of
Evangelical Friends Alliance, 178
Experiment in Depth, 201
Expiation, 158
Extracts, Book of, 42, 46–9

Family Service Units, 130
Farnsworth, Richard, 26
Fell, Margaret,
    convinced by George Fox, 27
    died, 1702, 36
    disagreement with John Story, 33

married George Fox, 33n
    protest against rigidity, 40, 137
Fell, Judge Thomas, 27–8, 33n
Fifth Monarchy Men, 127
Financial conservatism of Society of Friends, 141
Fisher, Mary, 29, 31
Fixed price dealing, 42
Fordham, Peta, 158
Forgiveness, 93
Fothergill, Dr John, 45
Fox, George,
    'Concerning the Antiquity', 32
    creator of organization, 177
    died, 1691, 36
    early life, 16–17, 71
    founder of Quakerism, 15–16
    fraudulent trading, opposes, 25
    Journal, 16–18, 19, 20, 21, 23–4, 25, 127, 128, 164, 246
    music and theatre, opposes, 25
    openings, 19
    Quotations:
        'Christ saith this . . .', 164
        'Hold fast . . .', 78
        '. . . took away the occasion of all wars . . .', 127
        'Walk cheerfully . . .', 11
        'Woe unto the bloody . . .', *see* 'Lichfield, Woe unto the bloody city of',
        refuses captaincy, 127
Fox, Margaret, *see* Fell, Margaret
French novels, scrofulous, of no concern to visitors, 220
Freud, Sigmund, 150

Friend, The, 95, 96, 154, 217, 232n
Friends Ambulance Unit, *see* Ambulance Unit, Friends
Friends Education Council, *see* Education Council, Friends
Friends Service Council, 181
Friends World Committee for Consultation, *see* World Committee for Consultation, Friends
Friends, *see* Quakers
Fritchley Yearly Meeting, *see* Meeting, Fritchley Yearly
Fry, Elizabeth, 58, 156
Fry, Joseph, 42
Fry, Margery, 156
Fun, unsophisticated, 235

General Meeting, *see* Meeting, General
God,
  experience of, 73
  in every one, 11, 69
  indwelling presence of, 72
  presence and love of, 243
God in Every Man, 246
Gorman, George H., 95, 183, 245, 246
Grace before meals, 208
Guardian, 231
Gurney, Joseph John, 55

Hardwick's Act, Lord, 225
'Harmless and innocent people of God', 128
Hazard, Tom, 44
Heath-Stubbs, John, 104
Heawood, Geoffrey L., 112
Hicks, Elias, 55
Historical Society, Friends, 233

Holy Office, visitors not a Quaker, 220
Home Service Committee, 145, 183, 213
Homeless, numbers of, 162
Hooton, Elizabeth, 25, 35, 185
Housebreaking, masterly, by Weighty Friend, 222
Howgill, Francis, 27, 38
Humanist Christian Frontier, The, 112

Ignorance and fear, unsound basis for ethics, 148
Immigrants in Britain, 152
Immortality, 103–4
India and Pakistan, conflict, 131
Indian Affairs, 61
International Voluntary Service, 130
Introducing Quakers, 95, 245

James II, King, 36
Jesus Christ,
  as mediator, 218
  followers of, 217
  light of, 217
  Quaker attitudes to, 95–6
  teaching of, 217
  the Living Christ, 218
Johnson, Dr Samuel, 185
Jones, Rufus M., 86, 214, 245
Jung, C. G., 98, 192

Kingston and Wandsworth Monthly Meeting, *see* Meeting, Kingston and Wandsworth Monthly
Kingston Monthly Meeting, *see* Meeting, Kingston Monthly
Kingston Preparative Meeting,

see Meeting, Kingston
  Preparative

Laing, R. D., 166–7
*Later Period of Quakerism,
  The*, 245
Law enforcement, cost of, 158
Lawrence, T. E., 71
Learning, lack of, 53
'Lichfield, Woe unto the
  bloody city of', 26
Lightfoot, J. B., Bishop of
  Durham, *see* Durham,
  J. B. Lightfoot, Bishop of
London and Middlesex
  General Meeting, *see*
  Meeting, London and
  Middlesex General
Loukes, Harold, 246
L.S.D., 117
Luffe, John, 29

Machin, John, 18
MacMurray, John, 149, 151
Madagascar, United Church
  of, 178, 187
Marriage, Quaker, 225
Marrying-out, 60, 223
Martin, P. W., 201
Masks of God, The, 98
Massachusetts, law against
  Quakers, 30
*Mathematical Psychology of
  War*, 132
McGlashan, Alan, 132
Medical Society, Quaker, 233
Meeting,
  Berks and Oxon Quarterly,
    196
  Colchester, 10, 122
  East Africa Yearly, 178
  for Sufferings, 35, 152, 181
  Friends United, 178

Fritchley Yearly, 57
General, 180
Kingston and Wandsworth
  Monthly, 180
Kingston Monthly, 152
Kingston Preparative, 180
London and Middlesex
  General, 180
London Yearly, 178, 181
  operation of, 185
  origin of, 41
Monthly, 41, 178, 220
Oregon Yearly, 178
Oxford, 191n
Preparative, 178, 180
Programmed, 179, 187
Quarterly, 41, 181
Recognized, 180
Richmond upon Thames,
  10, 179
Six Weeks, 179
Westminster, 10
Membership,
  a commitment, 222
  application for, 220
  basis of, 214–23
  by application of parents,
    224
  resignation of, 226
  termination of, 226
  World, by continents, 178
Methodists, 45
Middle-aged, symptoms of
  being, 235
Middle-class bias, historical
  reasons for, 241
Middle-class, Friends
  predominantly, 231
Minister, On First Rising to,
  197
Ministry, spoken, 189
Minority, sense of belonging
  to, 232

Minutes, drafting of, 204
Mission work, 55
Monthly Meeting, *see*
    Meeting, Monthly
Moral blackmail, weakness
    for, 233
Music,
    not approved of by George
        Fox, 25
    in eighteenth century, 50
    in nineteenth century, 136
Mystics, 74, 125

Nansen, Fridjof, 130
Nayler, James, 26, 171
    entry into Bristol, 29
    last words, 38
    recommended reading, 246
    trial and punishment, 30
Needles, *see* Camels, adept at
    slipping through needles
Nicholas, Henry, 23
Nicholson, Fred, 246
Noel Baker, Philip, 130

Objections to Quaker Belief,
    192
Observer, 231
*On Having a Sense of All
    Conditions*, 246
Oregon Yearly Meeting, *see*
    Meeting, Oregon Yearly
Origin of Species, 62
Outreach, 232
Overseers, 208, 209–11, 214
Oxford Meeting, *see*
    Meeting, Oxford

Pain and suffering, 100–103
Pakistan, *see* India and
    Pakistan, conflict
Parliament, first Quaker

Member of, 58n
Parker, Alexander, 188, 191
Passant, Norman, 96
Peace and International
    Relations Committee, 184
Pease, Joseph, 58n
Penal Affairs Committee
    (former), 184
Penington, Isaac, 31, 227, 246
    quotations:
        'All Truth is a shadow
            . . .', 111
        'And the end of words
            . . .', 92
        '. . . everyone learning
            their own lesson . . .',
            110, 169
        'I have met with the
            seed . . .', 76
        'Men keeping close to
            God . . .', 107
        'No variety of practices
            . . .', 193
        'The Light, Spirit and
            Power . . .', 34
Penn, William,
    buried at Jordans, 227
    founds Pennsylvania, 35, 44
    friend of James II, 36
    later years, 36
    recommended reading, 246
    Some Fruits of Solitude, 38
    son of Admiral Penn, 31
Perfect, Quakers not, 169
Perrot, John, 29, 33
Pickvance, Joseph, 131
Pictures, three acceptable, 136
Plainness, 47, 51
Plato, 73, 202
Plymouth Brethren, 57
Portraiture of Quakerism, 44,
    49–54
Poverty, numbers in, 162

Preparative Meeting, *see*
    Meeting, Preparative
Presence and love of God, *see*
    God, presence and love of
Priesthood of all believers, 8,
    92–3
Programmed Meeting, *see*
    Meeting, Programmed
Purcell, Henry, 42
Puritan ethic, 144
Purpose, divine, *see* Divine
    purpose

Quaker,
    synonym for Friend, 7
    term applied to Fox, 26
Quaker Bedside Book, The,
    245
Quaker International Affairs
    Representative, 130
Quaker Monthly, 197
Quaker Phrase Book, A, 232n
Quakers and the Arts, 246
*Quakers in Science and
    Industry,* 246
Quakers, The, 245
*Quakers, Their Story and
    Message, The,* 246
Quaking, still occurs, 26, 199
Quarterly Meetings, *see*
    Meetings, Quarterly
Questions relative to belief,
    219

Race Relations Committee
    (former), 184
Raistrick, Arthur, 246
Ranters, 23, 30
Reason and Emotion, 149
Recognized Meeting, *see*
    Meeting, Recognized
Relief Work, 55
Republic, The, 73

Resignation of membership,
    see Membership,
    resignation of
Retreat, The, 45
Revenge, 157
Revenue, not to be defrauded,
    48
Richardson Institute, 132
Richardson, Lewis Fry, 132
Richmond upon Thames
    Meeting, *see* Meeting,
    Richmond upon Thames
Robinson, William, 30
Rotch, William, 129
Rowntree, John Stephenson,
    60
Rowntree Quaker Histories,
    63

Sacraments, rejection of
    formalized, 9, 92
Saffron Walden Friends
    School, 43
Salisbury, Elizabeth, 197
*Savage and Beautiful
    Country, The,* 132
Schisms in Quakerism
    in U.K., 57
    in U.S.A., 55–7
Schools, Friends, 43, 45, 229
Second Period of Quakerism,
    245
Seekers, 25, 27, 105, 196
Service Civil International, 130
Sewell, William, 182
Sexual ethic, rigid, 148
Sherry, visitors not looking
    for, 220
Silent worship, *see* Worship,
    silent
Six Weeks Meeting, *see*
    Meeting, Six Weeks
Slack, Kathleen, 246

Slave ship, stowage plans of, 137
Slavery, 35, 44, 56
Social and Economic Affairs Committee (former), 184
Social Responsibility Council, 184
Social Workers, Guild of Friends, 233
Spiritual growth, lack of, 236
Spiritual life of the Meeting, 208
Stephenson, Marmaduke, 30
Storey, Thomas, 105
Story, John, 33
Story of Quakerism through Three Centuries, The, 246
Sturge, Joseph, 58, 61
Suffering, *see* Pain and suffering
Sufferings, Meeting for, *see* Meeting, for Sufferings
Swarthmoor Hall, 27
Swarthmore Lectures, 246
Sykes, John, 246

Table, the, 203
Teachers, disproportionate number of, 231
Teachers, Friends Guild of, 233
Temperance, 88
Temperance and Moral Welfare Union, Friends, 233
Testimony, 87, 88
Thought, significant aspects of modern, 237
Tillich, Paul, 108
Tithes, refusal to pay, 41–2, 48, 52

Toleration Act, 1689, 31
Tuke, William and Esther, 45
Turkey, Sultan of, 29, 31
Tyrol, South, 131

UNESCO, 130
Unitarians, 107
United Meeting, Friends, 178
United Nations, 130
Unprogrammed worship, 9

Vipont, Elfrida, 246
Visitation, 220

Wandsworth Meeting House, 227
War and violence, objections to, 52
Wealth of Society of Friends, 140
Weighty Friends, 122, 222
Wesley, John, 45
West, Benjamin, 136
Westminster Tuesday lunchtime meeting, 10
Whittier, John Greenleaf, 189
Wilbur, John, 56
Wilkinson, John, 33
William Penn House, 131
Women, equality of, 185
Woodbrooke College, Selly Oak, 229
Woolman, John, 44, 45, 232, 246
World Committee for Consultation, Friends, 184
World membership, 178
World Relationships Committee, 184
Worship, silent, 9, 52, 195

MORE ABOUT PENGUINS
AND PELICANS

Penguinews, which appears every month, contains details of all the new books issued by Penguins as they are published. From time to time it is supplemented by *Penguins in Print*, which is a complete list of all titles available. (There are some five thousand of these.)

A specimen copy of *Penguinews* will be sent to you free on request. For a year's issues (including the complete lists) please send 50p if you live in the British Isles, or 75p if you live elsewhere. Just write to Dept EP, Penguin Books Ltd, Harmondsworth, Middlesex, enclosing a cheque or postal order, and your name will be added to the mailing list.

In the U.S.A.: For a complete list of books available from Penguin in the United States write to Dept CS, Penguin Books Inc., 7110 Ambassador Road, Baltimore, Maryland 21207.

In Canada: For a complete list of books available from Penguin in Canada write to Penguin Books Canada Ltd, 41 Steelcase Road West, Markham, Ontario.

SOME OTHER PELICANS ON RELIGION

BUDDHISM *Christmas Humphreys*

Written by a leading Western expert on Buddhism, this volume covers its history and development, the teaching of the various Schools and its condition in the world today.

HINDUISM *K. M. Sen*

A guide to the nature and function of a religion that has been developing for five thousand years. As in Christianity there are several Hindu schools of thought, and *Hinduism* clearly outlines their common beliefs and particular differences.

JUDAISM *Isidore Epstein*

This short but comprehensive account of Judaism is presented against a background of the 4,000 years of Jewish history.

ISLAM *Alfred Guillaume*

With the great awakening of the Muslim world which is now in progress, an understanding of the spirit of Islam is essential to the informed Westerner. Professor Guillaume provides the essentials for such an understanding in this book.

THE FUTURE OF RELIGION *Kathleen Bliss*

'Dr Bliss's chapters on God and the Future of Man cry out for quotation, they are so full of insights' – *Church Times*